What *does* good education research *look like?*

Conducting educational research

Series Editor: Harry Torrance, Manchester Metropolitan University

This series is aimed at research students in education and those undertaking related professional, vocational and social research. It takes current methodological debates seriously and offers well-informed advice to students on how to respond to such debates. Books in the series review and engage with current methodological issues, while relating such issues to the sorts of decisions which research students have to make when designing, conducting and writing up research. Thus the series both contributes to methodological debate and has practical orientation by providing students with advice on how to engage with such debate and use particular methods in their work. Series authors are experienced researchers and supervisors. Each book provides students with insights into a different form of educational research while also providing them with the critical tools and knowledge necessary to make informed judgements about the strengths and weaknesses of different approaches.

Current titles:
Tony Brown and Liz Jones: *Action, Research and Postmodernism*
Gary Thomas and Richard Spring: *Evidence-Based Practice in Education*
John Schostak: *Understanding, Designing and Conducting Qualitative Research in Education*
Maggie Maclure: *Discourse in Educational and Social Research*
Lyn Yates: *What Does Good Education Research Look Like?*

What *does* good education research *look like?*

Situating a field and its practices

Lyn Yates

Open University Press

Open University Press
McGraw-Hill Education
McGraw-Hill House
Shoppenhangers Road
Maidenhead
Berkshire
England
SL6 2QL

email: enquiries@openup.co.uk
world wide web: www.openup.co.uk

and Two Penn Plaza, New York, NY 10121-2289, USA

First published 2004

A catalogue record of this book is available from the British Library

ISBN 0335211992 (pb) 0335212476 (hb)

Library of Congress Cataloging-in-Publication Data
CIP data applied for

Typeset by YHT Ltd
Printed in the UK by Bell & Bain Ltd., Glasgow

Contents

To Katie and Clara

Acknowledgements

This book grew out of an invitation to speak on this topic to staff and graduate students at the University of Tasmania, and I thank them for that invitation and the stimulating conference in which I took part. The book is built on many discussions with colleagues and students at the University of Technology Sydney and earlier at La Trobe University, both being places that have encouraged lively engagement and new thinking about educational research. The book was completed thanks to a period of PEP leave granted by UTS.

For this book, a number of people working in different fields of education generously made time to talk to me about their own insider experiences with different parts of the research field, though they should not be held responsible for the interpretations and arguments I make. I particularly thank Jennifer Gibb, Mez Egg, Geof Hawke, Nicky Solomon, Clive Chappell and Jane Gaskell for helping me with issues I discuss in Chapter 6; Deb Hayes, Evelyn Johnson and Lois Lazanyi in relation to Chapter 7; Eileen Sedunary in relation to Chapter 8; and Maralyn Parker and Wendy Bacon in relation to Chapter 9. Chapter 3 draws particularly on what I have learned from students whose doctoral work I have supervised or examined or have taught in Ed D programmes over the last decade. It also draws on discussions with colleagues on the AARE Executive and the AARE 'Exemplary Thesis' award committee. Some comments in the chapter draw more specifically on work and conversations with Steve Dillon, Jeanette Rhedding-Jones, Elody Rathgen, Kayoko Hashimoto, Margarita Pavolva, Georgina Tsolidis, Val Robertson, Kim McShane, and I thank them. Julie McLeod and Janne Malfroy provided helpful material and comment in relation to Chapter 4. Alison Lee developed a doctoral course on 'Research Literacies' that sharpened my interest in the textual forms that research takes. Sari Knopp Biklen, Miriam David, David Hamilton, Jane Gaskell, Sue Middleton, Alison

Jones, Harriet Bjerrum Nielsen, Jeanette Rhedding-Jones, Hildur Ve, Kathleen Weiler and Gaby Weiner have talked to me about experiences in countries other than my own, over many years, as well as more specifically in relation to this book.

Introduction

This is a book about two related questions: 'What *does* good research in education look like?' and 'What does good research in education *look like*?' It attempts to explore some of the reasons why the quality of research in the field of education is subject to such critique and dispute and why there seems to be such an ongoing problem about what good research is for this field. It also sets out to provide a way of looking at different parts of the field in which education researchers operate, how they make judgements about what is good, and have particular ways of addressing what good research 'looks like'. My aim overall is to generate a type of research methodology discussion that will be different from, and will complement, the types of discussion that are found in other books on this subject. It is not written to discuss epistemological, methodological, ethical issues internal to the construction of a particular research project or research design. It is written to discuss the contexts, relationships and conditions in which those engaged in such work are located. 'Contexts' here embraces both the large context – what kind of a field is education and education research? – and also the more specific locations that throw up their own criteria and ways of judging good research – the thesis, the grant application, the journal article, consultancy and partnership projects, schools and parents, the press and book publishers.

The field that is discussed in this book, and the examples and illustrations all come from education. My own background has been particularly in mainstream education (systems of schooling), and questions relating to this and a number of examples I use will reflect this. But I have also worked with women's studies and international students from a range of workplaces, and I currently work in a faculty that is as much concerned with adult, vocational non-formal and organizational learning as with school education. The discussion in this book is intended too for those in the broader field of education or learning or 'new learning spaces', not just those who work with schools. Most of it should also be pertinent to and usable by those who work in other fields of applied social research – in social work, nursing, physiotherapy and similar fields – at least as a starting point for discussion of particular contexts and agendas within those fields.

To begin then: What *does* good education research look like?

This is a question researchers struggle with each time we try to do a piece of research, or develop a thesis, or put in an application for a research grant, or try to get a research article published. If we are working with surveys or databases or with many forms of qualitative methods, we worry about whether our sample or focus is OK, whether we have used the right array of methods, whether we have written about it in a way that gets at the key points and that is convincing. If we are critical or feminist or post-structural researchers we worry about whether we have properly taken up and negotiated the minefield of critical points that the field we work in makes about what researchers do; we worry about whether we have served the right interests, been sufficiently self-critical, written appropriately.

But the question 'what is good research?' is also one that people other than education researchers also keep raising, directly and indirectly. Governments set up new committees, reviews, boards or other mechanisms to try to deal afresh with 'standards', 'accountability', 'quality', 'evidence', 'impact'. The media, politicians, teachers, academics inside and outside education all fuel highly public debates about the quality of education research.

Is education research rather shoddy compared with, say, medical research? Why do researchers seem to keep changing their minds about what research shows about effective teaching of reading, or about co-education, or about the best way to organize schools? Why are there so many debates in the field? Why is it possible for issues like class size, single-sex schooling, reading, vocational training or new technologies to bring out experts in favour of quite opposite practices?

Looking from within, this question 'What does good education research look like?' is one that the field itself (the professional field of education researchers) does seem to divide over and to keep recon-stituting over time. Quantitative and qualitative approaches, objective methods and engaged methods, action research and abstract decon-structions go in and out of favour. The field seems to turn at particular points to psychology, at others to anthropology, sociology, cultural studies, linguistics or economic theories to provide insights into education practices. New issues seem to take off and dominate research designs and discussions at various times: 'effectiveness', citizenship, race, gender, new technologies, unemployment, giftedness, vocational learning, international competitiveness and many more.

This is a book about education research as a field, and a book about research methodology and research writing. But it does not set out to repeat the terrain that is already well covered on the shelves of research methodology, or 'how to write a thesis'. It is not going to cover 'everything you need to know about research methodology'; and it is not going to discuss at any length the technical debates and paradigm disputes about methods and approaches. Rather it sets out to raise some issues that bear on all such discussions but that are not often evident: where those discussions of methodology or pragmatics are coming from; how they are located; what type of field of research we are talking about; and what types of pressures it works with.

The book is one approach to thinking about, judging and doing education research. It is intended as an argument, a guide, a perspective and something of a 'user's handbook'. As an argument, I want to make the case, very strongly, that education research is a human, situated practice itself directed at, as well as located in, a field of activity (education) that changes its form over time and place. Research practitioners, research agendas and the reception of research are contextually located; they are not timeless or universal. It is a mistake to treat this field as if it could be the same as experimental science or as medical research (though *some* aspects of it might well attempt to replicate or be measured against the methodologies and achievements of those fields, and those fields themselves are driven by their own networks and demands and are not simply technically and objectively driven). In the case of education research, its objects of study (people, cultures, national systems) are not timeless objects where a finding at one particular time can be assumed to hold in the same way at another place or at another time when different contexts hold. The argument on these points is developed in the first part of the book, by looking at particular issues and criteria that are held up for good research and discussing some examples of the debates and the changes of emphasis that can be found in particular areas of education research. This argument about the contextual and situated nature of education research is not new, and parts of it might seem like a truism. But the substance of debates and agendas in many countries today, particularly the new drive for 'scientifically-based research' and for 'evidence-based practice', and the new initiatives to find ways of producing standards or bodies to delineate what is reliable research knowledge in education, makes the argument worth revisiting.

My argument in the first part of the book about the situated nature of education research is a backdrop to the task I take up in the second part. Because 'good research' in education is not something that can be defined simply and technically, nor something on which we can expect absolute agreement, it is relevant to understand the pragmatics through which judgements of different approaches are nevertheless achieved or enacted. So in the second part of the book, I take in turn a number of contexts where judgements about research get made: thesis examination, accepting articles and manuscripts for publication, decisions about awarding research grants and consultancies, decisions made by practitioners and end-point users, media reportage, and I attempt to explore pragmatically what is going on.

What counts as good research for the purposes of a PhD thesis is not the same as what counts as good research for the purposes of what I as a teacher should do in my class tomorrow (though there may be overlap). What good research looks like for the media is not the same as what good research looks like when national research bodies are handing out funds (or at least, that was the case in the past, though the latter may be moving towards the ways of the former). Considering the different arenas in which education research is pursued, used and judged, as I try to do in the second part of this book, is not just about a 'how to do it' agenda – it is a way of seeing education research as a field of practice that interacts in complex ways.

But, I hope, there *is* also a 'how to do it' element to this book in the sense that, especially for researchers located in universities today, it will provide some useful starting points for positioning the work that they are often engaged in. In addition to my concerns to reassert arguments about education as a field with needs that are different from science, I do want this book to be something of a user's handbook for researchers, supervisors, readers and users of education research. What I hope will be useful for people trying to think about how to do it, is to get some sense of the explicit and implicit rules of the game in the particular arenas they confront. So I have tried, in various different contexts, to take the question 'What does good research look like?' not as an open-ended one, or some sort of wish list, or as a search for examples that meet my own particular criteria and values, but as one that we might approach empirically, and with particular attention to the texts, procedures and persons involved at the point where the decisions are made. I have started from the perspective that all the time judgements *are* being made, and have been made, about what counts as good research, about what is valued. They are made by thesis examiners, by journal referees and editors, by book editors and people who buy books, by policy makers and funding bodies, by journalists, administrators, teachers and parents. In other words, in this sense 'What does good research look like?' is not an abstract question, but an empirical one. To answer it, we need to look at who the people making the judgements are; what are the processes through which the judgements get made; and what evidence about the research and the researcher do they use when they make these judgements: what, specifically, are they looking at when they decide whether or not something is good?

Existing books on education research fall largely into variants of one of the following: methodological guides to research design, both general and in specialist areas; collections or sole-authored discussions of 'issues in education research' – debates about case study, post-structuralism, feminist research or anti-racist research; advocacy or elaboration of an author's particular approach to doing research, with both epistemological and technical emphases. This book offers something different. Instead of working directly on the methodological or political issues facing the researcher, and instead of offering an argument about a specialist area or about contending paradigms in the field, it sets out to consider education research as a broad field of *practice*, as activity done in particular contexts and for particular contexts, and in which judgements about the success or otherwise of research are also practices done by people with particular institutional contexts and histories, and able to be examined. It sets out to identify different contexts of education research and the ways that research is commissioned, accepted or judged as successful and unsuccessful in these. The discussion of these pragmatics includes, firstly, quite straightforward practical matters: what are the technical requirements required for a thesis or grant application or journal article to be legitimate? A second layer of matters are partly matters of 'fact' and partly insights based on experience and theoretical reflection: who are the examiners, journal referees, grant judges, and what stance do they take to what matters? Thirdly, to show how things work in practice, examples from my own and other people's experiences of types of work that was successful, and common reasons work failed to be successful.

I am writing this book as someone who has spent most of my adult life working in the field of education and doing and engaging with education research. I have written theses, and supervised students writing theses; I have edited and written for academic journals, written for teachers' and administrators' publications; and had my research reported and not reported by the press. I have talked to teachers about my research and about their own research interests; I have served on committees that allocate money for research; I have examined theses and taken part in deciding which thesis should get a prize. I have been president of a national professional association representing education researchers, and have served on its ethics committee, and responded to new policy agendas affecting education researchers as well as lobbying for researchers' interests. I have been a visiting researcher in other countries, taken part in more conferences than I can easily remember, mentored new academics about their research. The point of this shopping list of experiences is to reiterate one of the themes of this book. In all of these contexts, judgements are being made about what counts as 'good' research – and in all of them what is going on is something that goes beyond what traditional textbooks in research methodology deal with.

They are not simply concerned with the logic and justification and procedures for particular methods. Judging 'significance' and 'quality' also
brings into play issues of genres, networks, relationships, institutional
contexts and agendas.

'What is good education research?' is in some respects a trick question,
because the answer differs depending on where you are standing and
who is asking the question. The overall answer is 'It depends . . .' Often
the question and the answer have a political dimension, but it is not
simply reducible to politics.

As readers who are already engaged in education or social science
research will be aware, today the idea of giving any overview of research
or a research field, or of research methodology, is itself a quite contentious issue. The gulf is great between researchers who work with a
belief in the possibility of objective knowledge and proof, and those who
believe that all research is political, or is undertaken from particular
perspectives and with particular interests. Some textbooks try to set out
'comprehensively' the different paradigms with their associated beliefs
and methods, although their critics are quick to note that any typology is
not a simple description of what is, but a construction, a construction that
over- simplifies how actual researchers operate, and one that is designed
to point to the writer's own way of doing things (or at least their own
perspective on what kind of a thing 'research' is) as superior. For an
example of this, you might like to compare typologies of research
included in some different books on research methodology. Compare, for
example, the categorization of research types and setting out of tables in
standard textbooks such as Cohen, Manion and Morrison (2000) and Gay
and Airasian (2000) which discuss 'styles of research' to be drawn on for
different purposes; with Lather's presentation of different approaches in a
type of evolutionary and political grid (Lather 1991), with Lincoln and
Guba's (2000) overlapping but different version of 'paradigm controversies'. In recent years, even *Review of Education Research*, the journal
set up by the American Education Research Association with the specific
brief of publishing authoritative overviews of research on different
aspects of education has been debating whether such authoritative
overviews are now possible. *Review of Education Research* 69 (4) 1999
devotes its whole issue to articles on this matter and to highly reflexive
discussions of what it means to do a review of research in an area, and
the perspectives implicit in this activity.

So when people write about research today, one of the first questions
many readers ask is 'Who are you?' 'How are you situated in all this?' I
think these are legitimate issues, and I will say something about this
shortly, but I do not want to exaggerate the extent to which we are
condemned to talk only to those who share our own starting points and
values. This book is written from a particular perspective which reflects

the problems I have tried to engage with as a researcher in education, but it is not written only for those who share that perspective or my own concerns. It does try to give an overview, and I believe the overview I give is neither arbitrary, nor easily dismissed, nor the last word or only way of seeing what is happening.

My own background is that I first learned to do research as a historian – a discipline that tries to 'make sense of' a range of varied evidence and artefacts, rather than one that works with highly controlled or controllable data. In education, I have worked more as a sociologist and curriculum theorist, and have been concerned with issues related to inequality, and issues of knowledge and social change. A large part of this work has comprised attempts to engage with, to analyse and overview the research of others: to see the different ways that curriculum researchers have approached the issue of knowledge; to follow different forms of feminist work and see their assumptions, claims, impact and lack of impact; to research and analyse policy changes, influences, effects.

Another substantial part of my recent work has been an eight-year qualitative, longitudinal, interview-based study following young people from the ages of 12 to 18, investigating their changing identities, vocational paths, and the difference particular schools make – while also simultaneously attempting to engage with issues about subjectivity and research methodology that draw on feminist and post-structural perspectives that question what researchers do when they conduct interviews or draw conclusions from them. It was a project located against and attempting to talk to some quite different fields – the 'hard world' of factor analyses and school effects, and policy-making about schooling today; and the world of critical reflexive interrogations of gendered subjectivity, of how today people form particular types of identities, make particular choices, and so on. I have done some other work reviewing national statistical databases used to track education participation and outcomes for different groups; and some studies of education policy changes in Australia. Most recently I am engaged in projects using observations, interviews, document analyses to study uses of new technologies in school; and to study across a range of education sites (schools, technical and further education, workplaces, universities) pedagogies of the new vocationalism at work in programmes related to hospitality and information technology.

Even in trying to write this synopsis of the research I have done and how I am situated, I am aware of the tension between presenting this as a story that will make sense to readers whose understanding of research is located around beliefs in evidence, and interest in questions such as 'What are your findings?', 'What methods did you use?'; or presenting this as a story which needs to be told in more extended narratives, a story that emphasizes the complex theoretically located understanding we have been trying at different times to build up: what sort of a thing is 'identity' or 'subjectivity' or 'gender' and how does this help us to see what is going on in schools, and understand why reforms do not produce straightforward effects? Are people's positionings created by cultural discourse? or 'habitus'? (Yates 2000a, 2001b; Chappell *et al.* 2003).

The concerns that thread through my own history as an education researcher and that also shape this book are a dialogue between, on the one hand, questioning, raising critical perspectives, learning to see things differently and, on the other, an understanding of the 'real world' that is the context in which we work and operate in education – a world that wants research to be reliable, to have 'findings'; a world where decisions are made that some applications get grants and others do not; that some things get published and others do not; that some things have impact and others do not.

In pursuing my work I have been interested in and influenced by some of the ideas that newer research movements and research traditions offer: for example, research writing as 'inscription', the 'deconstruction' of policy concepts, 'the personal as political', 'reflexivity'. Like many others working in the backblocks of the Antipodes (or in the provinces of red-brick English universities, or in the mid-west of the USA) I have been rather taken with some new strands of French theory, and sometimes, in my academic writing, I use terms and take up ideas that David Lodge and a host of playwrights, the press and hard-headed politicians find easy to satirize, if not scorn. But I do not see that part of my work as operating in a different world from the 'real world' we keep being asked to 'live in'. In this book, I try as much as possible to avoid using jargon, and I am trying to write both for those who are excited by those bodies of work, and for those who are not. I believe there has been a tendency for the hard-headed advocates of evidence-based, quality research to take too little account of the *type of phenomenon* education research deals in, and that these contemporary critical ideas are more attuned to. Equally, I believe there has been a tendency for post-structural researchers in particular to dismiss too quickly work that does not signal its belonging by the use of certain jargon, and to write as if they operate in a totally different world to the traditional researchers they scorn, as if they themselves have no location, do not have to meet certain standards (or operate in certain ways) to get articles published, get grants, get a thesis passed. It is the argument of this book that they do not – that, at least at the level of algorithm and judgement practices, very similar things come into play in relation to thesis examination, refereeing of articles, assessing research grant applications, whether the researcher is working with realist epistemologies or is playing with words.

Readers who are working in particular disciplinary and/or theoretical paradigms for examining research or academic practice more generally –

for example with genre, or discourse analysis, or situated practice, or communities of practice, actor network theory, materialist analyses and others – will see elements of my approach that could fit within these theories, and might wish that I had carried through one of these particular approaches more tightly. But the book is not trying to set up a tight *model* of how research operates; it is attempting to set up a discussion about the field.

In the first part of the book, then, I want to show how research is, like all fields of human practice, a social, historically-specific, culturally-situated activity: what matters changes over time, and in different places. In this part of the book I discuss some of the current debates about good and poor research and take issue with some widely-held popular views about what good education research is – for example, that good education research must contribute to the improvement of learning; or that good education research must be research that teachers can use; or, more generally, that there is a single and obvious way of measuring it; or that it is obvious that education research is poor because it cannot show the achievements that medical research can show. I also discuss here the issue of the different paradigms and fashions that are evident in academic research in education, and argue for an appreciation of situatedness and change as the context in which they operate. In this part of the book I make an argument about what kind of a field *education* is, and what kind of parameters this might set up for thinking about, reading, judging, or embarking on research.

In the second and longer part of the book, I want to take seriously the issue of the different contexts and genres in which education research and researchers operate, the different ways it and they are judged, and to try to provide some guide for practical and pragmatic thinking about those contexts. Here I take in turn different arenas in which education research is asked to measure up: the doctoral thesis; the academic journal article; the book; the grant application; the consultancy or commissioned research; the partnership or action research with schools; research subjects; the press and journalistic assessments of research. In each of these I discuss examples and characteristics of research which has been successful or which, in some way, has failed; and insider experiences of myself and others about how the processes of judgement work in that particular arena. I look at issues such as: *who are the judges* in that field?; what are the *explicit and technical criteria* that come into play?; what are the *implicit and/or hidden criteria* that come into play?; what does good research actually *look like* here?; and, what are some *common failings* in the research that is deemed not successful in this arena?

My discussion (and the summary tables that accompany each arena) is intended to be both helpful and provocative, and to be a starting point for further discussion and specific exploration (how do these rules work in your particular university or country or journal?) rather than the final word on each. For newcomers, it is an attempt to lay out some of the rules of the game held by insiders. For all readers, the intention is to provoke further discussion. You may not agree with all the claims I make about how a particular institutional context is operating, and of course these change over time as well as between countries – but I think there is a lot to be gained by trying to talk about the questions I have raised.

Part 1

Political and paradigm disputes, historical change and the field of education

Introduction

What is *good* education research is a much debated topic, both inside universities where researchers are trained, and in more public arenas. Why certain forms or examples of research are not good is an even more common topic of discussion. This part of the book discusses these debates.

In Chapter 1, *What does good education research look like? Some beginnings and debates,* I argue that people do bring to their discussions of education research some reasonably common and meaningful formal criteria (they are concerned about what it contributes to knowledge, about the quality of its methodology, and about the type of contribution it makes to the field, that it does something that matters), but that the attempts to more narrowly prescribe these agendas are, rightly, disputed. To illustrate this, I take three currently popular attempts to delineate more specific criteria for 'good research' in education and show the problems in accepting any one of these as the mandated answer. All three examples appear to make some good sense. The first is to say that 'good research' in education must contribute to learning. The second says that 'good research' in education must speak to, and be usable by, practitioners. The third, now being rapidly taken up by important government bodies, is that 'good research' must mean 'scientifically-based research'. My discussion of each position tries to show some of the agendas at work with those who promote the criteria and some of the agendas or issues important to education that are not met by working tightly within that particular framework. More broadly, this discussion shows the interplay of normative, technical and contextual issues that shape various debates and various approaches to education research.

In Chapter 2, *History, fashion and academic research in education,* I take two arenas of education research activity, research on reading, and research on gender, to discuss why research approaches (theories, methodologies, types of claims) change; why education researchers do not appear to make the same kind of progress as medical researchers; why disputes about research approaches persist rather than being resolved. I argue that careful research is being done, and builds in ways that other research fields do, but that the engagement between researchers and the broader field of education policy and practice gives a different overall shape to their activity than researchers who work in a 'pure' research field.

What does good education research look like? Some beginnings and debates

or, why education research is not as straightforward as finding a cure for cancer...[1]

When I teach a course on research methodology, I often begin by asking students to give me examples of work they have come across previously that they consider to be good research. Over the years I have put this question to people who have done a lot of previous study in academic research and to those who have done little; to people whose academic/disciplinary background is 'education' and to those whose degrees are in linguistics, sociology, psychology, or women's studies; to people who are schoolteachers or university teachers, or administrators, and to those who are nurses, or who work in community centres or in adult vocational education, or are returning to study after a long time out of the workforce. The examples they give are varied, diverse, and sometimes at odds with each other. In a recent class, someone had been impressed by the research they had seen on television about genetic mapping; another mentioned some research that had gathered a number of older women's stories about their early lives; someone had been impressed by work on how men and women have different ways of talking; someone else had been impressed by some action research they had participated in as a technical college instructor.

What are we to make of these answers? And why start in this way – asking people in the class or at a seminar what *they* happen to think is a good piece of research – when it is my task to teach them about research? Is this setting them up to show them that they do not really know what good research is? Or, alternatively, am I suggesting they already know what good research is, that anyone is entitled to decide for themselves? What can I, or they, make of the quite different and often apparently contradictory types of answers people give to this question?

When I begin in this way, it is not because I believe everyone is already an expert on the issue of good research, that they have nothing to learn; but nor is it about showing that they have somehow got it wrong, that they do not know what they are on about. Rather, I think that this initial snapshot of the ideas and values people bring to discussions about education research sets up something important about what type of a 'thing' this research activity is – at least in a field like education.

The first thing that can be said in relation to my starting point is that the instruction 'give me an example of a piece of good research you've come across' is a *meaningful* one. Whether or not they can explicate their reasons, in giving me examples people show that they have some criteria by which they decide what counts as 'research', and some further criteria by which they judge some research as 'good'. Moreover the question is meaningful both to those who have spent time studying research and research methodology and *also to those who have not*. A second evident point is that people come up with very different actual examples of 'good research': their answers are diverse. What to some members of the class seems like an example of good research (gathering older women's stories, for example), to others can seem like second-rate research or as not 'research' at all.

A straw poll of how a varied audience of non-experts think about education research is one useful starting point for recognizing the context in which education research operates. This is not a field in which the quality of one's work is judged only by one's academic peers; neither is it a field in which the success of research is established in only one way (finding a cure; making a bomb). Public debates rage about what issues matter in education, and these mediate and are mediated by political decisions, funding, emphases in academic appointments. And politics and values are part of these debates: people have *different* views about whether a topic is important; whether an argument or finding is an 'advance'.

But neither are the examples of good research that people furnish simply free-floating expressions of personal preferences. Not everything counts as 'research'. When I ask people to say a bit more about why they chose their particular example of good research, three themes tend to recur. Sometimes people consciously choose all three; sometimes they emphasize only one or two of them. The three themes are:

1 that the research was *technically good*: it did something very systematically, was 'tight and convincing'; or was impressive in its design; was ingenious and creative in its methods;

2 that the research made a *contribution to knowledge*: that it established something that was not previously known in this way; for example, it proved something convincingly; or it showed something that changed our understanding of things; or it successfully put on the agenda a new

type of question or set of questions; it changed our way of looking at certain things;
3 That the research achieved *something that mattered* – either universally, or specifically to the person giving the example (for example, it had obvious benefits to health; or it disrupted racism; or it generated useful evidence about the value of one approach to a particular area of teaching compared with other approaches).

Judgements about education research involve judgements about research and about education. They commonly involve some consideration both of the methodological (how well it was done) and of the substance (what it achieved). At the heart of the fierce debates that rage currently about education research, both in the community and in the research literature, are attempts to make claims for particular criteria or particular standards in relation to both of these. The debates and disagreements in themselves are not signs of the impoverishment of education research, but of the kind of thing it is. In the next section, I want to argue this point further by taking some very popular (and to many, uncontentious) positions where people have tried to define 'what is good education research' in terms of a single particular criterion, and to show why I consider that these do not work. It is not, precisely, that these ideas, which have a lot of 'common sense' appeal, are wrong. It is more that they obfuscate, or that they try to tie up an answer by setting up one aspect of the broad agendas of education research as if it could adequately legislate for the whole. But the claims themselves are useful illustrations of some of the ways that judgements about good research in education are made, and allude to practices apparent in different contexts that will be discussed in the second part of this book.

Claim I: We can measure 'good education research' by its contribution to learning

A few years ago, the Director of the Australian Council for Education Research made this claim:

> The purpose of medical research is to create and disseminate knowledge and tools which can be used to improve human health ... The purpose of education research is to create and disseminate knowledge and tools which can be used to improve learning.
>   The improvement of learning is the objective that drives (or should drive) all education research.[2]

This statement of a criterion for good education research has a very powerful appeal. Who would possibly disagree that in education we should be trying, ultimately, to improve learning? It certainly has had an immediate appeal to people in classes I have taught – and you can see how it would appeal to politicians and the public. It seems straightforward, practical, getting to the heart of the matter, proposing a criterion which lends itself to clear measures of whether progress is being made. Needless to say, it accords nicely with the currently fashionable 'evidence-based' view of what should drive education, that I will discuss further shortly.

My concern about this statement is not that 'the improvement of learning' is an improper criterion, but about the consequences of treating it as the sole or ultimate criterion. My own work in education has mainly focused on inequalities and social change and its implications, so I am concerned about the way it works to narrow education to the type of individual operation one might test adequately in a laboratory. Here are some examples of the type of things it leaves out:

- Schools do not just teach students things, they select and sort and produce differentiated outcomes. We can improve all students' learning without changing the fact that in *relative* terms some will fail – and indeed some aspects of the current concerns about boys losing out relate to this: overall retention and achievement even for boys *has* improved over time – but in some respects their *relative* achievements and retention have declined (Yates 1997a; Arnot *et al.* 1999). The selecting and sorting are not just an accidental side issue of systems of schooling, or there would not be such fierce debates about forms of examination and university entry.

- In schools, students do not just learn the things that schools and teachers set out to teach them, and that are measured in their final exams – and this too affects their future. In my own recent long-itudinal research project, we followed young people from different backgrounds at four different schools from the ages of 12 to 18, and we found many examples of different values and aspirations and self-assessments that they learned at those different schools (Yates and McLeod 2000; Yates 2001b; McLeod and Yates 2003). For example, in two ordinary high schools, with demographically comparable student populations and comparable participation and higher school certificate results, and a broadly similar formal curriculum, we found that one school tended to produce students who were quite practical and vocationally oriented, and who saw their future as their own responsibility. When we interviewed these young people the year after they had finished school they were very much involved in their post-school courses or jobs, and planning what they would do over the next few years. At the same time, this school produced a strong sense of 'keeping up with the Joneses' and a considerable lack of sympathy with bullying, racism and the unemployed. At the other school, the young people at the end of school were as likely to be drop-outs as not: they were still 'finding themselves', not strongly career active. But this was also a school where the school leavers we interviewed expressed appreciation for what their teachers had done for them, in taking an interest in them as individuals and giving them second chances. It was a school that had developed in the students we interviewed a general sensitivity to and acceptance of difference, values where they would speak up about racism even after they left school. These two schools had had a short- and long-term effect on their students, but it was not a simple picture of the kind one could measure by the end of school statistics. This form of qualitative longitudinal study gives a rather different perspective on 'school effectiveness' than researchers who use that term or who work with a focus on 'learning' and medical models tend to think about. But it is researching effects that are a relevant part of assessing what schools are doing, both short and long term, to the people who go there.

- What counts as 'learning' (that is, *what is to be learnt*) is a debated, contested issue. The Director's statement encourages us to treat the end-point as a given, and suggests we are mainly working with technical questions. A moment's thought or reading of the newspapers would show that this is not the case. In recent times, while there are certainly outbursts of concern about the effectiveness of learning or the standards being reached in a particular subject and in a particular country (the International Education Achievement (IEA) studies are designed to produce just such a reaction), there has been equal attention to concerns about what young people should be learning today: How much do they need to study contemporary culture as well as older literature? Given the pace of technological change and change in the form of work, what are the learning foundations for entry to work in the future? What story of the nation, the globe, social values is to be approved for the compulsory years of schooling?
- In relation to technical, vocational and professional education, while some issues are rightly about 'learning' (how to promote competency, for example, or how to develop 'new workers' with the right dispositions to be flexible, self-disciplining, lifelong workers (Chappell *et al.* 2003); there are many equally pressing questions about the wide-ranging effects of different ways of providing education and training (the relationship between certain forms of certification and what pay and conditions can be claimed, for example).

The idea that good education research must be directed to 'improvement of learning', just like other attempts to insist that it must be directed to 'effectiveness' or 'employability' or 'developing every child's potential', is an attempt to define and restrict what can count as education research, whereas the field of education itself comprises a broad arena of practices, institutions and problems. It is possible, and observably so, for governments or universities or education departments or funding systems to make a political decision that at a particular time and context only certain ways of addressing education problems will be eligible for funding, but this is not the same as establishing that, in principle, only certain problems are part of the agenda. The latter statement appears to be making a claim about the scope of the field of education research, but is in fact making a claim for particular agendas of research or kinds of research within the field relative to other kinds. The analogy to medical research is a common vehicle used in such arguments about education research and what it should be doing, and I will return to that shortly.

Claim 2: Good education research must make sense to/be usable by teachers (or instructors or parents or the lay reader)

A different starting point in many debates about education research begins not with what good research does, and what topic it should be directed to, but by talking about why much education research is *not* good. Some of the tropes of this discussion are widely shared: the problem with education research is that it is irrelevant, too academic, poor quality, jargon ridden. It is not producing new knowledge that speaks to teachers or instructors. It is not useful.

All of these are salutary comments. They direct our attention to what sort of a field this is: a field that is not simply characterized by some abstract search for knowledge but a field of practice where different players have their own sense of what is needed or desirable. These comments air the questions of how, in this particular arena, we are going to judge traditional research issues such as 'significance of outcomes', 'contribution to knowledge'. These are good questions, but Part 2 will try to show that they are not at all straightforward, and are given quite different enacted meanings in different parts of the education arena.

Taking the 'usability' criterion first, most people are aware that the questions and knowledge relevant to a teacher or instructor interacting with their class are not identical with those of a school administrator or a system policy maker. To some extent then, the claim about how too little of the research seems to speak to practitioners is a complaint about the relative funding and attention given to large-scale concerns rather than small-scale ones, or to the interests of some practitioners in the field (policy makers and administrators) rather than others (classroom practitioners).

Alternatively, the claim here might be seen as speaking from one position within a range of paradigm differences and points at issue in the field of research itself: how much of what happens to participants in an education system is a result of large resource allocations, accountability systems and other processes and checks that can be instituted at system level; how much is it explicable by social changes and movements and relationships beyond the field itself (processes perhaps not immediately accessible at a 'common-sense' level); how much is it revealed by laboratory-based experiments on the mechanics of cognitive processes; and how much are outcomes essentially produced by what happens in particular and complex relationships between teachers and learners? Some of these paradigms claim that 'useful' knowledge about teaching/ learning process can begin with serious research on basic mechanisms that are later applied in ways that can be used by teachers (or used to manage teachers); others say that real insights are only found in research that works in real-life contexts with the collaboration of the teachers.

Now consider the criterion that good research must, at least, 'make sense' to a broad class of readers, that research that is jargon-ridden and 'too academic' is poor, and helps account for the poor reputation of research in this field. Later in this book, I illustrate two different dimensions of why this accusation might be less transparent than it seems (which is not to say that it is never warranted). Firstly, personal testimonies from practitioners about what they find meaningful and useful indicate considerable *diversity* in this (see Chapter 7). Some teachers choose to do doctorates on formal and jargon-laden academic themes, and later claim that these areas of intellectual interest have been relevant to their own practices, while other teachers have little time for research which takes the forms necessary if it is to be deemed respectably technically 'valid' as research. Some practitioners look for research to provide new ideas rather than ways to do it; others are critical of research not directly framed to the latter ends. And some ideas which once were the jargon of a few researchers can eventually enter the 'common sense' of a wide range of practitioners or even the broader domain of public discourse.

Equally importantly, university-based researchers do not simply choose idiosyncratically to conduct and write research in ways that practitioners dismiss as academic: it is frequently a requirement of how they must operate if they are to gain a doctorate, hold down a university job, win money to do research. The specific ways that 'contribution to knowledge' or 'significance' are judged in contexts discussed in Chapters 3, 4 and 5 (the thesis, publishing in refereed journals, winning competitive research grants) force choices that may well compromise the achievement of a researcher in relation to these same criteria as judged in the contexts discussed in Chapters 6 and 7 (commissioned research; schools, teachers and other practitioners). Some of the tensions here are likely to be exacerbated by the movement to 'evidence-based' policy-making and its corollary of favouring for funding only the research that meets 'scientific' standards of design, particularly large controlled trials and comparisons. This latter direction of course draws on another widely held common-sense notion of what good education research needs to look like, and that is the next claim I want to consider.

Claim 3: Quality education research must be scientifically-based research

In the USA, a number of federal initiatives since the late 1990s have been enacting in legislation the requirement that research funding for education be 'scientifically-based': that only SBR (scientifically-based research) designs be eligible for federal funding, and only initiatives based on such research be eligible for the billions of dollars of federal aid. Subsequently, the Education Sciences Reform Act (2002) was passed, creating a new Institute of Education Sciences to replace the previously named Office of Education Research and Improvement in order to 'advance the field of education research, making it more rigorous in support of evidence-based education'. It specifically aims to promote 'more rigorous' and more focused randomized trials, and other effectiveness studies, and to circulate the results of such research evaluation and review through mechanisms such as its 'What Works Clearinghouse'.[3]

In other countries too, there are some parallel moves to encourage a research organization and set of criteria that attempt rigorously to review the state of knowledge on a particular area, and fund only projects that meet standards of rigorous research design to take this further. In the UK, for example, the Department for Education and Skills (DfES) works in collaboration with the National Foundation for Education Research (NFER) and the EPPI Centre (the Evidence for Policy and Practice Information and Co-ordinating Centre of the Institute of Education, University of London) to produce a database on current education research in the UK (CERUK).[4] The EPPI Centre's publicity emphasizes its 'systematic' approach to reviews and research appraisal, in contrast to 'traditional literature reviews' and suchlike. *Systematic* reviews 'use explicit methods to identify what can reliably be said on the basis of these studies'.

These moves are different from the longstanding practices of having a range of 'experts' in a field assess the quality of work, as discussed in Chapters 4 and 5. The particular developments here are moving to pre-scribe particular technical qualities that research must meet to be considered legitimate.

The case in favour of such a move is heard repeatedly across national contexts and different arenas. Like the ACER Director's argument earlier, the arguments make lavish use of analogies with medical research (its immensely greater achievements compared with education; its much higher funding; its higher public reputation), and promote an approach that elevates controlled comparison as the basis for rigorous knowledge.

Here is one version of the case that indicates the ready appeal of this movement to improve education research by making it operate more like research that has been successful in other areas:

> This process [of Scientifically Based Research] could create the kind of progressive, systematic improvement over time that has characterized successful parts of our economy and society throughout the 20th century, in fields such as medicine, agriculture, transportation, and technology. In each of these fields, processes of development, rigorous evaluation, and dissemination have produced a pace of innovation and improvement that is unprecedented in history. ... Yet education has failed to embrace this dynamic, and as a result, education moves from fad to fad. Education practice does change over time, but the change process more resembles the pendulum swings of taste characteristic of art or fashion (think hemlines) rather than the progressive improvements characteristic of science and technology. ... If Rip Van Winkle had been a physician, a farmer, or an engineer, he would be unemployable if he awoke today. If he had been a good elementary school teacher in the 19th century, he would probably be a good elementary school teacher today.
>
> (Slavin 2002: 16)

At the heart of a wide range of research is the attempt to build in some systematic way on what has gone before, and there is an intuitive appeal to current moves to try to pull together more systematically and on a larger scale what research has so far established, especially given that such moves have been accompanied by increased government funding for education research. The current debates in the education research community about the moves are also of interest because they make explicit some of the implicit benchmarks that are widely held about good research, particularly the appeal to medical breakthroughs, and attempt to set down what it would mean to do similar quality research in education. But therein lies the problem: what, precisely, is the 'scientific' characteristic of research of those fields that have made widely-recognized 'research' breakthroughs? What would it mean to do this in education? And how appropriate is it to take such an approach as the single benchmark for good research in education?

The first point to notice is that the move to prescribe certain forms of 'scientific' research as the benchmark for good research in education, is not one that has been reached by a developing consensus within the research community, but one that comes into being only because much of the education research community has apparently come to different conclusions, and has developed directions that are not sufficiently science-like. In the UK, for example, the debate sparked by David Hargreaves and James Tooley (Hargreaves 1996; Ball and Gewirtz 1997;

Tooley 1998, 2001) in the late 1990s was that the research community itself had lost its way, that 'peer-reviewed' journals were accepting research articles that do not meet good standards of research (as defined by Tooley).

In the USA, developments were driven by decision making in the political sphere. For example, the 1998 legislation to allocate a large sum of money for school reform on the condition that funds were allocated only to models 'proven' in terms of experimental-control comparisons on standards-based measures, was an initiative of two congressmen (Slavin 2002). The subsequent and much cited 'No Child Left Behind' Act (2001) mentioned 'scientifically-based research' 110 times, defining this as 'rigorous, systematic and objective procedures to obtain valid knowledge' which includes research 'that is evaluated using experimental or quasi-experimental designs', preferably with random assignment (Slavin 2002). But this particular operationalization of what it meant to do 'scientific' research *preceded* the commissioning of a report by scientific experts on what they thought doing 'scientific' research entailed (the report on *Scientific Principles in Education Research* produced by a sub-committee of the National Academies of Sciences, of Engineering and of Medicine) (Feuer 2002 *et al.*). And, despite the legislative intent to fund only scientifically-based initiatives (SBR), Slavin, an advocate of the new directions, notes that the bulk of the federal money on school reform initially at least has gone to approaches that do not in fact meet high standards for evidence-based approaches, partly because so much exist-ing research does not fit the technical form required, and partly because 'state officials who review CSR [Comprehensive School Reform] propo-sals still have broad discretion' (Slavin 2002: 16) – that is, they may have a different way of judging what they think is quality research.

So what does good 'scientifically-based' research look like?[5] In Acts like 'No Child Left Behind', and in bodies associated with the US Institute of Education Sciences and the UK EPPI Centre, it means research that has a particular methodological form: research that looks like an experiment or a quasi-experiment or clinical trial because it uses careful controlled com-parisons. Only such research is deemed 'valid' or 'proven' and only such research is taken account of when panels are commissioned to review research in particular areas of education to identify what is 'known' and 'not known'. Yet when scientific experts are asked to say what it means to be scientific, it appears that the issue is not nearly so clear cut.

According to the report by scientific experts from the National Aca-demies in the USA, 'scientific' research describes a 'culture of inquiry'. It involves certain norms or principles, and self-monitoring by the research community. It does not involve 'an algorithm, checklist, or how-to guide' (Feuer *et al.* 2002: 7). The report lists the norms or principles shared by 'all sciences' as follows:

- Pose significant questions that can be investigated empirically,
- Link research to relevant theory,
- Use methods that permit direct investigation of the questions,
- Provide a coherent and explicit chain of reasoning,
- Yield findings that replicate and generalize across studies, and
- Disclose research data and methods to enable and encourage professional scrutiny and critique.

And even here it qualifies its list by noting that it 'is very unlikely that any one study would possess all of these qualities although a successful programme of research is likely to embody all of them' (Feuer *et al.* 2002: 7).

There is nothing in this list to declare that only controlled comparison studies measure up to these principles, and it is at least arguable that all streams of education research that participate in the culture of peer-reviewed journals do work with these norms, depending on how one defines 'replicate and generalize'. My argument, discussed further in Chapter 4, would be that even postmodern articles could be interpreted as meeting these standards in that they are accepted for publication only if they are seen as linking to and building on some existing lines of this developing body of theory and empirical analysis.

Nevertheless, scientifically-based research in education *is* normally interpreted as 'random or matched controlled studies', and the case where Feuer, Towne and Shavelson explain what these principles look like for education helps to show why this is the case. In particular, the argument constantly blurs and shifts between (a) a consideration of how scientists in other fields operate; (b) what *people* say about *the reputation* of education research; and (c) the problem of whether it is the education research 'peer' community itself, outside research experts such as the National Academy, politicians, or people in general who are relevant judges of good practice here. I now want to look a bit more closely at what types of appeal are being made, what source of legitimation the arguments refer to at different points.

Scientific culture vs technical standards for methodology

The National Research Council (NRC) report emphasizes that scientific method is not a single set of methodological techniques as are defined in the earlier legislation. For one thing, scientific method requires attention to and methods appropriate to the *contextual specificity* of the phenomenon being investigated: 'No method is good, bad, scientific, or unscientific in itself. Rather, it is the appropriate application of method to a particular problem that enables judgments about scientific quality' (Feuer *et al.* 2002: 8).

The specificity of education as a field is drawn on heavily by critics of the imposition of new standards for what 'valid' research is, and here the authors and advocates of the case for a 'scientific' approach in education appear to share at least some of the starting points of such critics. They say, for example, 'many have argued – and we agree – that the complexities of education are not analogous to the physiology of disease and thus the expectation that any single intervention could adequately "cure" an education "ill" is misplaced' (ibid. 2002: 12). But the authors bury this particular point in a footnote, and, having noted it, retreat immediately from their own opinion as experts, to the court of appeal of what politicians and the community think: 'We include the reference here as an illustration of public perceptions and policy rhetoric; we do not intend to take on the underlying substantive issues' (Feuer *et al.* 2002: 12, fn 14).

Nevertheless, among education researchers and in the practitioner community there is an ongoing debate about the implications of the *specific* nature of education for methodological approach (for example, Loughran 1999; Lagemann 2000; Rist 2000; Berliner 2002; Edwards 2002; Erickson and Gutierrez 2002). Among the reasons for the widespread shift in the late 1970s and beyond to qualitative and case-study based work was that this seemed to address better the complexity of the real-life classroom situation, and that it is 'methodolatory' to insist on laboratory-based or artificially simplified experimental programmes that may well generalize and build on themselves in other similar laboratory or other artificially simplified contexts, but that are not 'generalizable' in real-world settings. Others, such as Berliner (2002), point to a range of empirical evidence from past research and education reform that would question a faith in quasi-experimentalism and controlled comparative trials as a definitive answer:

- Findings do not stay stable over time (for example, the starting point assumptions of researchers about gender or race in the late twentieth century are different from those of 'good research' done earlier in the century);
- Attempts to replicate a programme of research have frequently produced inconsistent results;
- Within broad 'scientific' findings about education there are frequently many individual classrooms or schools that show directions of effect in confounding directions, that is, context and specificity appear to be of as much interest as the 'general' pattern.

There are practical and ethical problems too as to whether or how far education research can replicate controlled methods, even if it wanted to. Some of the problems are described by one of the enthusiasts for these new standards, recounting his own difficulties in setting up research that is appropriately controlled. In one case he found, not surprisingly, that schools were not prepared to participate in a study where they might be randomly assigned to experimental or control groups – even though they were being offered $30,000 to participate. The researchers had to increase these incentives enormously before schools would participate, meaning that the study became so expensive that it was very unlikely ever to be replicated (Slavin 2002: 18).

Another point emphasized in the NRC report (a report produced by Academies with experts from science, engineering and medicine) was that the scientific work is not guaranteed by the techniques used but by the peer scrutiny that takes place by the members of *the research community in that field*, and that this is what makes possible 'disciplined, creative and open-minded thinking' and produces researchers who 'can engage differing perspectives and explanations in their work and consider alternative paradigms'. However, in the case of education, this soon produces a circular problem for these experts: taking peer scrutiny as the court of judgement appears to be acceptable only if the community of peers is already acceptable. Once again, the scientific experts retreat and appeal to the fact that 'education research is *perceived* to be of low quality', not by themselves (that is, they decline to make a pronouncement on this matter), but by 'lawmakers', community and some education researchers. This perception is used to justify certain standards of method or structure being imposed as the criteria of good quality.

Analogies and courts of appeal

Medical research is repeatedly invoked in arguments about education research, usually in ways reminiscent of the old song, sung by Rex Harrison as Professor Henry Higgins in *My Fair Lady*, 'Why can't a woman be more like a man?' Why can't education research have the prestige, the obvious history of progress of medical research? Why can't it attract the same money and produce an aura of awe and expertise? Why can't it produce the same outcomes and breakthroughs? Why can't it look the same?

One approach in these debates has been to keep exploring the analogy until you find the illustration that will support the direction you wish to argue for in education. On the one hand, Robert Slavin, quoted earlier, argues that the take-up of scientific methods in medical research produced 'a pace of innovation and improvement that is unprecedented in history' and tenders a Rip Van Winkle contrast to show how little teachers have been advanced compared with doctors (Slavin 2002: 16). In riposte, Frederick Erickson and Kris Gutierrez counter with the example of thalidomide:

> We are concerned that premature conclusions about 'what works' in the
> short term without careful consideration of side effects that may appear

downstream, can provide false warrants for the education equivalent of thalidomide. That was a medical treatment that was shown scientifically (i.e. by means of randomized trials) to have clear positive effects. [...] What a tragic irony; thalidomide prevented morning sickness very effectively but it was also effective in causing deformities in the fetus growing in the mother's womb. The latter effects were only discovered after the babies were born, and it took years to trace the cause of the deformities back to the mothers' use of thalidomide. Will our current desperate attempts to discover 'what works' to raise standardized test scores in the short run have analogous effects on our children and teachers in school...?

(Erickson and Gutierrez 2002: 23)

Some use medical research to justify only experimental laboratory work or randomized clinical trials; others point to the way medicine itself has been impacted on by movements that bring in more complicated criteria, theories and forms of research to take account of doctor–patient relationships in new ways: for example, from the women's movement, from consumer rights, from cross-disciplinary developments in psychology, from studies of minorities and power.

What is interesting is why medical research is such a ubiquitous point of reference. The fact that breakthroughs have been made is undeniable, but, as the NCR expert report makes clear, this is only part of the story, even in medicine. Most of the arguments explicitly use medicine to associate arguments about method and design quality with arguments about status and money. But if the phenomenon is not the same, there is no guarantee that replicating the methods will have such an effect – either that it will produce similar outcomes or that, even if it did, it would acquire the same prestige or attract the same funding. *Every* aspect of education (training, salaries, conditions of practitioners and so on) is funded differently from medicine – not just research. And funding is committed or not committed (both by governments and by individuals) for many reasons in addition to a rational calculation that it will produce particular outcome effects. To give a simple example of this, in the mid-1990s state government elections in Australia were dominated by politicians promising that they could spend less on schools than they were currently doing. State premiers scrutinized each other's education funding and it was a matter of shame and a task for reform to be spending the most per head. Efficiency and small government rather than education spending were the dominant discourses. After some period of this and some unexpected losses by parties that had most successfully run with this platform, the discourse has changed. In more recent elections, politicians compete to show how much they care about education, including how much they are prepared to spend on it. In an election campaign in 2003, one party began with material promising that certain of its proposed education reforms would be 'cost neutral' but removed this part of the boast from its election material as the campaign progressed[6]. Presumably, the party's polling had told them that this boast about restrained spending on education was not helping them seem attractive to the voters.

It is also interesting how the 'poor reputation' of education research is frequently used as a court of appeal that establishes its low quality, rather than as something that needs to be investigated and unpacked. The issue of what produces 'reputation' is a far more complex matter than most of the debates assume, and an issue that would require some attention to structures, communication, multiple demands and how fields of research are or are not made visible.

Like hemlines?

We have seen that currently, in a number of countries, governments, research offices and organizations, and at least some researchers are getting excited about the potential for education research to be made more rigorous and systematic and to produce the results and transformations that have been apparent in other fields. In the passages above, I have focused particularly on the case being made by the advocates of such an approach, with some briefer references to other parts of this debate. Here is a slightly more extended case by two researchers, David Hamilton and Malcolm Parlett, against the controlled evaluations and trials that are increasingly favoured:

> The most common form of agricultural–botany type evaluation is presented as an assessment of the effectiveness of an innovation by examining whether or not it has reached required standards on prespecified criteria. Students – rather like plant crops – are given pre-tests (the seedlings are weighed or measured) and then submitted to different experiences (treatment conditions). Subsequently, after a period of time, their attainment (growth or yield) is measured to indicate the relative efficiency of the methods (fertilizers) used. Studies of this kind are designed to yield data of one particular type, i.e. 'objective' numerical data that permit statistical analyses. Isolated variables like IQ, social class, test scores, personality profiles and attitude ratings are codified and processed to indicate the efficiency of new curricula, media or methods.
>
> Recently, however, there has been increasing resistance to evaluations of this type. The more notable shortcomings may be summarized as follows:
>
> 1 Education situations are characterised by numerous relevant parameters. Within the terms of the agricultural–botany paradigm these must be randomised using very large samples; or otherwise strictly controlled. The former approach entails a major data-collection

exercise and is expensive in time and resources. . . . The latter procedure – of strict control – is rarely followed. . . . is dubious ethically,
but also leads to gross administrative and personal inconvenience.
[And even if it was used] rarely can 'tidy' results be generalised to an
'untidy' reality. Whichever approach is used, there is a tendency for
the investigator to think in terms of 'parameters' and 'factors' rather
than 'individuals' and 'institutions'. Again, this divorces the study
from the real world.

2   Before-and-after research designs assume that innovatory programmes undergo little or no change during the period of study. This
built-in premise is rarely upheld in practice. . . .

3   . . . the concentration on seeking quantitative information by objective means can lead to neglect of other data, perhaps more salient to
the innovation, but which are disregarded as 'subjective', 'anecdotal'
or 'impressionistic'. However, the evaluator is likely to be forced to
utilise information of this sort if he is satisfactorily to explain his
findings, weight their importance and place them in context.

4   . . . tends to be insensitive to local perturbations and unusual effects . . .

5   Finally, this type of evaluation often fails to articulate with the varied
concerns and questions of participants, sponsors and other interested
parties. . . . diverts attention away from questions of education practice
towards more centralised bureaucratic concerns.

(Hamilton *et al.* 1977: 7–9)

One reason I have chosen to report this particular argument by Hamilton
and Parlett at some length is that although published in 1977, it can be
read as a rejoinder to the case for concentrating on large controlled trials
that are now being treated as such an exciting new discovery. Some of
the current debates imply that the main reason education research has
not been making progress is that it has not been bright enough to think
about trying to be systematic and to do big studies. The sub-text is that
the field had not been able to get its act together, has not been able to
recognize what might be possible – that no one had previously come up
with the idea that concentrating on big scientific studies would be a good
thing. But reading the history of debates about research suggests something other than either ignorance or simple 'fads' is at work.

I have reported these arguments about scientifically-based research
and the counter-arguments in favour of qualitative and anthropological
styles of research not because I think the latter disposes of the former (or
vice versa), or that there is no place for large controlled studies, but
because I think attention to the different arguments and location of
arguments helps to show what debates about education research look
like. Education research might look like 'fads' or 'changing fashion in
hemlines' to use Slavin's words, but there is some logic in why different
types of arguments keep recurring rather than one disposing of the other
once and for all.

One obvious issue is that there are different end-point users for the research, and what some want to know differs from what others want to know – with implications for methodology and also for what a research design and a research publication should look like. Another is that the phenomenon itself has different conditions at different times. Parlett and Hamilton were writing to contexts where decentralized curriculum was common and school-based innovation was favoured. Slavin and others are writing in a context where governments are attempting to bring more centralized control and steering of what happens in the research community generally, not just in education. It is *not* the same as simply finding the mechanism that causes a disease.

Definitions and enactments

Many of those who participate in debates about education research, even where they disagree strongly about the importance of different types of work, allow that there is at least some place for large data-gathering studies that attempt to do some controlled comparison, and some place for other kinds of work – interpretive, philosophical, case study (though there is less agreement about this in the case of post-structuralist work and in arguments by post-structural researchers). But the debates about the moves to tie federal government funding to one particular form of work, even if they formally acknowledge that there is room for a range of other styles of research, are heated because funding rules can begin to define in practice what is able to be done as research, and to define what is counted as legitimate well beyond the context in which it is initially enacted.

Even in the account of the National Academies, this difficulty is apparent. Feuer *et al.* are clear that scientific education research is *not* to be read as being the only legitimate form of education research: 'we do not intend to minimize the significance of humanistic, historic, philosophical and other non-scientific forms of study in education' (Feuer *et al.* 2002: 5). But there is an ongoing slippage in how both the specialists and the broader community react if important bodies decide that only certain *methodologies* will be considered 'scientific' or 'valid'.

Context and timeliness as issues in education debates

Examining recent debates about the quality of education research draws us into issues about the scope of the field, the questions and audiences (or courts of appeal) that are considered important, and about what analogies and types of arguments carry weight for whatever reason. They draw attention to issues of context in what is being said and done, context both in the sense of historical context – what matters at this time – and in the sense of the particular and broader setting of the discussion. Here, using some further examples from my own involvements in research, I want to draw together a number of the themes that have been flagged in the preceding discussion as part of the 'thing' that makes up education research.

1   The *phenomenon under study* is not static, whether it is about students, teachers, schools, vocational training, higher education. One of the reasons Julie McLeod and I began the 12 to 18 Project was to investigate how teenagers see themselves, schooling and their future *today*. These young people have grown up with different cultural norms from their parents; different kinds of parents, technological artefacts, kinds of experience, school curriculum policies, even different words in the language. Research done on their parents' generation when that generation was at school does not necessarily hold today in terms of who girls or boys are, what motivates them, what would best engage their interests in learning, or what trajectory they are following or need to follow to end up with a good job or life.

Similarly consider the old single-sex versus co-education debate. It is highly debatable whether 'single-sex' or 'co-education' is the same phenomenon where it exists now as it was in the 1950s. We can choose to see co-education as an abstracted 'factor', where research done several decades ago can give us a foundation for what to do today. But we can choose to see it as something that is, at least potentially, done differently and experienced differently according to what purposes teachers have in mind, how they actually set things up, what the girls or boys and their parents *believe* about it, even what the media says about whether or not it is a 'good thing' – and that might need some new research rather than taking old research on trust.

2   The range of *questions* thought to be worth answering are not static, though some questions do endure. At the beginnings of national state education systems, the major issue was often how to get good attendance in schools, and what types of pressure to put on families to achieve this. When nations become concerned about their international competitiveness, the emphasis turns to achievement comparisons of various kinds. At some times, and in some countries, there is a particular interest in identifying different types of aptitude and providing appropriately for different types of students; at other times and in other countries, levels of basic achievement, or mass outcomes, are the focus of concern. In vocational education, the concern has sometimes been with how to train effectively for existing jobs; currently, there is a concern about how to educate in a way that will allow people to go on to do other types of jobs

in the future. Sometimes the key interest has been how to operate a system in a way that costs less. But some questions, of course, are more enduring ones. What is an appropriate way to develop mathematical or scientific or literacy knowledge and skills? What is the relationship between particular ways of teaching and particular learning outcomes?

3 The *material support to do or publish research* changes, and along with it there are different *opportunities and pressures* in relation to doing particular types of research. In Australia, in the 1970s, the government made available money for school-based partnership research, both through Innovations funding, and through its Disadvantaged Schools Program. This effectively encouraged styles of research that were local, action-oriented and collaborative. Now major funding primarily comes through national competitive grants programmes or through consultancies to state and commonwealth authorities or national associations in different fields of education. The former encourages research that is seen to be big: to have national and preferably international impact. The latter encourages research that is policy oriented.

This changing funding and political context affects not just methodology and the types of research that seem desirable, but the substantive agendas of that research and its presentation. In the 1970s, in both Australia and the UK, attention to 'innovation' was encouraged, and attention to disadvantage or inequality was also encouraged. In the 1980s and 1990s, disadvantage went very much out of favour, and politicians were enthralled by 'effectiveness'. If you wanted to get your research funded and listened to, it needed to be couched more in terms of winners and effectiveness, and less in terms of elucidating the problems that losers were facing. One side effect of this was that sociologists, in danger of being removed from education faculties because they were seen as critical and not contributing to good teaching practice, began to rebadge themselves as 'policy researchers'. Similar changes affect publishing and readership. In Australia, in the 1980s, books on girls and gender were selling well; now they are not.

4 Changing *social agendas and knowledge* also directly affect the research field and what counts as adequate or good research in terms of a thesis, or a journal article, or a book. When I did my Masters degree in Bristol in the mid-1970s, Paul Willis came and gave a talk on the study he was doing in Birmingham, which later became the book *Learning to Labour*. The advertised title of his talk was something like 'An education ethnography of youth, and the reproduction of class', and what I remember from the discussion was Miriam David giving Paul Willis a hard time for advertising his talk as being about youth (or young people), when in fact his research was solely about boys. (In the end of course, Willis did take account of this and his book is now remembered as much for its con-

tribution to understanding working-class masculinity as to class reproduction, the tradition where he began.)

Up to about the mid-1970s, it was quite legitimate for researchers to do
research on all-male samples and to write about it as if it included
everyone (Kohlberg, on moral thinking, was another well-known
example, which spawned Carol Gilligan's body of work to ascertain if the
hierarchy looked the same if you took girls and women as your starting
point). And the same thing applied to a lot of quantitative research on all
sorts of topics published before the 1970s. Another way of putting this is
that in that earlier period, across a whole range of different methodologies (quantitative and qualitative), research could be judged as good
research without having any fine attention or sensitivity to gender – it
was not picked out as an essential factor for investigation. Today, however, if you propose an education study and do not include gender as
something you will mark or note, there is a reasonable chance your
research will be seen as inadequate. Note that this does not mean that
you have to be compellingly interested in gender, or to *find* that gender is
an important differentiating feature in a particular area of investigation,
but you are expected to be alert to the possibility that it may be, and to
take account of this in your methodological design. This is not about
whether you, yourself are particularly interested in gender issues: it is a
sign that debates about this have become socially prominent in relation
to debates about young people, and about what is happening in education. Whether you are dealing with quantitative research and factor
analysis, or interpretive, case-study work, an awareness of gender as a
possible aspect differentiating or influencing the phenomenon you are
studying is expected. (However, empirically, one would have to say there
seems to be no similar imperative to be required to take account of the
theories and previous research that people who have worked on gender
issues have produced!)

What good research looks like – reflecting on the debates

Looking at these debates, and taking education research as an arena, I
hope it will be apparent why I think we are not dealing with something
as simple and straightforward as a cure for cancer. It may indeed help to
make progress if we devote greater resources to research, call for larger
studies that attempt to pull together expertise and build on it, do more
'rigorous' research, replicate what seems to help progress in finding the
building blocks for a cure for cancer. But in education we also have a
field whose end-point parameters and questions are much more diverse,
whose setting and agendas change. It is a field where an individual
student (or teacher or administrator) is located in a bigger setting where

the culture and the things they are exposed to change; where parents' and teachers' thinking about what they are trying to achieve changes; where policies are introduced and change each time there is an election, often for reasons relatively unrelated to technical research results on 'effectiveness' and at least as related to how modes of doing education fit or conflict with the prevailing political philosophy of the day. Different participants have different demands on what types of research knowledge about education they need, and how this should be delivered. Researchers are engaged in debates both about what is possible and about what is desirable and whose interests should be served. Researchers are also positioned within decisions, processes, structures created by others, decisions that directly and indirectly define good research and the consequences for researchers of taking certain research paths rather than others.

2

History, fashion and academic research in education

or, why hasn't education research discovered the magic bullet on literacy?
and why did a lot of gender researchers go off into the airy-fairy realms of postmodernism?

One reason medical research is so favoured as the benchmark for research activity (apart from its prestige and the fact that so many governments and corporations are willing to throw large amounts of money at it) is that, whatever the arcane debates that medical researchers may be pursuing in laboratories and academic journals, their activity overall does seem, to the untutored eye, to be making progress. Against this backdrop, education researchers seem to suffer a double burden. More of their theories and debates reach the public and are scrutinized along the way, not just by peers with similar expertise in that area of research but by bureaucrats, politicians and the wider community. And the question of whether this research activity has produced 'progress' seems as much to throw into question the value of what education researchers do, as it does to underwrite the value of this activity. In this chapter I take two examples of areas in which there has been a large body of education research by academic researchers, to discuss the shape of changes in them over time and to illustrate further some issues about the field of practice that constitutes education research discussed in the previous chapter.

The areas I have chosen for discussion are research on reading, and research on gender and schooling. I have selected these two examples because they highlight issues that are often at the heart of attacks on education research as a quality activity: respectively, that it is not making progress or that it is not relevant or rigorous. In both cases, what I want to suggest is that the research *is* engaging with its field or object of enquiry, *is* making a contribution to the practices of that field, but that the field and object of enquiry changes, as does the point of *what is worth doing as research at particular times*. This discussion is not an attempt to examine, far less to defend, each piece of research in those fields. It is an attempt to show something of the logic of how and why research in a particular area moves its direction over time, and why the matter of reputation or perception of quality in relation to education research needs to be treated with some caution.

I have chosen research on reading, an area in which I am not an insider of the research community, because it relates to the problem that research findings and practices in education often seem to go in swings or cycles rather than to be evidently on a trajectory of cumulative progress. If research was doing its work, why would practices and theories go back and forth, rather than build? In this core area of activity, such swings are found in debates about phonics versus whole language, and experimental versus interpretive methodologies. We could equally take as examples swings in other areas, on such perennial education topics as learning multiplication tables versus conceptualizing mathematically; academically selective schools versus comprehensive ones; co-education versus single-sex grouping and many more. All are areas which have seen movements of emphasis in 'what research shows' not just in a single direction, but in opposing directions, including apparent reversals in the story of the relative outcomes of adopting one or other approach.

My second example is taken from a field I have worked in, gender research, and is chosen to discuss the problem that certain types of research approach seem, to outsiders, to be sensible and high quality, and others do not; some research seems rigorous, other research seems tendentious; some seems broadly convincing, other work seems to fly in the face of common sense. I will trace some moves in the types of questions and theories researchers, including myself, took up and try to show something of the logic of this – both the technical logic in the sense of building on what was already known; and the contextual logic in relation both to the state of the reform enterprise at a particular point, and also to the ways academic research is judged.

The reading wars: why hasn't education research established the magic bullet on literacy?

In our first editorial, we boldly stated that the paradigm debate was over as far as *Reading Research Quarterly* was concerned. As a result of this goal, we moved away from laboratory studies to a rich mix of articles that drew from rigorous quantitative and qualitative designs.

(Readance and Barone 2002: 369)

> The evidence-based methodological standards adopted by the Panel are essentially those normally used in research studies of the efficacy of interventions in psychological and medical research [. . .] Unfortunately, only a small fraction of the total reading research literature met the Panel's standards for use in the topic analyses.
>
> (from National Reading Panel reports on *Teaching children to read: An evidence-based assessment of the scientific research literature on reading and its implications for reading instruction*, quoted in Cunningham 2001)

> You have yourself acknowledged, in 1997 testimony before the House Committee on Education and the Workforce, that 'failure to learn to read adequately is much more likely among poor children, among nonwhite children, and among nonnative speakers of English' (Lyon, 1997:2). But of the fifty-nine studies on reading currently funded by the NICHD, virtually every one, with marginal exception, is on some aspect of phonological processing reading, including the supposed genetic, brain morphometric, eye movement and neuroimaging correlates. None are on the role that race, ethnicity, and socioeconomic stratification in America plays in denying children access to literacy.
>
> (Strauss 2001: 26)

If there is such a thing as 'core business' in schooling, literacy is certainly in there, and a huge amount of research and contending theories have been produced on this area over a very long period of time. Why, then, do we still have some illiteracy, and why does a new presidential administration in the USA announce as its mandated new approaches to this area some approaches that would fit very comfortably with those of 50 years, or even a century, earlier? Has the huge body of research in the meantime been a waste? Are the researchers simply not very bright, compared with medical researchers? My discussion of this is by no means a comprehensive one, and I write as an observer rather than an insider. My aim is to illustrate some issues of changing socio-political contexts and how it affects what researchers do and achieve, but, even more, what they are seen to have achieved and not achieved.

If education research, or rather, judgements about education research, really operated similarly to those in medical or scientific research, we might not be so quick to assume that research on reading and the teaching of reading has not made progress. Taking any of the specialist journals of the field, we could see much evidence of how (like science) the published contributions refer to and build on previous research, how they attempted to extend and refine previous work and to move to new approaches and theories to overcome limitations in existing approaches and theories. We could find progress of this kind both in studies attempting to take a cognitive and experimental approach to what reading is (for example, work on dyslexia), and in teacher-focused studies taking contextual and anthropological approaches to the classroom and building up insights into how teacher practices produced good out-comes for their students. We could find examples of practitioners and systems using this work to reform their practices.

But reading research is more often used as evidence of 'lack' in the education research community than of its achievements. For one thing, no schooling system appears to achieve 100 per cent literacy. For another, the research field is vigorously divided over such fundamentals as what literacy is, how it can be researched, and what teaching practices are effective in relation to it. And, capping this off, the topic is of per-ennial interest and highly visible to politicians, school administrators, teachers and parents. In this context, the fact that 100 years or more of research have not produced the equivalent of penicillin is, not surpris-ingly, taken as prima facie evidence that education research is not doing the job. However, each of the three issues mentioned above – outcomes; paradigm and territory disputes; and agendas, receptiveness and interests of the non-researchers in the area – are also illustrative of the specificity of this particular arena, and help to explain how research, research uses, and perceptions of research quality in education take the form they do.

Outcomes and achievements

> In 1995, for every dollar spent on education in the US, less than 1 cent
> went to research.
>
> (Lagemann 2000: 212)

The broad sense of what a research field is achieving, or how well it is making progress, is measured by visible improvements in outcomes: we (in affluent countries) live longer and recover from diseases that were once fatal; scientific research feeds new technology and enables forms of communication that were previously unimaginable; agricultural pro-ductivity is measurably enhanced. Of course there are also less progressive effects of all these processes: unemployment related to automation; iatrogenic and affluence-related illnesses and deaths; mad-cow disease and farmers in some countries starved of crops because they cannot afford the technologically developed and commercially protected new seeds; but these do not detract from a broad sense that we can *see* what such research can achieve. In the case of education research, the macro-judgements about what has been achieved conflate education *research* achievements with education *practice* achievements, that is with the outcomes of a complex set of policies, practices, personnel involve-ments and resourcing, and particularly with teacher education practice.

When George W. Bush was Governor of Texas, he used evidence of a decline in Texas scores on a particular literacy test to argue that the problem lay in the state's teacher training and its 'philosophical quagmire' about the best way to teach reading. But, as one critic points out, there is no evidence that those producing the poor results were the ones who had been exposed to such training, let alone were the fault of the research from which it might have drawn:

> In a state with an extreme teacher shortage and where as many as half the teachers in major urban districts are hired with emergency certification . . . many rural and less affluent school districts – districts with the highest number of at-risk students – hire individuals with 2 or 3 years of college as long-term subs (and so skirt the law that teachers must hold a bachelor's degree) [yet] there has been no accounting made to date of how many such teachers have been hired, what their assignments are, or how many of their students passed the third-grade TAAS in reading each year.
>
> (Dressman 1999: 23–4)

It is well understood that if you are poor or live in the wrong country you do not necessarily benefit from the achievements of medical research, but that is not taken as evidence that the research has not made progress (though it is used, quite appropriately, in arguments that too much medical research is devoted to exciting technological breakthroughs for a wealthy few). In education, however, the conflation of the two is less easily disentangled.

And there is a further complication in relation to literacy, and many other education enterprises: outcomes are not transparent. In terms of the measures of how a country or a state education system is doing, what it means to be a literate adult changes over time, and so do the measuring instruments, even in national testing programmes. In terms of parents, however, their perception of how their child is doing relates partly to whether the child has competency in expected areas, and partly to whether their child does what they themselves could do at that age, regardless of what other things and other world that child is now part of. I realize that this discussion is beginning to sound like an apologia for education, a charge that any criticisms of education and education research are mistaken, and this is not what I intend. My arguments here do not mean that it is not possible and appropriate to look for measures of where and whether particular approaches succeed and fail, or to have arguments about the quality of methodology of particular pieces of research design. Administrators and teachers have to make judgements about how to proceed, and education research is one potential and appropriate source of this judgement. But I am trying to draw attention to the fact that judgements about what has been achieved are not simple, straightforward 'objective' ones. They draw in emotional and psychological components, memories of one's own biography, political values about how citizens should be formed.

The issue of how broad outcome measures of reading achievement for a whole school population relate to research in reading then is complex, and it is one of the points of contention in the ongoing paradigm debates about research methodology.

Paradigm differences

'Paradigm' is a concept whose ubiquitous status in debates about research was generated by Thomas Kuhn's work on scientific research (Kuhn 1996). Kuhn's book, *The Structure of Scientific Revolutions*, originally published in 1962, ushered in a new way of looking at scientific activity, in which equal attention was paid not just to the obvious points at which a single experiment was done and carefully observed and controlled, but at the assumptions that would govern what counted as proof at that point, what factors needed to be controlled at that point, and whether, in the face of unpromising results, the theory and programme of research should be modified in minor ways or should be abandoned and replaced by a new programme. Paradigm was the word that described the amalgam of theories, assumptions, conscious and unconscious decisions within which scientists worked at a particular time, until they began to cease to make progress, at which time it might be replaced by quite a different theory (and paradigm) to give guidance as to what might be tested. At the time when he originally wrote this book, Kuhn specifically saw social science research as *not* having this form because it did not proceed with such internal paradigm agreement.

The disagreements quoted at the beginning of this section as to how reading research can make progress is a good illustration not just of the fact that there are opposing sets of assumptions at work, but of some of the logic of why these continue to battle rather than one knocking out the other and getting on with the job. Some people are focusing on what makes sense to teachers and others on what makes sense to administrators; some are focusing on achievement in international test scores, others on how to change the experience of those not doing so well; some come from backgrounds in psychological research and can see what the approaches of that discipline might offer, others come from anthropology or sociological training and believe in a different way of understanding how individuals learn and might learn better. In what follows, I am also simplifying this whole discussion as if there were only one central point of contention, whereas any of the methodology textbooks now show clearly the expanding differentiation of the field and points of divergence, but my concern is only to show that the nature of this field makes it understandable why opposing types of research, with different implications for practice, continue to find a place.

In the quotes that introduce this discussion of reading, we hear echoes of the debates about what counts as good research that I canvassed in Chapter 1. The National Reading Panel (NRP) report and the National Literacy Strategy in the UK (Wyse 2000) want to build up an approach by only taking account of evidence that is 'rigorous' in that sense of 'objective' and 'replicable' that is associated with the evidence-based policy movement. This tends to produce two main ways into the topic. One attempts to build basic knowledge about isolated mechanisms via experimentation and theory. The other attempts to gather reliable (valid, systematic) evidence evaluating the effects of interventions. Both are widely used forms of research in other fields, and well understood by policy makers and other readers.

On the other hand, the announcement by the *Reading Research Quarterly* (*RRQ*) editors that they believed the 'paradigm wars had been won' and that this meant moving *away from* laboratory-based research to a 'rich mix' reflected a different starting point, one that focused on the specificity of the problem and from that, a belief that the topic should not be artificially simplified or controlled, but that a range of methods were appropriate in trying to understand actual practices, classroom and social settings, and parameters and the outcomes these produced. This form of research had gained popularity because it spoke to many teachers and because it began from an attempt to understand the experiences and characteristics of those who were not doing well. Comparing the NRP report with the editorial discussion of criteria for good research on reading, we see approaches that not only use different methodologies and have different standards for rigorous research and good evidence, but that frequently focus on different measures of outcome success (short term versus long term; test-based versus broader competencies; overall success rates versus distribution of demographic groups).

The differences here are not like Kuhn's example of a scientific paradigm dispute and revolution (Newtonian to Einstein's physics for example), but ones that have a long history. Lagemann's history of education research in the USA discusses it in terms of the different legacies of two major figures. Thorndike trained as a psychologist and advocated the forms of scientific measurement as the form of reliable knowledge; Dewey also believed in scientific experimentation but in a way that moved its methods somewhat closer to anthropology or action research, believing that for education, the unit of research must be the whole school, his laboratory school, and look more like action research. In Australia, a long-standing history of different approaches to the field can be seen in the development of the psychology-based testing-oriented research institution, the Australian Council for Education Research (Connell 1980); compared with the legacy of other curriculum-oriented, humanistic and action-research-oriented traditions that were associated with high-profile teachers' associations, some journals and some education faculties (Hannan 1985; Bessant and Holbrook 1995). The different legacies that Lagemann discusses can be seen in ongoing differences among important education theorists and researchers as well as among the community in general as to whether the work of the teacher can best be approached as a set of skills or is more like a set of knowledge, abilities and deliberative engagements; and in arguments about whether teaching is more like being a mother or being a psychologist or being a Socrates or an F.R. Leavis.

In Kuhn's sense of paradigm, each approach has some potential to solve problems that the other approach cannot solve, but they are not simply complementary – particularly at a policy and administration level, they generate different approaches to how education should be seen, how it should be managed, and what types of research are of use. There is no reason to think that these differences will ever be decisively resolved.

One final irony on paradigm wars and the scientifically-based research movement is that the justification for instituting such an approach is to advance education research, to produce the high-powered, rigorous work and breakthroughs that have characterized other fields. Yet its enactment in relation to reading research has been to underwrite the forms of practice (phonics) that characterized the nineteenth-century schoolroom, as compared with the attention to ethnic, racial, class and gender diversity that has characterized many more recent approaches.

Slavin's point about Rip Van Winkle (Slavin 2002) was actually made to justify what a difference a more scientific approach would make, but in this field it would make Rip Van Winkle comfortable in ways that he would not have been in terms of the research approaches that the reading research scholarly journals had been developing. Additionally of course, we should note that in any case many more children are literate than 100 years ago – in this respect schools (and researchers) are succeeding.

Gender research: what does 'making progress' look like?

Research on reading has been a long-standing core arena of education research, one whose object of enquiry seems evident and which seems to lend itself well to the comparisons with 'scientific' research, even though, as I have argued, influences on and differences in the construction of what that object of enquiry is are not so widely understood. Research on gender and sex differences reveal even more clearly some of the complexities of research and research enquiry in the field of education. In this arena politics and values have been more evidently part of the construction of what counts at a particular time as a problem for education researchers. It is also a field where we can see, in a more compressed timescale, how research agendas build and change, both for individual researchers and across a field of research enquiry and indeed, community and policy debate.

In broad terms, the issue of 'who gets what' out of education is widely accepted as one key agenda of education research: as much the subject of statistical data collection by UNESCO and government agencies as of those who set out to study learning, institutional processes, student identities. But the specific attention to gender in research is an interesting case study for the discussions of this book, because it has shown such marked visibility, development and change over recent decades, because there has been much debate and counter-charge about different research claims and approaches in the area, because it is an area where politics and values are explicitly part of the debate rather than hidden, and because, in recent times, we have seen a rather strange phenomenon where *critics* of a particular research approach (the 'what about the boys?' lobby, talking of feminist research) have been claiming that feminist research has made progress and it is time to borrow from it. On the other hand, researchers associated with this apparent progress (feminist researchers on gender who have been working in the area for a long time) have not been trumpeting achievements but finding more and more difficult problems to address, and often jumping in to dispute stories about the progress and achievements they are said to have made (Yates 1997a, 1999a).

In half a chapter I am not going to review this field or provide a definitive statement of its achievements though, of course, these are many (Arnot *et al.* 1999; and Collins *et al.* 2000 provide two good reviews of issues and developments). What I want to do here is again to take up the issue of 'what kind of a thing is education research?' I want to show that what people are often critical of in relation to education research – either its political flavour, or its use of theories and jargon that seem removed from the day-to-day concerns of the field – are not signs that it is poor research, but that it is engaged in what programmes of research in other, very respectable fields do: attempting to delineate its object of enquiry and problematic; and engaging not simply in a one-off investigation but a *programme* of research that attends to and builds on what has already been investigated in previous enquiries. But, as with reading, both the construction of the investigation, and the way progress is judged, is not confined by the specific field of education research activity – it is permeated by many developments outside the field, and by many practices and judgements about the institutions that are its object of enquiry.

Let us begin by considering a reflection by Alison Kelly some time ago about her experiences with one specific field of research enquiry: why so few girls compared with boys choose science. She begins by noticing that a question that had been one that few people seemed to be interested in, in the space of six years grew globally: 'In 1981 the first international Girls and Science and Technology (GASAT) conference met with 27 participants from eight Western countries. In 1985 the third conference had more than 100 participants from 20 countries, covering the First, Second and Third World on five continents ...' (Kelly 1987: 1).

She also notes that she and other researchers had, in a similar time, been changing how they were approaching the topic. They moved from a 'psychologistic' search for explanations, looking for the individual atti-tudes and perceptions that led girls to avoid science, to a 'sociological' one, looking at what schools or the society or science was doing and how this constructed the curricula in a way that cut girls out. They moved from focusing heavily on survey evidence, to ethnographic studies, and histories of science and curriculum.

Or again, in a number of attempts to develop an overview of move-ments of both policy and research on gender in Australia (Yates 1997c, 1998, 1999a), I noted that in the space of two decades both research and policy seemed to go through a number of phases in the types of work and approach that were dominating. In the first stage, in the 1970s, the reform agenda was equal opportunity and counter sexism; and research was occupied with gathering facts and figures on inequality, exposing curriculum and language practices that treated girls and women differ-ently, contesting past research theories that saw girls' lesser achievement as innate. In the next stage, in the early 1980s, there was a focus on 'girl friendly schooling'. Researchers now were studying patterns of inequality in the co-education classroom ('who does the talking?'), and were engaged in attempting to identify girls' and women's 'ways of knowing'. By the mid-1980s, researchers interested in gender were confronting a more full-scale challenge about difference, especially in relation to race and ethnicity; and were now seeking to investigate how power and exclusion operated in schools not just to marginalize girls as a group but, more specifically, to deal poorly with cultural difference, to repeat stereotypes that limited the chances of girls from different back-grounds. Now the Australian policies started talking about the importance of 'inclusiveness' and difference. Meanwhile, researchers were investigating what was happening on the ground when reforms were being attempted: why were pre-schoolers not responding to non-sexist fairy tales in the ways that had been predicted (Davies 1989), what did girls, boys and teachers do when they encountered reform strategy? (Kenway *et al.* 1997). Taking up such questions, researchers were now writing about 'non-unified subjectivity', 'discursive constructions' of identity and the role of pleasure compared with rational reform projects. Readers interested in following some similar changes in research ques-tions and theories and methodologies in the UK could compare the readers used in Open University courses over a similar period; or they might compare changes in the types of papers on gender appearing on the AERA Conference programme during the 1980s, 1990s and today.

Taking up questions about race and ethnicity in relation to gender, or following through questions about why girls continue to like old-fashioned stories about boarding schools, or are unenthusiastic about certain reform agendas, led to much more complicated theories and forms of research than simply counting how many female illustrations were included in a textbook, or identifying some forms of explicit discrimination in career counselling of girls compared with boys, or in the admissions policies of education institutions and training possibilities beyond school.

Georgina Tsolidis, for example, discusses some of her own problems in trying to work as a researcher concerned with both ethnicity and gender, both equality and difference. Her first research was carried out in the early 1980s, and was a study of the experiences and aspirations of girls and boys of mainstream and 'non-English speaking background' in their schools:

> [at this point] being positioned as a feminist researcher working within schools on the education experiences of minority girls was, theoretically, relatively unproblematic. I was working to voice the hitherto silenced. My research was school based, enacted through teaching, and was guaranteed a policy outcome by virtue of its sponsorship by a government body.
>
> (Tsolidis 2001: 103)

A decade later, the academic theoretical context had moved on, and so had the conditions of policy making and research funding. Theoretically, the debates of feminist and other researchers had challenged the researcher's confidence in being able straightforwardly to represent the voice of the oppressed:

> Gone was the comfort of speaking for and from the margins. Instead the scepticism surrounding the constitution of such locations and the privilege implicit in the inversion of hierarchies of worth – that is, the epistemic privilege of being relatively more oppressed – had consolidated itself.
>
> (Tsolidis 2001: 103)

And government funding policy no longer supported the small-scale case study and modified action research of the earlier project, so methodologically too there were new challenges: 'How was I to frame a project, funded by a government body that insisted on a quantitative component to the study, around categories that were determined by the language of the bureaucracy, and maintain some semblance of theoretical dignity?' (Tsolidis 2001: 103).

As a researcher, Tsolidis is unable to simply ignore new theoretical challenges and questions raised in her field, nor to ignore the material constraints that decide what work will be funded. Instead she tries to work out how to proceed given both developments, what type of theoretical and practical approach now makes sense with regard to her own ongoing agendas and commitments.

A national conference on gender equity in Australia in 1995 brought together researchers and participants from parents' organizations and education departments who had worked on gender issues for a long time, and I described one aspect of this meeting in a later analysis of Australian developments:

> There was considerable sophisticated discussion of post-structuralism, a taken-for-granted understanding not to talk about 'girls' as a unified phenomenon; concern about homophobia, and so on. Meanwhile, in schools, teachers were facing such funding cuts and increased work pressures that in many cases it was felt that any attention to gender issues was a luxury. The professionals have become concerned with subtle and complex issues affecting the possibilities of change via education: the workings of desire as well as of 'rational' ambitions; the differences of race, ethnicity, class; the cultural 'discourses' which regulate current possibilities. These are much more difficult issues to attract support for, and to give a practical form to, than some earlier claims about restricted access, biased representation of women, encouraging female students and their teachers to aim higher.
>
> (Yates 1999a: 561)

Around this time too, in policy circles and in public debates, there was a quite abrupt change of agenda: a gradual attention to how boys were being placed in schools and what might be done about this. A new range of revisionist reading of facts and figures, and a whole new range of masculinity research got underway, much of which looked methodologically more like the simpler research that had been done on gender and girls in the 1970s than the work that had built from this in the 1980s and 1990s (Yates 1997a).

What is good research here? Again, what I want to draw attention to here is not my own evaluation of particular pieces of research, the quality of particular methodologies, the power of particular theories, but to some issues of the shape of this research arena, the 'logic' of its development, which is one component of the ways that research is judged.

The first thing to note (again) is the permeability of education research to broad social movements, agendas and shifts. Gender issues became prominent in education research in the late twentieth century not because these were the research-generated next step in tracking down some long-standing riddles about how education functioned, or how it could do better (compared, for example, with the ways that science researchers discover DNA, or begin to map genes). Nor was it that girls in the 1970s were suddenly achieving worse results in education than they had been earlier in the century. Instead a range of social developments (a women's movement, the UN Year and Decade for women, the spread of capitalism and its standards of making money and status the prime measure of lifetime achievement) framed new agendas for what education systems *should* be achieving. In some respects good research achievements at this point are finding appropriate ways to show what this problem looks like.

The re-entry of boys as an important issue in the 1990s was also one whose parameters arose as much from outside research programmes as from inside any of these. Admittedly, researchers now were tracking 'who gets what' with attention to gender, and could note some new problems in relation to boys. Admittedly too, the academy encourages researchers to be finding new problems to address. But the voices that put the boys' issues more prominently on the agenda (around the world!) from the 1990s also came from concerns about race, violence and disaffected youth; concerns about powerful males losing their entitlement; changes in social patterns and expectations regarding men and women, and many more. Research questions for education researchers are a moving target, and are generated both inside and outside theories, paradigms and research programmes.

A second point about the 'logic' of research development in this area is that, from the point of view of a research *programme*, broad moves of emphasis, theory and methodology among researchers do have an understandable logic. They move from what is known, they generate strategies, they revisit theories and ideas in the light of what has been achieved and not achieved, they respond to challenges arising from projects and research questions that overlap with their areas of interest. In the first phase in which a new issue has been raised ('equal opportunity' and why are girls ending up with different education outcomes than boys?), researchers spend time gathering data about the shape of the problem, especially using existing statistical collections, and they revisit the disciplinary theories they have been working with, to see where those might be extended, challenged or replicated using a new focus on the experience of girls and women. Examples of this strategy included sociological work on 'reproduction' and 'codes' (Arnot 1982), mathematical research on assumptions about innate capacities (Leder 1976), philosophical work on 'the educated man' (Martin 1982), psychological research on hierarchies of moral development (Gilligan 1982). Sometimes existing theories can be pursued and brought to bear on this problem: exploring the 'hidden curriculum' of textbooks, for example; or looking at what is made available differentially to girls and boys before they start school (as had previously been done in relation to poverty and disadvantage). But sometimes the theorists move on because their empirical object of study suggests limitations in the theories they are working with; or other theories have developed outside their own discipline that seem to offer some new purchase on their problem.

So the researchers themselves may have explored a problem in depth through particular perspectives, recognized certain limitations in working with those perspectives, and moved on to new approaches that attempt to give a more powerful or complex or effective insight. But others who are also involved in deciding what is a good approach in this area – parents who have not thought about this issue until they themselves had children, government bureaucrats who have been moved on to this area from another – may be seeing the problem in ways that resemble more those of the researchers twenty years ago.

Education research is an arena where some interaction between 'insider' and 'outsider', and semi-insider and semi-outsider, perspectives is an ongoing part of the territory. Policy makers readily accept that, in order to build an eventual treatment for a recognized medical problem it will be necessary to sponsor some programmes of more fundamental investigation about mechanisms, as well as trial initiatives and explore how well and for whom they work. But in education, it is widely assumed that researchers' work on mechanisms should be as accessible as their recommendation of strategies. Non-researchers in the gender area hang on to understandings of mechanisms in terms of 'roles' and 'role models' long after most researchers have decided that these constructs are badly flawed (these constructs do not explain how young people relate to a diversity of 'roles' and 'role models', why they take up some and not others, why they frequently reject well-meaning attempts to offer different ones, and so on). Conversely, the idea that discursive construction of identity and institutions may shape inevitable conflict in how girls do mathematics and science is not widely understood, though it is seen by many researchers to offer one promising means of exploring the observable behaviour and outcome of girls at school (Walden and Walkerdine 1982; Walkerdine 1988).

One reason then that education researchers engage in bodies of theory and ways of seeing that seem 'academic', that use language and concepts that are open to ridicule, is that they have engaged at length with some of the more accessible down-to-earth explanations and approaches and concepts and found them wanting, that they are looking for new ways to come to grips with issues and outcomes that are readily seen in the field, and that to do this requires new ideas and theories, not just new experiments or data collection within existing approaches.

To take one example, after a decade or so in which many researchers and associated reform initiatives had recommended that parents and schools provide 'equal opportunity' and develop girls' sense of a more expansive future by providing 'non-sexist' readers for young children,

Bronwyn Davies begins a new account of 'gender' and pre-school children by discussing her own experience that young children were not simply absorbing the new 'messages' in the ways that adults expected. A 'non-sexist fairy tale' that adults generally find amusing, the young children were finding puzzling: 'I then began to talk to her about the story, and discovered that the meanings which seemed to me to be readily available to any listener were not necessarily available to her, that the story she was hearing was different from the one that I was hearing' (Davies 1989: viii).

In her book, Davies goes on use her detailed research with young children to argue for a view of gender as 'discursive practice' and to explore some of the difficulties involved in trying to develop new teaching materials for young children, when the categories of the language and culture they are part of constrain meanings in certain ways. Her concluding chapter uses concepts and arguments that would seem very unfamiliar to many people: critiques of the idea that people have a 'unitary and coherent identity formed during childhood', arguments that we need to accept and work with contradiction, references to 'post-structuralist discourse'. Other researchers took up similar concepts in an attempt to explain more broadly how they saw students responding to new 'equal opportunity' policies in schools (Kenway *et al.* 1997), or to show how there was a 'double bind' in a legal case in which 'equality' was posed as necessarily antithetical to 'difference' (Scott 1990).

Of course there are contending theories and debates about all of these issues. But what I am trying to show here is the 'logic' of the research programme and that theories and types of programmes that may be ridiculed or rejected as having little connection with arenas of 'practice' have, in fact, arisen from and are connected to quite recognizable problems of practice and earlier research approaches.

A second explanation might also be given about why there have been shifts in the types of theories gender researchers work with, the type of language and concepts they use: that their own conditions of employment as academics encourages them to move in certain directions, in particular to be developing 'original' contributions and taking up 'current' theory rather than replicating past work. Policy makers, teachers, consultants, and academics get judged and rewarded for different types of things (which is not to say that the same person may not take on all of these persona, and indeed most people working in the gender area do so). I discuss this further in the second part of this book. In relation to three central areas in which academic researchers are assessed (the thesis, publishing in refereed journals, and gaining competitive funding grants), there is a premium on being 'cutting-edge', moving into new areas of theory, finding new bodies of theory and approach to apply to an area, rather than simply replicating existing work. And in academic work, writing that sounds most like common sense seems less like the-ory, low down the status hierarchy. There *is* an element of fashion in theories that are taken up, but researchers can lose face, fail to be pub-lished, fail to win grants if they persist with theories whose sins have been (or appear to have been) recounted by many writers.

So, critics of post-structural work on gender are not necessarily right when they dismiss this work because it affronts common sense, or uses difficult language. 'Common sense' may be precisely a central part of the problem that produces patterns of gender inequality, and researchers who understand well the limitations of older theories have the right to look for more fruitful directions in terms of the issues they pursue. Equally, the widespread moves one sees in the research community in taking up particular theories (and theorists) and lines of enquiry at particular times, are not necessarily guaranteed to be a way of making progress, in the way that moves on a more tightly circumscribed scientific problem might be. They may indeed be simply conforming to what is judged as significant theory at a particular time.

And research contributions and theories may be important, without being important to every audience at every point. One prime example here is the move to reflexivity and more extreme forms of self-criticism and self-reflection by researchers. Many methodology writings now emphasize the need to see research as 'constructing', not 'finding' truths; to examine the embodied relationships between researchers and researched; to critically scrutinize acts of writing up the research. In my own longitudinal research on young people, we have argued that these critical approaches are, paradoxically, an important source of new insights compared with research that is not sceptical and reflexive. We write about this in journals for other academics who grapple with similar problems (McLeod and Yates 1997; McLeod 2003; Yates 2003). But the project overall is one of educational research, one whose purpose is also to speak to and contribute to concerns about what schools do, and interests in how young people today shape their identity in the course of particular schools. In many of the contexts in which we wish to speak, we need to curtail our own fascination with methodology and its pro-blems if we are to be heard as even a critical voice, regarding practices and policies and inequalities.

Final comments

Education problematics are particularly difficult ones in the ways they bring together far-reaching normative and technical questions against a backdrop where changes in the social world are also highly relevant. Within particular programmes of research, researchers do make progress, and there is also change over time in the theoretical frameworks that dominate a particular area. In part this can be understood in terms of a working through of the scope of the problem. Education questions and agendas are only partially shaped from within the research field, and judgements about the quality of the research similarly reflect changing imperatives inside and outside the research community. At times concerns about research having relevance to particular communities or practitioners are given more prominence than concerns about 'rigour'; at other times the reverse is the case. Some researchers seek new fields to conquer and aim to dazzle; others to demonstrate the greatest 'reliability'. But education researchers do not have the luxury of sealing themselves away and working on a problem cut off from all other developments.

Taking the debates about reading research, or following changes of emphasis, theory and methodology in gender research as I have done here does not directly answer the question 'what does good education research look like?' What it does do is show that education research is always an engagement with a field and a situation, not just with a research question.

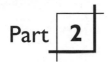

Part **2**

Arenas of education research:
contexts, genres and the rules
of the game

Introduction

What would an *empirical* answer to the question 'what does good education research look like?' look like?

What I am going to attempt to do in this section of the book is not so much provide some 'empirical' answers to the question, but to take an *empirical and pragmatic approach* to the question. I am not going to replicate in any detail some of the types of discussions – albeit relevant discussions – commonly found in research methodology textbooks: what makes a good case study, survey, genealogy, or piece of action research. This is not directly about how you design your research, or what techniques are appropriate within particular approaches, though I do think such discussions also matter (Yates 1996, 2000a, 2003). Nor is this section concerned with providing reviews and lists of the work that has been successful in different areas. That is an interesting exercise but one that already takes place elsewhere: in periodic reviews of grant schemes; in journals in particular areas; in content analyses of media reports; in critical reviews by dissenting voices about the dominant form of a particular arena. This part of the book is not even centrally about my own criteria for deciding as a researcher or an examiner or a member of a grants committee why I think particular pieces of research or research approaches are better than others. What I am going to try to do here is to look at different places where education research gets judged, and to try to show as an insider and as an observer *who* are the people making the judgements, *what types of criteria* come into play and what are the indicators or markers or *appearance features* of the research application or report they draw on. My aim is to try to give an approach to thinking about how the judgements about good research happen; how this question is meaningful; but how it is not the same in the different arenas I will discuss. It is a type of discussion that is intended to help researchers and intending researchers position themselves better in various contexts; it is intended to supplement rather than replace the other types of discussion that normally characterize the research methods arena.

The more common way to discuss 'what is good research?' is not empirical but normative and technical. Often a particular methodology is legislated as the 'gold standard' (currently RCTs (randomized controlled trials), or replicas of 'scientific method') and the question is how well does a particular piece of research meet the standards (this approach is implicit rather than explicit in the Tooley report (Tooley 1998)). Or a particular outcome criterion is nominated as the standard, and the research is measured against this. In recent years, for example, both the UK and Australia have commissioned enquiries into the 'impact' of education research, with the implication being that good research is research that can be shown to have produced effects on its field of practice. But even in these cases the task of turning the normative criteria into technical empirical assessments is a tricky task. Ian Stronach has argued that few of the RCTs in education can actually meet the standards normally expected of a 'control group'.[7] And in the case of impact, the highly-funded review sponsored by the Australian government (Australia. Research Evaluation Programme. Higher Education Division 2000) ended up commissioning five different groups, each of which had a different take on what 'impact' looked like and what type of study would be needed to provide empirical evidence about that. The first group surveyed schools and school systems about the dissemination of research. The second took specific policy/programme initiatives and 'backtracked' these to determine what (if any) research base they were built on. The third took a more close-up study of teachers' practice and the sources they drew on. The fourth reviewed the influence of research on decision making in vocational education and training policy formulation; and the final study used a bibliometric analysis to trace through citations how particular researchers impacted on their fellow researchers throughout the world.

'Empirical' is a tricky concept: what you find depends where you look and what you look for. In the first part of this book I have given some background to the question I have set up here by looking at changes over time, political disputes, different parts of the field. I started out as a historian and later was educated as a sociologist, and noticing what is produced in what *contexts* is part of that training. Recently I moved to a new faculty and encountered a strong 'Language, Discourse and Policy' group whose interest and training are much more strongly directed to *textual* practices. This form of disciplinary training foregrounds texts and 'discourse' as the way in which all practices are constructed. One of my first tasks was to teach a subject in the Ed D programme, originally designed by Alison Lee around the idea of 'Research Literacies' and research as writing (Lee 1998; Richardson 2000). What the 'Research Literacies' approach assumes is that we need to see education research as writing; we need to see it as *textual practices*. We need to think what makes good research not in terms of a philosophical answer, but as an empirical examination of *the places where judgements about good education research are made, and, related to that, the textual strategies of the work that is successful.*

I had long taught my own postgraduate courses on research, and had developed a different way of having students look at the field and its issues,[8] and I continue to think that one can overemphasize textuality as an approach to social life. But it did seem to me that the concept of Research Literacies also provides some appropriate starting points for approaching the question I have set out for this book. People coming from a literacy and cultural studies perspective take very seriously the idea that we can get a long way in understanding how the world works if we take more literally the investigation of what things 'look like' – that is, if we see the practices as texts, and we examine those texts. This part of the book then is an attempt to approach contexts both in terms of their institutional constraints and shaping, material foundations, identities and networks; and also to begin to look at the textual characteristics of what good research *looks like.*

In this part of the book I will take some of the different arenas where judgements about what counts as good education research are being made, and look at the textual agendas that shape them, as well as at issues not directly represented textually: *who* gets to make the judgements, and how. The arenas I shall discuss are: thesis writing and examination (and best thesis prizes); consultancy and partnership research for education departments or schools; articles for refereed journals; book publication; competitive research grants; national higher education policy; and the public press.

In each of these cases I will discuss what I see as the key elements of this context and the genre, including examples or markers of successful and unsuccessful work in the area. I draw on illustrations from my own experience; from published documents such as thesis guidelines, instructions to examiners, journal submission instructions and guides used by referees; from published research about the area; and from stories and illustrations from colleagues around the world.

This part is intended to illustrate an approach that I see as a useful way to think about what is going on. Even within my own terms, this is not a comprehensive coverage of all the places judgements about research get made. I do not, for example, attempt to deal here with judgements about research as it is being carried out, or 'in the field' – judgements by those on whom the research is being conducted, for example, including judgements by particular communities such as indigenous communities. Nor, except in passing, do I discuss the issue of citation indexes, and the ways these construct particular, selective, judgements about the research field. I do include a chapter on judgements by schools, teachers and other practitioners, but that chapter is no more than a starting point discussion of a complex area on which much has been written elsewhere. It will also be clear from what follows that I have had much more extensive personal experience in some of these areas than in others.

The chapters that follow then do not claim to offer a definitive account of how each of these different contexts work. It was part of my argument in Part 1 that research is situated or contextual: doctoral thesis examination, for example, shows some regional variation in its forms and practices and some changes to its practices and formal requirements over time; the composition and emphases of research grant committees is not the same in different parts of the world; some school systems are much more devolved than others and this affects how research is generated and judged. My examples are intended to be evocative rather than definitive – to provide starting points for further discussion, not to assume that every assertion I make will apply to every context.

3

The thesis

The pragmatics: how does the thesis work?

Arena	Judges	Explicit criteria	Implicit criteria	What does it look like?	Common failings
PhD	Licensed academics;	Literature	Can self-consciously locate relative to academic community	Formal language	Looked sloppy
Ed D (thesis)	University committee	Methodology		Precise conventions (front pages, referencing)	Aims unclear
Masters (thesis)		'Original' contribution to field	Up to date		Not 'systematic'
				Hyper-correct grammar, error-free presentation	'Poorly presented'
		Correct presentation (conventions and grammatical expression)	Mastery of conventions plus potentially publishable addition		Ignored X or X's theory
				Voice: modest but authoritative	References are dated (too old)
			Clear aims, boundaries	Claims: neither over-sell nor under sell 'contribution'	
			Critique important		
			Mastery of English important		
			Thesis introduction and conclusion of disproportionate importance		

One might think that this chapter should be the most straightforward of the arenas where I try to examine 'what does good research look like?' A thesis, after all, is a defined entity with defined specifications. University regulations set out in explicit and microscopic detail what physical form, including textual form, it is to take; who can be a producer of such research (that is, what one needs to demonstrate to be accepted as a candidate, demonstrate satisfactory progress, allowed to submit a thesis for examination); and who can be examiners; what the processes of examination entail; what criteria examiners are asked to answer; how the final decision about the acceptability of the thesis is made. Departments in universities often produce their own guides and regulated practices which the student and supervisors and thesis committees are required to follow. Commercial publishers and experienced academics produce 'how to write a thesis' books and manuals, and these are widely circulating best-sellers. And university libraries and web-based collections contain large pools of successful examples – past work that has met the criteria, that has been judged to be 'good' or at least acceptable enough to be awarded a doctorate or a masters degree.

And yet, the doctoral thesis is also often a field of 'trauma', to quote a recent research project on now successful academics about their own past experiences of doing a PhD (Lee and Williams 1999). Recent research on supervision would seem to suggest that neither students nor supervisors find the task of accomplishing a good final product to be a straightforward one (Holbrook and Johnston 1999). In a number of countries in recent years, government bodies have imposed their own interventions into the desired processes and outcomes of the thesis work, trying to add ideas like efficient progress and national benefit or of being located in a 'research concentration' to the emphases seen to hold sway in universities. Academics and professional bodies attempt to debate and contest the new definitions of what a good research student and a good research outcome in this context looks like. Some researchers suggest that the imperatives of the thesis definition of what good research is are biased by gender (Leonard 1997, 2001; Lee 1999), or by cultural norms (Yates 1999c; Popkewitz 2002), or are broadly too conservative, backward, rather than forward looking (Lee et al. 2000). The rise of professional doctorates has been accompanied by academic and policy debates arguing that new modes of knowledge are important today, and not sufficiently catered for by previous PhD processes (Gregory 1995; Brennan 1997; Lee et al. 2000).

In this chapter I want to draw attention to both elements of the agendas I have set out here: the highly-defined technical specifications and processes through which the judgement of good research is made in relation to a thesis; and the networks, disciplinary and university contexts, and cultural specificities and political changes that also impact on what is judged to be good.

A note before continuing: my emphasis in this chapter, as elsewhere, is on unpacking certain aspects of the pragmatics and modes by which judgements about quality take place, and this might be mistaken for cynicism. In fact, in relation to the issue of good research and the PhD, I am not someone who joins the now fashionable disapproval of this exercise; who complains about its producing things that are only read by three people; and dismisses it as 'academic' in that word's everyday pejorative sense of meaning irrelevant to the real world ('that's an academic question'). The doctoral thesis is a human invention, culturally specific, and judged by people in certain ways. That does not mean that it is simply a cynical exercise. I do think there is something about being forced to pursue research in a 'pure' way over a substantial period of time, and to be challenged closely on methodological adequacy as you do it, that is a good training. I also think there is something about the scope of the task that does transform how you see yourself, and the questions you get into. Even people who start off saying that they intend to be totally pragmatic about their doctorate, often find that they are forced to work out just what really are their own assumptions about what counts as good knowledge, what type of contribution they are really interested in making to their professional field, and so on.

Most people, including those who take on academic jobs, never again pursue research with the thoroughness that they did in their own PhD – and most continue to draw on lessons and knowledge they learned while doing it. And while it is true that there are major paradigm differences in education, there is also considerable overlap in how people from different backgrounds judge what is good – and committees in research organizations such as AERA and AARE that award prizes are examples of that. Although I focus in this chapter on the conventions by which a PhD or Ed D or Masters thesis is examined, this does not mean that a thesis project cannot produce knowledge that 'makes a difference', that is important for a much wider audience, and that is able to be conveyed (in different forms) to that broader audience.

What is a PhD?

A PhD is a form of accreditation that certifies that the holder has proved himself or herself as a researcher and warrants admission to the community of licensed academics or competent scholarly independent researchers. This form of accreditation is not timeless: the doctoral thesis did not always hold the same importance or popularity for certification of one's suitability to be an academic or a researcher; and the rise of professional doctorates, greater interpenetration of 'industry' and 'public' agendas; institutions competing for students across the globe; interest in new forms of knowledge, all indicate that its significance is likely to change again in the future (see Gibbons *et al.* 1994; Garrick and Rhodes 2000; Doecke and Seddon 2002; McWilliam and Singh 2002).

In Australia, New Zealand and the UK, for example, the doctorate is a qualification which dates primarily from the second half of the twentieth century; and for the humanities and education, it was not a common qualification for academics to hold until the last quarter of the century (Middleton 2001). In those countries, as recently as the 1970s, leading professors of prestigious history or English departments were likely to hold a Masters degree as their highest qualification – though at that point the characteristics of the research Masters thesis were similar to those which now result in a doctorate – whereas the doctorate had been taken on as the normal qualification for researchers in science. In the USA, however, with a differently structured higher education sector, with far greater numbers proceeding to graduate school, the doctorate was established earlier as a more common qualification for academic employment across the disciplines; while in northern Europe, the more extended period of doctoral work, and, at least in some countries, formal status of doctoral students as academic staff, frames the meaning of the doctoral accreditation in a different way.

In the professional disciplines, the demand for a doctorate as a necessary accreditation basis for academic employment is often an indicator of a march to higher status on the part of the particular professional field, a claim regarding the advanced knowledge base of the field in question. Education, social work, nursing, physiotherapy, occupational therapy and other fields can be seen following some similar patterns in this regard. Interestingly, the highest status professions, medicine and law, are less subject to this demand: there the outstanding practitioner can more readily be granted professorial status without the doctoral thesis attesting to their mastery of a certain type of research knowledge.

As well as there being different patterns in the extent to which the doctoral thesis was historically required as a basic certification for academics and researchers in particular fields, there are also field differences in what was expected of the thesis, what it was seen to represent. In all cases, it was a core requirement that the doctoral thesis be a 'contribution to knowledge'. But in the case of science, doctoral students normally worked in a team with professors, lecturers, post-doctoral fellows and other students. They were working on different parts of a problem, and their work fed the whole as well as the individual 'discovery' or theory of the thesis. The thesis itself was expected to attest to the individual's ability to design and theorize; but when the research was broadcast to the outside world in the form of publications (and even more so, if the research led to applications for new patents), it was normal that not only the doctoral researcher, but their academic supervisor and possibly others in the same team, were also credited as co-producers of the research.

In the case of the humanities, single-authored publication was more the norm. Here the doctorate was seen not so much as part of normal business (as in the science laboratory) but more as an individual opus. Originality was highly valued. The process of producing such research might take many years. Diana Leonard (1997) contrasts the different perspectives on what the qualification is expected to mean in her criticism of moves by governments to use financial regulation to ensure that research is more directed to areas of national need, and that completion rates are improved:

> In the current debates, the dominant – government – discourse concerns the need to make the PhD a training for high quality generic researchers (to make sure young students become skilled in choosing and using appropriate methods) and relevant to the needs of employment and the nation's economic growth and competitiveness. The PhD is apprenticeship work which should be completed promptly.
>
> Against this, debate is finally being joined more systematically by those who take an 'education' stance: who say a PhD is about personal development, growth and satisfaction; and that unlike a PhD in science or engineering, a social science or humanities thesis produces important original work, which takes time.

One of the reasons both students and supervisors located in education often find the question of what constitutes a good PhD to be a difficult one, one where they find themselves at odds with other supervisors and students in the same field, is that this field and the types of questions it generates, draws on disciplines and research traditions both of the science/engineering type and of the humanities/creative type (and similar strains can be found in fields such as social work). In some parts of education (particularly psychology and science and mathematics education; some types of sociological research), it is common to find a group of researchers working on a related problem, as a team, and frequently producing multi-authored research texts. Sometimes the funding of the PhD student here is directly tied to the research grant for the larger project, where the area on which they must work is decided in advance as part of the conditions for gaining funding. For PhD students in such settings, the task of designing their research question and the array of methods they will use in answering it are comparatively straightforward issues and derived from their research team or supervisor: the emphasis in distinguishing good students from more mediocre ones is on how well they actually do the work, and how powerfully and creatively they theorize what they find. In other parts of education (some types of policy and sociological research, cultural studies-based research, philosophical theses), the task of designing an original problem for the thesis to address assumes almost equal weight with the work of addressing it, and occupies quite a lengthy part of the period in which the student is enrolled. Clandinin and Connelly (2000: 41) discuss the tensions this can pose for students involved in narrative forms of inquiry in the North American system where a committee rather than a single supervisor oversees the work: 'it is expressed in the different advice given by different committee members: Go to the library. What experiences have you had with this? Read Gadamer. Go to a school.'

For the 'humanities' concept of the thesis, the emphasis is on origin-ality and creativity. It involves putting together an approach that is recognizable and defensible in terms of existing literature and meth-odologies, but also, in some way, being creative, doing something that is original. Some supervisors here, as in the quote from Diana Leonard, see their task as nurturer or midwife to a development that is a personal, creative act on the part of the student. Other supervisors see their role as technical adviser, or project manager, or master to apprentice, and understand the task of doing good PhD research to be one of learning the ropes, being inducted, mastering an approach.

Further discussions about what a doctorate means have been gener-ated by the development of professional doctorates, as well as broader discussion about new modes of knowledge formation and 'mode 1' and 'mode 2' knowledge (Gibbons et al. 1994; Gregory 1995; Brennan 1997; Lee et al. 2000; Brennan et al. 2002; Doecke and Seddon 2002; McWilliam and Singh 2002). Currently in Australia the 'professional doctorates' (Ed D) take many different forms, in terms of the specific type of written work that is required, and the logics and models that are appealed to when these degrees are represented to university hierarchies and to potential students. Regular conferences and publications are committed to debating the extent to which there are real changes at work in terms of what is to be counted as good practice in terms of such doctorates, the extent to which they are to be seen as assessing research, and whether research in the professional context means the same as research in traditional uni-versity terms. It is still common for the actual assessment of research to take the form of a thesis and of examining practices that are similar if not identical to PhD theses, and it is the latter that I am taking for the main focus of examination in this chapter. However, the issue of professional doctorates as compared with research doctorates, as well as the issue of national and institutional differences in what any of these categories mean, can be pursued in similar ways to those I adopt in this chapter by scrutinizing the regulations, forms, personnel and the relationships through which the judgements about what is 'good' come to be made.

At one level, the issue of what a PhD is, is straightforward: it is the highest level of qualification in the training period, as compared with later honorary doctorates, or doctorates of science and so on, which are awarded, more like prizes, to practitioners who have made a special contribution to their field, usually involving a number of different projects, or a whole programme of research, rather than the single, focused study of the PhD. It is unambiguously a research degree and is in some countries contrasted with other degrees that are seen as more directed to an amalgam of research and practical ends (professional doctorates, for example). But the issue of what it means to attain that mastery of research in one's field, or to make an original contribution to it, is put differently by people speaking from different disciplines, sets of interests, national contexts, and times. In some cases, the emphasis seems to be on the technical: showing that the research has been done properly, in accord with the approved methodological procedures of one's field. In some cases, there is attention to the substantive nature of the 'contribution to knowledge' that the thesis has made. And in others, particularly the humanities, the thesis is read as if it is to furnish evidence about something else beyond the thesis: what sort of person is doing this, what sort of mind is at work here – good research is research that demonstrates an original voice and an original perspective, that is in some way 'creative'.

Who are the judges?

> The examiners shall be expert in the field of the thesis and be able to make an independent assessment of the student.

(from University of London *Instructions for the Appointment of Examiners for the Degrees of MPhil and PhD* 2000)

Whether explicit in the regulation or not, the starting point as to who is an appropriate expert to judge good research in relation to the doctorate is that the judges themselves should normally be people with doctorates, licensed academics, and people who are active producers of research in the area that the thesis addresses. What then do they bring to this particular judging of good research?

Their own disciplinary training and experience; their position and authority

Examiners who are themselves licensed academics bring to their judgements their own training and experience of what a PhD meant at the time they accomplished this. Some institutions have formal or informal rules that examiners should not themselves be *recent* graduates. This is for two reasons. As I argued in Part 1, even within an area, the issue of what is appropriate methodology is the subject of change and debate. It is believed that those who examine theses should have some breadth of experience in this regard, and should have had the opportunity to see the research of people working in areas other than that of their own training.

The second reason is that even in this most regulated of arenas, expert judgements are not entirely free of psychological emotional investments. A very new graduate, fresh from his or her own struggle with the demands of producing a successful doctorate, is likely to see the standards required for the PhD as very high, requiring high levels of perfection of methodology, and very high levels of contribution to knowledge. There is a 'gatekeeper' element in their response. An eminence in a particular field, a 'grand old man' of the field, may look like a more impressive judge of the research, but, paradoxically, often has a more relaxed standard of what a good contribution is. They are secure in their own position, having supervised many PhD students themselves, and being more likely to see it as a starting point, are prepared to take competency as sufficient, or to recognize how a small contribution in this thesis can be seen as a real 'contribution to knowledge'.

Their own particular research commitments

All things being equal, examiners are likely to rank as good research that which explicitly or implicitly validates their own research or reputation. One problem here is that the more extensively the thesis engages with the research of the examiner, and signifies this as important, the more, in order to make a contribution themselves, the doctoral candidate will have to take issue with at least some part of that work.

Their own particular relationships, particularly with the supervisor or department

The thesis offered for examination is seen by many not just as an item of research that is the product of the individual whose name is attached to it, but as an artefact that reflects in some degree the quality of the supervision and the department from which it is offered. These considerations may influence how an examiner formally judges a thesis. If they are severe in their criticisms this may harm their relationship with the colleague who supervised the thesis. Conversely, if they are very uncritical in their response, they may fear being seen by that colleague as insufficiently knowledgeable about the areas they are reviewing.

The institutional structure of the examining/judgement process

In the North American tradition, doctorates are produced by students who must also study and pass a range of related coursework subjects as part of their degree; and whose thesis research is overseen by a committee that acts as both examiner and guide to what needs to be done at each stage of the work (usually annually, but certainly at the proposal, as well as the final stages, when the committee is sometimes supplemented by an external examiner). In the British tradition, the student's ongoing relationship is usually free from compulsory studies and involves an individual relationship with a supervisor who acts as the guide, with the examination of the research being conducted only at the endpoint. In Sweden, students formally have many of the conditions of staff members in the department, and are treated as members of that department, and usually the acceptability of the thesis is effectively decided at the point of the (gatekeeper) judgement by the supervisor that the thesis is ready for formal examination, rather than by subsequent examination. So in some countries the supervisor becomes one of the examiners of the research; in others they act as advocates for the research; in others again, they are formally excluded from the process once the thesis is submitted. In each case, the particular institutional structure can shape the judgement itself.

For example, in one university where I spent time, the system seemed to be designed to treat supervisors with some suspicion. The examination process was handled by a cross-disciplinary university committee; the supervisor had no formal rights to nominate the examiners; there was no oral examination; and neither the student nor the supervisor had a right to see or comment on conflicting examiners' reports before the committee made its decision. That is, those with no close expertise in the particular area of the thesis, and who know nothing about the standing or prejudices of the examiners and status of the type of critiques they are making, controlled the process. Here the prejudices of staff about education as an inferior field to other disciplines, or the status and networks of the supervisor in the university community, may play a part in how the examiners' reports are judged.

In Scandinavia, where there is a substantial and public interrogation of the thesis, there is some pressure on the examiner to demonstrate their own expertise and perform well. This leads to a different sort of display than where examination takes the form of a oral with only examiners, student and supervisor present; or is based wholly on a written report, or is made by a committee that has seen each step of the process and any adjustments in the research along the way.

The institutional processes say something about how institutions judge their own standing in the research hierarchy. For example, in many Australian universities, it is still a requirement not only that examiners be external to the university, but desirably that they are external to the country. This might be seen as a sign of institutions or national contexts that are immature, or unconfident of their place in the world of research and higher education, that feel they need external validation about the standards of research internationally. By contrast, the University of London regulations say that an examiner may be appointed from over-seas 'only in exceptional circumstances', and in that case the Panel 'must be satisfied that the examiner appointed is familiar with the British higher education system'. In the USA, the most prestigious institutions (Princeton, Yale, Harvard) use committees comprised solely of academics within those institutions. Smaller institutions are more likely to bring in external examiners as part of the process. In some countries (USA, Australia, France) a right to be free from external scrutiny of matters involving academic decision making (such as thesis examination) was something that historically differentiated universities from teachers' colleges, colleges of advanced education, or technical colleges. England, however, has had more long-standing traditions of university teams reciprocally scrutinizing standards and examining practices – and the idea of some external overseeing or involvement of external examiners is an established practice.

The practice of involving external examiners in thesis judgement might also be seen as a sign that breadth or scale of judgement matters in relation to good research in scholarly work, and that the highest level of achievement is that which appears most robust when subjected to critical scrutiny. In Scandinavia and northern Europe, the idea that a final doctoral 'defence' should be both public and involve structured forms of expert attack to which the candidate must convincingly respond, reflects this sense. The Australian obsession with examiners outside the country might be seen as reflecting the idea that scholarly academic work is ultimately judged by the international field, so that the highest prestige in science goes to work that has the broadest international recognition. Such work may lack immediate local relevance and application (this will be discussed further in Chapters 4 and 5). The US system, by contrast, places most emphasis on judgements by practitioners from *inside* the USA, and contributions to the literature and professional field of *American* educa-tion, and this flows through judgements of good research at every level there: grant applications, publishing and doctoral examination.

Explicit and implicit criteria

Here is how one university website[9] sets out in detail the explicit criteria of PhD examination (emphases are mine):

The format and style of PhD theses can differ as it is expected that a thesis be written to the convention of that field. However examiners are asked to consider, where appropriate, eight questions. These are:

- Does the candidate show sufficient *familiarity* with, and *understanding* and *critical appraisal* of, the *relevant literature*?
- Does the thesis provide a sufficiently *comprehensive investigation* of the topic?
- Are the *methods and techniques* adopted *appropriate* to the subject matter and are they *properly justified and applied*?
- Are the *results* suitably set out and accompanied by *adequate exposition and interpretation*?
- Are *conclusions* and implications *appropriately* developed and clearly *linked* to the nature and content of the research framework and findings?
- *Has the research question(s) in fact been tested?*
- Is the *literary* quality and general presentation of the thesis of a suitably *high standard?*
- Does the thesis as a whole constitute *a substantive original contribution* to *knowledge in the subject area* with which it deals?

Examiners are also asked to consider the following attributes:

- The thesis demonstrates *authority* in the candidate's field and shows evidence of *command of knowledge* in relevant fields;
- it shows that the candidate has a *thorough* grasp of the *appropriate methodological techniques* and an awareness of their limitations;
- it makes a distinct *contribution to knowledge*. Its contribution to knowledge rests on *originality* of approach and/or interpretation of the findings and, in some cases, the discovery of new facts;
- it demonstrates an *ability to communicate* research findings effectively in the *professional arena* and in an *international context*;
- it is a *careful, rigorous and sustained* piece of work demonstrating that a research 'apprenticeship' is complete and the holder *should be admitted to the community of scholars in the discipline*.

This is a particularly detailed summing up of a number of the issues I have discussed, and try to summarize in my table. It captures many of the issues that are common across judgement of good research in this context, though universities do not always spell out their expectations in such detail, and sometimes select a smaller number of the above elements as their explicit criteria. (Students and supervisors would be advised to look carefully at any criteria specifically issued to examiners within their own institutions for any variations of emphasis.) The set of instructions to examiners makes clear the following characteristics of PhD examination.

- Judgements of research quality at this level are expected to have some disciplinary variation, and to require judgements from experts within the discipline as to adequacy of methodology and contribution to knowledge.

- Nevertheless, across disciplines there is expected to be some broader common understanding of what this degree represents (indeed in many if not most universities, the final decision to pass a PhD involves some input from a university committee including academics outside the particular field), one that makes it possible for the university to set out this common set of guidelines for PhD examination.

- It is in all cases understood to be research or an investigation that is technically good (methods and techniques 'properly' applied, well justified, their limitations understood); that represents 'a substantive original contribution to knowledge' (specifically 'in the subject area with which it deals'); that shows a high level of correctness of presentation; that is a 'careful, rigorous and sustained' piece of work.

- It is also to be understood as a certification that one now has 'authority' in one's field; has 'command of knowledge', has demonstrated ability to communicate such both within one's professional field and internationally, and above all has demonstrated 'that a research apprenticeship is complete'.

On technical matters of presentation, it is common for university doctoral regulations to prescribe such fine details as word limit, page size, type of binding, contents and order of opening pages (for examples title page, abstract, declaration of authorship, and so on), *exact* wording of the title page, number of copies to be submitted, and other matters. I have known cases of students not being permitted to lodge their thesis for examination because the clerical assistants at the graduate studies office detected one or two minor inaccuracies in the wording of the title page; or of the graduate studies office or a thesis examiner refusing to accept a thesis for examination because it exceeded the word limit (by a substantial amount). On the one hand, a central criterion of 'mastery' here is 'originality'; on the other hand, the student proves that he or she has completed the apprenticeship and deserves to be certified as a member of the community of scholars in that discipline by demonstrating very high levels of ability to conform to the technical modes of that discipline, and to follow instructions in fine detail. This ability is in fact a very appropriate apprenticeship for applying for grants (see Chapter 5) – but precisely the wrong sort of training for making an impact in the media (see Chapter 9).

Broadly, then, instructions to examiners of PhD research mark out as important:
- the writing and presentation of the work;
- relating it well to the research literature;
- satisfactory methodology;

- making a contribution to knowledge in that field.

In contexts where examination is by written report alone, the report forms commonly ask examiners to tick a range of different boxes as to whether corrections or resubmissions are required in addition to giving an overall judgement about quality and acceptability for the degree. Examiners are often asked specifically whether the presentation and grammar of the thesis was good, and to include a list of typographical and other errors. Some universities ask examiners to state whether the work is publishable in book or journal form.

This then is what is formally set out as the criteria: what are the implications of this for the research tasks of the doctoral student (and their supervisor) in education; and also for the examiner?

For the producer of research in *this* arena, the student, all of these explicit criteria point to an implicit criterion of what good research looks like here: *showing that you know your professional community and appreciate what kind of contribution you are making to it.*

For the doctoral thesis, good research is judged relative to a particular, existing research community

Showing that methods are adequate, that writing presentation is appropriate, that the research has been conducted with 'care, rigour, and made a sustained contribution' all carry a sub-text: *as judged by a particular community* and *relative to the current standards of your discipline/sub-discipline.* Learning good methodology involves more than going to a traditional research methods textbook; students should, at the same time, be learning to understand what their field is and to understand the state of play in it, to demonstrate some self-consciousness about how that community will judge the new work and evaluate what is being added. Because education is a wide-ranging and hotly contested arena of research activity, one which draws on people of different disciplinary trainings, and in which within a particular set of research questions ('learning', 'inequalities') some very different ways of understanding and investigating the issues are possible, there is first of all a need for the thesis to define the community to which it is addressed. In *Narrative Inquiry* (2000), Clandinin and Connelly point out that 'some precision of naming' is likely to be important in explaining the 'logic of justification' of a thesis – for example, to distinguish phenomenology from ethnography, or ethnomethodology, or grounded theory.

The issue of defining boundaries and allegiances is intrinsic to the thesis task and to the examination process. The literature review, for example, is not merely there to show that the writer has done some background reading, but to set up *what type of a thesis* this is; to show which discussion he or she is aiming to make a contribution to. A good discussion of the field sets up a story of why the particular topic of the thesis matters, as well as why it is appropriate to embark on it in such a way. As the University of London Institute of Education advice to students puts it, 'Ideally, the problem to be tackled in the research should emerge naturally and inexorably from the literature review.' But to 'emerge naturally and inexorably' actually requires considerable work of discrimination and constructive writing on the part of the student.

This is one reason why the initial stages of embarking on a project are often so difficult for a student who comes to doctoral study in education from an interest in an area or problem, rather than from an extended disciplinary training in a particular network of research theory (for example in history, or sociology) that over four years has led them to refine their knowledge of the broad field, and focus on the details of a particular area of research from which they build their own topic. Often such students (that is, students who may have studied a range of education courses, and who have some general understandings of different research methodologies, but are not directly building on a previous honours or Masters thesis) begin, in recommended fashion, by searching for literature on their topic. But it is often hard to make sense of this literature, which is not simply a matter of adding and comparing findings, but understanding some of the research agendas and definitions of boundaries and appropriate approaches given complex problems. Students often need some induction by supervisors and by attending conferences, to get a sense of the practices and agendas that are not always explicit in the writings, but that frame how the discussion develops. A field such as 'learning' or 'inequality' has within it a number of quite distinct research communities – communities which emphasize different literatures and methodologies. Putting a literature review together is not simply a matter of being comprehensive, whatever that might mean. The following 'helpful' advice comes from the University of London Institute of Education guidelines:[10]

> The literature review should not be over-inclusive. It should not cover non-essential literature nor contain irrelevant digressions. Studies recognised as key or seminal in the field of enquiry should not be ignored. ... A good literature review will be succinct, penetrating and challenging to read.

The problem is more difficult in countries where the doctorate does not incorporate substantial specialist coursework that helps the student to understand some of the different strands of their field, and to examine more specifically the research conversation they are trying to join. In my current university in the Ed D programme we use an early exercise that helps students to understand this issue of the different histories and communities that may be hidden behind a common label fed into the library search engine. We ask them (as an assessment task) to take the initial outline of their proposed topic, and to interview a number of different academics, and a number of people in the proposed site of the study about their own reactions and suggestions in relation to how the student initially framed their problem and proposed approach.

So, good research in relation to the doctoral thesis means 'good ... relative to a particular research community'. Some people might interpret what I have said quite cynically, as if I am saying that good research is mainly an exercise in deciding that you get the right examiners, and say the right things about them, and as feeding the broad criticism that I discussed in early chapters, that education research is 'ideology-driven' rather than rigorous and productive. But to interpret it this way would be seriously to over-simplify and misrepresent what is at work here. As I argued in Part 1, good research in education involves discussions both about 'research' and about 'education'. Different paradigms develop, and different values about what matters in education are often part of this: but with regard to a given problem or area of concern, paradigms neither stay static, nor are self-contained. At the PhD, as we have seen, you are being judged both on your ability to conform and on your ability to be different. The 'normal' PhD is expected to challenge. One common way to make progress on a problem (now vaunted in the sciences as well as the social sciences) is to bring together theories and perspectives about an area that have formerly been kept separate; or to contribute to a current research body in a field by seeking a different type of theory and research approach to bring to it. It is common for PhD projects to be constructed in such a way that appropriate examiners come from different areas (that is, different sub-disciplines) of the broader research field, and that part of the task of the thesis is to explain why the new move/approach/combination that the student/writer/researcher wishes to pursue is a good one.

My broad point is that students writing doctoral theses need an understanding of research methodology and contribution that is broader than understanding the debates about particular research methods and appropriate tests of these. They have to defend the appropriateness of the overall logic of the project: of the selection and combination of approaches, as well as micro-methodological validity/reliability/trustworthiness issues of the steps they take within this; and that *doing this involves some understanding of what research conversations have been going on in different research networks and literatures of the field*.

The current period is a particularly difficult one for students, supervisors and examiners. Not only are there increasing numbers of people doing doctorates, attempting to mark out new 'contributions to knowledge', but with the advent of postmodernism and the rising significance of the text in forms of social science research, many currently favoured theories are being very reflexively critical about norms such as those that make up the doctoral writing (see, for example, Rhedding-Jones 1997). The imperative for theses in this mode is to produce something that shows you have mastery of the norms at the same time as breaking through and doing something different.

For the last few years, I have been a member of a national committee that makes an 'Exemplary Thesis' Award. All universities are invited to submit one thesis for consideration, together with the examiners' reports on it. In 2001 and 2002, on the testimony of examiners' reports, *at least half* of the submitted theses had chosen to use formats that in some sense were unconventional or novel. Another way of putting this is that the breaking of format conventions has become a new convention.

But I have also been involved in a few cases where there has been disagreement as to whether a thesis should pass and the point at issue has been whether it sufficiently included what, I think, are still basic expectations, no matter how novel the overall format. These are: that the thesis be seen to systematically address what academic literature has been done to date (though 'systematic' means different things for a poststructural thesis than for a quasi-experimental one); that it in some sense be seen to set up or retrospectively justify some aims and boundaries for the project (an issue of the written logic of the final product, whether or not such aims and boundaries represent the actual historical story of how the work came to be developed). In one case in which I was involved, both examiners essentially agreed on what the thesis had done well, and what was not in it that they would normally expect. Both examiners themselves worked in a similar field and used similar theories, yet one argued that the thesis needed to be rewritten to include more of the conventions of marking out aims, boundaries and literature, whereas the other argued that it could pass as it stood.

Here are some of the comments examiners made of theses that were submitted by their universities as the best of that particular year (emphasis added by me):[11]

> This is an impressive *contribution to knowledge* and understanding in the area.

> The *complexity and integrity* of the candidate's response to these two issues are impressive and engaging.

> Outstanding in every respect ... a remarkable *scholar* ...

> her *writing* is a joy to read

> the thesis provides ... *a challenge to the field* to think more clearly about

these critical issues in the future

this is an *elegant* thesis

What could have been a patriarchal, paternalistic enquiry became instead a *profound* analysis.

a *sophisticated* grasp of relevant literature

I would judge the study to be *especially sophisticated* ... because it employs both quantitative and qualitative methods and because the quantitative methods employed ... are clearly *state of the art* methodologies. Such methodological sophistication gives the reader considerable confidence in the robustness of the findings.

a *marvellous* piece of research

Its contribution to the knowledge of this difficult subject is substantial and *original*, and the research has been conducted meticulously, *avoiding* both the *superficiality* all too common with qualitative studies and the proving of the obvious which is so often the result of quantitative research.

The topic is an under-researched one and the approach that the author takes is *innovative and virtually unique.*

is to be commended for his *mastery of the subject* and for applying a methodology that is both appropriate and *revelatory*

what is really credible is the manner in which he has integrated all three areas into an *original, fascinating* study

Scholars of cultural capital and of 'research as writing' would have much to say about such comments. I think they illustrate well a number of the points I have been emphasizing in this chapter: that the best theses are seen as meeting the standards of the masters but clearly adding some new contribution. Their mastery is indicated as more than a matter of getting methodological techniques correct, but is seen in 'elegant' writing; 'sophisticated', 'state of the art' work that knows what the field has been saying and doing and that can convincingly argue for an approach that goes beyond that. The judgements are of form (especially the quality of the writing), of methodological quality and appropriateness, of substantive contribution, and of what the written text is assumed to indicate about the quality of the person who produced it, 'a remarkable scholar'.

Whatever critical points the examiners might also make in the reports on which I drew here, their overall judgements stress that these very good theses demonstrate sophisticated mastery and the making of some real contribution to the field. By contrast, a recent study (Lovat *et al.* 2000) has examined examiners' reports on theses that were judged to be not yet adequate, and to require rewriting and resubmission. The researchers here argue that what was notable about the reports was the way in which they adopt a strong 'gatekeeper' voice; that they did not write as if the writer of the thesis was a peer member of the community of scholars, but adopted the voice of a supervisor or tutor telling the writer what they had done wrong, and what they needed to fix. Frequently the issues raised by the examiners in these reports are about writing (not presenting a 'sufficiently detailed' or 'coherent' account of the overall study); flaws of methodology or logic of the thesis as a whole; or are about not having sufficient mastery of the relevant literature.

But we should also not forget that examiners' reports are themselves a genre, written for specific purposes. They are useful ways to consider some of the modes of judgement in this arena, but are not a transparent window as to how the examiner judged the thesis. Let us take one example. It used to be the case that I would expect reports to be written for and read by two limited audiences: the university committee that decided whether the thesis would pass; and the student and supervisor involved in producing it. I used to make sure I began my report with an unambiguous story to the committee of what my overall judgement was (that the thesis should pass, was a good one, and so on), and why. I would then discuss the thesis in some detail, speaking as an academic colleague to the writer who had often spent five or more years of their lives dwelling on that work, discussing what was enlightening and so on, but also mentioning any problems I could see, or things I would want to dispute, sometimes raising other areas or literature that might be relevant. A context of that examining was that most theses were, when I was first engaged in examining them, 'ungraded'. The required judgement was whether the thesis should pass, require amendment, or fail; the narrative report was a discussion or justification of that decision, as well as feedback to the writer regarding the further development or publication of their work. The judgement about whether to tick the 'top box' (pass as it stands), or the second box (pass after attending to minor corrections listed) was not seen by me as a major differentiation of the judgement I was making about the quality of the thesis, but simply as useful editorial feedback to the writer before the volume was placed in the library for others to read. More recently, however, it has become more common for the reports to be used for other purposes, such as competition for 'best thesis' awards inside and outside the institution where it was submitted. Here the temptation may be with a thesis where the overall judgement is that it is very good, to minimize or omit any criticisms that may reduce its chances in this competitive sphere, even if they might be useful; to see the boxes as a hierarchy of quality; and so on.

Let us again consider the comments of Lovat *et al.* (2000) regarding the 'gatekeeper' voice detected in the reports. Structurally, what is happening here is an examination. Just as a priest or other state-accredited person declaring you 'husband and wife' makes you married, the words of the examiners are a legal component of the judgement. If an examiner's report were to adopt an exceptionally modest and egalitarian tone, to stress his or her own inadequate knowledge, as a prelude to praising the superior work of the PhD writer, this would be to risk having the report rejected as an appropriate judgement on the worth of the PhD research. The judgement is whether the research here shows mastery of a particular field, and it is inherent that those chosen as examiners be accepted as insiders and experts in order for such a judgement to carry weight.

What does good research here look like?

The PhD is an interesting arena in which to consider arguments about 'research as writing' (Lee 1998; Richardson 2000). As we have seen, the explicit criteria in university examination regulations often specify many features of what the thesis must look like; commonly make reference to the requirement of a 'high standard' of expression or literary quality; and often ask examiners to provide a specific list of grammatical, spelling or typographical errors they detect (although this latter may be a form of examining the examiners, to check that they are reading it carefully – a growing problem as academic workloads and numbers of theses for examination are both rapidly increasing). In the PhD guidelines of one university from which I quoted earlier,[12] the very opening sentence of the handbook on the PhD thesis says this: 'Candidates are strongly advised to discuss with their supervisors the style of writing to be used in the thesis *before* writing begins' (emphasis in original).

Later, preceding the discussion of the instructions to examiners I quoted earlier, there is a lengthy section on 'editing of theses'. This section makes a distinction between 'providing guidelines about problems with style and accuracy' which is seen as appropriate work for a supervisor to do, including referring students to other units to improve their skill in this area; and editing that involves 'detailed and extensive correction' of the writing, especially of the final thesis, that is seen as not appropriate. It makes clear that learning to write in an appropriate way (acquiring expertise in writing and editing) is part of the research learning apprenticeship that the PhD is intended to provide. 'Supervisors should advise students about structure, style, and general editorial issues and should guide their candidates accordingly.' However, it distinguishes this advice from detailed correction of the thesis before submission by another source:

> 'A thesis must express the candidate's voice. ... The integrity of the work relies on the thesis as demonstrably the candidate's work, and must indicate that the candidate has the ability to write and argue with clarity.'

At least three different issues about writing are raised in these instructions and guidelines.

i   *Disciplinary differences concerning what is an acceptable style and structure of a thesis*

The fact that the very first sentence in this particular set of guidelines warns the student about the need to discuss 'style of writing' reflects a context where there is growing diversity and divergence in what different fields and disciplines consider acceptable. To take a common example: in styles of research that work with assumptions about the possibility of 'objective' inquiry and inquiry that is replicable (that is, able in principle to be done by another researcher, and to produce the same findings) the use of a passive voice in which the particularities of the researcher are not present in the writing would be common.

> This study takes advantage of the availability of data sources held in the state education department. It has gathered data through diverse methods, including surveys and interviews with key personnel. A method of bivariate analysis was utilized to explore associations between variables.[13]

The authority of this type of research relates to issues such as adequacy of sampling, use of appropriate statistical tests, construction of surveys or attitude scales that are properly tested and validated. The thesis is seen as a work of reporting what was done, including the findings, and offering some objective theoretical interpretation of those findings. Whether the researcher was a man or a woman, a liberal or a conservative, is not seen as important to the judging of the quality of the work that was done. In principle, the work reported should be replicable by someone else, so the particularities of the researcher are not present in the text. The writing uses passive voice, or de-personalizes the actor in the research to be 'the study'.

Alternatively, in qualitative case study or ethnographic study, it is part of the methodological assessment of quality to know more about who the researcher was, how they entered the field; how those they studied might have seen them and their purposes and adjusted their own behaviour or answers as a result.

> I began this research with these kinds of thoughts, experiences and
> questions in my mind ... I have spent over seven years working at the
> case study site discussed in this thesis ... Throughout that time I kept
> records in diary and journal form, collected video and audiotapes of
> music within the school and documents describing the curriculum...[14]

The readers need to see how aware the researcher was about these
matters, and the way to demonstrate methodological quality is usually by
including some first-person account in which incidents of the fieldwork
are discussed, so that some picture is offered of both what the researcher
was doing (what steps they were taking), and what were their thinking
processes (what types of awareness preceded and accompanied the
steps). In studies like this, first-person accounts would usually be seen as
essential, because a passive voice would indicate that the researcher was
not thinking enough about their own impact on the object of study and
was not scrutinizing sufficiently critically what happened in the field.

Or again, research that is working with postmodern concerns about
disrupting common sense, and finding other ways of opening up perspectives on a particular arena, is likely to have a structure of chapters
that is not simply linear, but involves bits of empirical work and reflective
discussions, other ways in, and revisiting earlier discussions, and so on.

> I cannot/will not deny that this section is part of the revision of the
> thesis. It was not part of the original document. It has been impossible
> to write it naively as if it was.[15]

Creative writing, photographs, video or computer records may all be
included within particular logics of research approach.

In the instructions quoted earlier, one large and prestigious university
(Melbourne) begins its PhD handbook with a warning that writing style
needs to be discussed from the beginning with one's supervisor. This is an
indication that today, divergent forms of writing have proliferated and
been accepted, but that these are contentious between different groups of
experts.[16] There is no longer one single formulaic style or structure to the
acceptable doctoral research, but this does *not* mean that judgements
about appropriateness of the writing have ceased to be important.

ii   *The distinction issue*

The university is the institutionalized, visible form of the highest level of
being 'an educated person' (Bourdieu 1998), and within this, the doctoral thesis is the highest form of examination. The thesis regulations
traditionally appear to have an obsession with being 'error free' in terms
of expression, often asking the examiner to comment specifically on the

quality of the writing. In this regard the writing or 'looks like' aspects of the doctorate exemplify an expression of the cultural hierarchy within which the degree is located. It is the highest level whereby the visible accomplishment of the educated person is demonstrated, so high levels of ability to speak and write correctly in educated or formal language are expected. This requirement is currently under some strain, partly from the globalization of universities, and the presence of many students completing doctorates not in their first language; and partly because of the infiltration of the world outside the universities and greater presence of market needs. In the latter case, there is some new questioning of why expectations about writing mode should be so different for a university degree from that required in the fast-paced world of business and electronic communication.

iii   *The issue of 'voice': if the study has been extensively rewritten by an editor, can examiners judge its quality as research?*

The section on 'editing of theses' from which I have quoted above would once not have been present in the guidelines of this university on doctoral work; it would not have been considered necessary because it would not be envisaged that writers might use an editor. That it is present now, and the particular line that is taken on voice, reflect both the changing student body and practices; and also the particular history of this institution. In most Western countries, university postgraduate populations have changed considerably in recent times. There is a much larger international student population; and a much larger group of people undertaking their studies as employed and relatively senior professionals, rather than the young student immediately proceeding from an honours degree who is the implicit doctoral student of so much policy-making. Both the internationalization, and the drawing into graduate study of part-time mature people employed in relatively senior positions, has given rise to the visible pressure to use editorial assistance. International students and their supervisors struggle to produce an extensive document in a second language, in the same conditions and timescale as local students. Part-time students whose other life in the workplace makes extensive use of secretaries or personal assistants; who see themselves as busy professionals; may simply see this final form of editorial checking and polishing as a sensible division of labour on a technical task, akin to having someone else do the typing and layout of the work.

The key question is how closely correction and improvement of grammar *is* akin to having a document nicely typed and laid out; and how much it is presenting a 'contribution to knowledge' that is not simply the work of the researcher, but is really a co-production of what the research 'is'.

Issues of 'voice' and 'research as writing' have a different significance in different areas and styles of research. It is certainly arguable that with qualitative, post-structural, philosophical, highly theoretical and policy research, the writing is inseparable from the contribution being made. Conversely, it is also at least arguable that with some kinds of research that use highly structured methods, quantification and computer modelling, that some distinction can be made, and that the thesis can be seen as a report on the research rather than the research itself: that the heart of the contribution is not in the words in which it is presented in its final product. I discussed these different traditions of doctoral work in an earlier part of this chapter. In the case of Melbourne University, the university quoted, which has a strong position on having access to the 'candidate's voice', it is not accidental that it is one of the oldest universities in Australia, with a very strong humanities faculty, and a marketing mode that wants to emphasize its elite qualities – including its association with social elites. In this case the emphasis on 'voice' has some of the qualities that Bourdieu (Bourdieu 1984, 1998) has written about: it is a way of distinguishing those who 'belong' from those who come from different classes or cultures.

A further issue about voice in the good thesis flows from the earlier discussion about explicit and implicit criteria. The thesis is being judged on its ability to acknowledge the existing field adequately as well as on its ability to add something new. It is being judged in terms of whether this newcomer deserves to be seen as a peer. In the face of these tasks, a tone of arrogance can be a problem and so can a tone of excessive modesty. The writer must not dismiss sweepingly what has gone before, but must demonstrate appreciation as well as critique. But they must also make the case that they have something to add. Inability to offer any criticisms in the literature review is a problem (as the University of London says, it should be 'succinct, penetrating and challenging to read'). Being self-conscious about how the project adds to the existing work means, in textual terms, neither grossly exaggerating, nor underselling what has been achieved. Gender, class and cultural differences in what students bring to this task mean that for some the achievement of this voice is a much more difficult accomplishment than for others. (For some examples of approaches to thinking about this problem, see Leonard 1997; Mahoney and Zmroczek 1997; Bourdieu 1998; Lee and Williams 1999, Popkewitz 2000; Middleton 2001.)

Common problems or failings

The PhD version of research, then, requires a particular type of writing that demonstrates particular types of knowledge (relation to a research community), with particular types of textual qualities. Students who embark on such work in education, often as mature students, can easily not recognize the specificities of such requirements. Problems I have noticed (and that are often reflected in critical examiners' comments) include the following:

- Especially for mature students: working to discourse or genre conventions they are familiar with (teacher judgements, TAFE reports) and not recognizing that this is a particular *academic* discourse convention which has highest levels of expectation regarding systematic and self-critical methodology.

- 'Unclear focus': a lot of this practice is about *being self-conscious* – about being able to say what it was you are on about, and why these were adequate ways to do that. Students are often stronger on particular bits they want to say, or do, on justifying particular methodological steps within their project, than on being able to think about how the whole package hangs together so that the methodology is judged adequate to the aims and the final claims. As one set of advice to doctoral students puts it 'there will be an intellectual wholeness to the submission'.[17]

- Competing cultural specificities. Few things have made me as aware of some of the assumptions of the 'discourse' or conventions I work in as having foreign students to supervise. The expectations in Australian social science research place a high value on critique, specificity and careful steps of argument. In recent years I have worked with foreign students whose own higher education and cultural criteria of good research gives prominence to different things: for example students from Russia, oriented more to big overview claims and theories, to working with a range of literatures, and being expected to know research written in at least three languages, coming into a department highly concerned with small and careful steps of validation, interested in case study and qualitative work and largely discussing Anglophone literature; or from Japan and advancing an argument in much more implicit and subtle ways rather than explicit statements of the critiques that were common in Australian work in the same area.

- Competing disciplinary specificities. In education it is not unusual for people from one disciplinary background to do a thesis in another – for example, to move from linguistics to policy research; or to have done a degree in science but now be studying classroom behaviour. But different traditions and paradigms of research in education have quite different expectations about how one establishes one's methodological adequacy. For example, as I discussed earlier, some forms of research which focus on producing large-scale, quantified testing disapprove of the use of the first person. Other forms of qualitative, interpretive research see knowledge as grounded in the relation between researcher and researched, and would find it methodologically inadequate if the writer did not use the first person and explore their own positioning.

- In terms of students doing qualitative research: thinking they can interview six people and write out what happened and get a doctorate – and not thinking enough about what makes this count as *research* or as a *contribution to knowledge*. (You can do a thesis on a very small scale – but you need a sense of why your research contribution is different from simply bumping into someone and asking them the same questions.)

- In terms of students doing quantitative research: losing the big picture – focusing on fine statistical differences, without enough interpretation of whether these are educationally meaningful.

- In terms of students doing postmodern or post-structural research: claiming originality for something that is now both highly fashionable and a cliché.

So:
What does good research look like in terms of the PhD?

At the heart of the PhD is *mastery of the conventions* (literature, methodology, 'staging') and *adding something recognizable for the existing masters or gate-keepers of those conventions* (the examiners). Technical adequacy is a necessary condition here, and the basis for a 'pass'. The basis for being judged as a good piece of research is the scale of the original contribution: either (or both) that it is going to have some impact on the professional field, or that it redirects or adds in a significant way to the ways that researchers are currently framing their problems for that field. However, compared with other arenas of our social world, simply having something important or transformative to say does not make this a 'good piece of research' – it has to meet conventions for defending claims and being systematic. A major issue for doctoral students in education is that, in relation to any particular project, 'the field' in the sense of the particular bodies of appropriate theory and methodology and expertise, is not simply a given but has to be constructed. Good research writing in the case of the PhD is hyper-correct and simultaneously modest and authoritative.

4

Academic journals

The pragmatics: how do academic journals work?

Arena	Judges	Explicit criteria	Implicit criteria	What does it look like?	Common failings
Academic journal	Editor (named)	methodologically sound	'voice', writing style	abstract dispassionately sets out	neophyte voice
('refereed' or 'peer-reviewed')	Editorial Board (named)	contribution to knowledge	ratio of article quality relative to size of backlog	specificity of contribution	not linking to that journal's previous articles/
	Academic referees	appropriate for *this* journal	timeliness	literature references are prominent	authors
			recognizable citations		not demonstrating succinctly contribution being made
				writes as equal in the research literature	
				usually sequence of 1 where-this-is-coming-from (including previous work); 2 why-my-approach-is-authoritative; 3 my findings or theory and why they matter	
				carries journal's house style ('voice' as well as citation conventions)	

Publishing in 'refereed' academic journals is a central concern for people seeking academic jobs or jobs in government-funded research organizations, lecturers seeking promotion, new PhD graduates applying for fellowships, academics proving annually that they are operating effectively as researchers and for university departments proving their relative research performance. It is a key criterion, possibly the major one (together with winning research grants and referees' reports) of whether they are doing good research. Put another way, in university contexts, a pragmatic indicator of what 'good research' looks like is that it is research that has been published in or is publishable in academic refereed journals.

What is a refereed academic journal?

This journal publishes academic articles from throughout the world which contribute to contemporary debates in the cultural politics of education. It adopts a broadly critical orientation, but is not tied to any particular political, disciplinary or methodological position. In order to ensure a journal of the highest quality, all contributions are submitted to at least two referees before acceptance for publication. Apart from the main articles and book reviews, the journal will also, from time to time, contain review essays, symposium on emerging issues and interviews and policy interventions.

(*Discourse: Studies in the Cultural Politics of Education* journal – cover and website statement)

Education Evaluation and Policy Analysis (ISSN:0162–3737) is published quarterly by the American Educational Research Association ... *EEPA* publishes manuscripts of theoretical or practical interest to those engaged in education evaluation or policy analysis, including economic, demographic, financial and political analyses of education policies; syntheses of previously completed policy studies, evaluation theories, and methodologies; results of significant evaluation efforts; retrospective views of evaluation studies; and book reviews related to education evaluation and policy issues. ... Four copies of the manuscript should be submitted ... and must conform to the guidelines of the *Publication Manual of the American Psychological Association* ... Manuscripts are accepted for consideration with the understanding that they are original material and are not under consideration for publication elsewhere. The review process normally takes 4 months.

(*Education Evaluation and Policy Analysis* journal, statement on inside cover)

A refereed journal is a publication to which writers submit articles reporting their research, and where those articles are then sent out by the editor to be assessed by two or more people who themselves hold academic positions and are considered to have expertise in the area of research with which the article is concerned. Another term for journals of this type is 'peer-reviewed', meaning that it is assumed that both the writers of the articles submitted and the people who assess these articles will be recognized as qualified people in the same academic field, usually, though not always, holding doctorates; and usually, though not always, holding a position in a university. But while it is true that both submitters of articles and assessors of them may be peers, the two categories are not identical. Referees and editors also write and submit research articles, but not all people who write and submit research articles, particularly people starting out, would be used as referees. I will discuss this further below.

Here is a description of a typical process by which articles are submitted to, assessed and published in an academic journal:

1   Author sends in the article (following instructions on the journal inside cover or journal website as to the number of copies required, conventions, abstract, title page, anonymity, and so on).
2   Editor may or may not send letter of acknowledgement.
3   Editor reads title and abstract and selects appropriate referees. (Occasionally the editor may decide on the initial reading that the article is inappropriate or of such poor quality that they may reject without sending out to referees.) Journals usually use two to three referees, but may use more. Usually referees are contacted first to check that they are available to do the task.
4   (Three to twelve months' delay while editor tries to extract reports from referees.)
5   Editor reads referees' reports and makes a decision on the article, which is sent to the author. Editor will either
    • accept article as is;
    • accept article subject to revision as specified;
    • ask author to revise to address the criticisms in the reports, then resubmit and we *may* accept [article will go through the review process again];
    • reject (editor may suggest alternative journals).
6   If accepted, or 'accepted subject to revisions', the letter will normally give instructions and a time-line for the final submission. Normally both disc and hard copy are required at this stage. With the large journal publishers, the author is now also required to sign a contract and supply a list of copyright permissions to the publisher, and certify that they will take legal responsibility for the content (in relation to plagiarism, defamation, and so on).

7   Author submits corrected hard copy and disc.
8   Around 4–6 weeks before publication, author *may* be sent proofs to check and correct for typographical errors (not all journals do this). Author is not permitted to make changes of substance at this stage. Normally proofs have to be read and returned within 7–14 days.
9   Some 1 to 2 years after initial submission, the article appears in print (or in 'published electronic form').
10 Sometimes immediately, sometimes 1–3 years after the article appears in print, it becomes accessible through database and citation indexes.

In recent times the operation of academic journals has been markedly reshaped by two related developments. The growing importance of the Internet and of electronic sources for libraries and literature searching and retrieval has led to the development of new journals that are solely disseminated in online form (and whose time-line may be much compressed compared with the 'typical' process outlined above). For existing journals, the growth of new technologies has resulted in an expanded significance of being placed on availability in online form, and being indexed in and searchable through key online search engines. Libraries increasingly purchase access to online versions of journals instead of, or in addition to, the print form. Accompanying this growth of new forms of access, there has been in recent decades a marked consolidation (concentration) of the publishing firms which deal with academic journals, as well as an expansion of their activities in terms of range of titles carried and global reach. Where once many professional associations or local publishers were involved in publishing and marketing certain journals, most are now published by a relatively few global and commercial publishing houses, particularly Carfax/Taylor & Francis, Elsevier, Sage, Kluwer, Triangle. (The very large American Education Research Association also still self-publishes and distributes its own range of journals.) The form of publishing, the economies of scale they encompass in relation to procedural matters, and the commercial value of expanding the lists which they can offer to libraries, means that the number of specific journal titles in a given field has expanded enormously. So there are more 'niche' opportunities for publication of particular types of research interest. Taylor & Francis, for example, in April 2003 was listing 30 different journals in the general area of 'Education Policy' and even more under 'Education Research'. Even within the header 'Sociology of Education' it offers 16 titles! Some consequences of these changing contexts and agendas for 'refereed publication' will be discussed below.

Situating refereed publication as a marker of good research

To many readers, it might seem strange that I would take time to spell out definitions and the process of journal publication in the way that I have done at the beginning of this section – equivalent to telling university level essay-writers that sentences need to begin with a capital letter. But the centrality and the practices of journal publication as a means of adjudicating good research are neither timeless nor uniform, and there are understandable reasons why awareness of this arena is quite unevenly spread among those who work in education faculties and in similar fields of professional research.

Science and non-science

'Refereed' journal publication draws its status as a marker of research quality particularly from the practices of scientific and medical research. In the world of scientific discovery, at least until recently, peer-reviewed publication was the normal mode by which advances were communicated and built. One of the characteristics of science is that researchers in different parts of the world are working on the same problems, attempting to advance the next insight, theory, findings, applied achievement. For science to advance it needs a background of communicated knowledge about what is already reliably known or has been experimentally investigated (although this too is under some transformation given the growing significance of research being done within or sponsored by rich commercial enterprises that do not allow free publishing). In principle, in any field of science, there is a hierarchy of journals, with those that are seen to be of most significance (for example, *Nature, British Medical Journal*) using the most rigorous processes of refereed judgement from the most expert sources. In the sciences, publication in book form is necessarily of less recent discoveries. That form of publication is normally either for textbook purposes or to serve as a review or collation of a field for reference purposes, and, especially in the case of textbooks, can be of lesser status than the publication of refereed articles on the original research itself.

In the humanities and social sciences, the history of research and its communication is different. Often it has been particular important or landmark books rather than journal articles that have had a lasting impact, that attract major discussion, that continue to be cited and to shape future work. For example, taking history as a field, a typical research project or agenda involves a range of investigations (archives, texts, and so on), but equally important is the way that those investigations are put together as an argument or narrative. Journal-length articles may make important points about particular debates or issues of interpretation; or they may provide a historical account of a relatively restricted object of investigation – but a book-length publication is likely to be necessary to put together an account that is seen as of major significance. Consider, for example, the wide impact in the USA of a sociological book such as Robert Putnam's *Bowling Alone* (2000), or of E.D. Hirsch's *Cultural Literacy* (1978). Those fields do not automatically see journal publication as more important than book publication. However, here too, when university promotion and grant committees assess the quality of published work, they place weight on the concept of peer review and peer testing of the research. In the case of books, this will often come in the form of 'serious' reviews and discussions of the book in the refereed journals of that field.

Education as a field encompasses both types of the research traditions discussed above. It includes research that is science-like (experimental reporting and theory building), and research that is humanities-like (building a broad and interpretive case from a range of evidence, such as the book-length examples mentioned above). But education has a further complicating issue: its prime audiences and its forms of publication are not only directed to research peers. Books are not necessarily 'scholarly' nor intended as examples of good research – but they may be! In terms of university purposes of assessing research quality, however, the issue of peer assessment or review is a central issue. (The issue of 'impact' or outcomes or 'contribution to the professional field' may be others.) In the case of book publication, promotion and grant committees often have to do further work to decide what weight they will place on that as evidence of research achievement (is it 'merely a textbook'?). Refereed journals have a more ready currency, and articles published in them can be taken as a signifier of prior judgement of quality by those who *are* expert in the field of the research.

The debate raised by Hargreaves and Tooley in the UK raised a further matter. They argued that the journals of the field were not being rigorous in the articles they accepted. Effectively (as discussed in Chapter 1) they were arguing for a form of supra-expert judgement of what methodological quality looks like that would supersede the type of peer judgement that has been the norm in the sciences. As I also noted earlier, the authors involved in producing the recent US report on *Scientific Research in Education* appear to fudge the problem that the Tooley and Hargreaves-generated debate raised. That report argued that peer review is 'the single most commonly used mechanism for nurturing a scientific culture' and should play a central role in ensuring the scientific status of education research, but then concluded this section of their argument with the following comment: 'The key to peer review, of course, is competent peers, and understanding what *competent* means in scientific education research is complex given the diversity associated with the field' (Feuer *et al.* 2002: 10). In other words, education as a field is asked to take peer review as a central marker of research quality because this conforms to some sense of how good research in general (scientific research) does this, and because it is a mechanism readily used as a proxy by promotion and grant committees. But at the same time there is some reluctance to accept that all the directions that peers have taken education research are appropriate.

Nevertheless, although I argued earlier against those who would want to impose a single methodological form or set of criteria in relation to education research, the issue of the current proliferation of journals, together with the debate generated by Tooley and others, does raise the matter of how a field of expertise becomes defined and accepted for the purpose of being an appropriate tool of peer judgement. On the one hand, it is the characteristic of all fields of research knowledge and theory to change and generate new foci of interest, new combinations of methodological approach, and to generate internal debates with rival theories and paradigms. In the 1960s and early 1970s questions about curriculum became prominent in many education systems and within about a decade from 1968, four new journals naming curriculum as their field of interest were founded (*Journal of Curriculum Studies*, which was UK-based; *Curriculum Inquiry*, founded in Canada; *Journal of Curriculum Theorizing*, in the USA; and *Curriculum Perspectives* in Australia). At other times 'policy' burgeoned as a field of interest and new journal titles; and other new journals arose to publish articles on gender, race or 'pedagogy' (indeed a journal with which I was associated changed its name in this period from *Curriculum Studies* to *Pedagogy, Culture and Society*). Changes of this type are an indicator of changing problems, conditions or agendas that have become important, and these usually relate both to issues of the field of professional practice (education systems, schools) and to new directions of theorizing (for example in sociology, or in psychology or social theory). On the other hand, those who wish to use the criterion of peer review as a mechanism of quality want to see that more than vanity publishing or cult-like status is associated with a particular journal.

A different but related issue for peer review as the measure of education research is found in the problem that grant committees and university hierarchies and the general public frequently expect *education* researchers to have demonstrated an appropriate dissemination of research to education practitioners. Writing for academic journals and disseminating well to a general audience are not the same task, so there are choices to be made about time allocation. Gaskell and McLeod (forthcoming) discuss this problem in relation to a major initiative of funding by the Canadian Social Science and Humanities Research Council, which was to set up large inter-disciplinary networks, specifically including industry partners, to address major applied problems. A condition of funding in this programme was for ongoing communication with different partners, practitioners and the lay public. Gaskell and McLeod found that academics in one network at least felt caught between the need to 'bury' results in top academic journals – the 'bottom line' not just for promotion but for further funding from the SSHRC – and the need to undertake the wider dissemination that was a formal requirement of this project.

Electronic journals, electronic access and the research quality issue

The issue of whether specialist peers are the appropriate judges, or whether education research is better judged and validated by the community as a whole is being given new life in the debates around moves to open access and online forms of publication. Writing in relation to The Public Knowledge Project and Open Journal Systems, at the University of British Columbia,[18] John Willinsky argues strongly in favour of journals being freely available rather than copyrighted. He argues that such 'open access' serves both public interest (democracy) and the interests of writers 'by giving them the widest possible readership, and contributing to reputation-building with its direct salary benefits within the university job market' (Willinsky 2002). Nevertheless, his case assumes that editors and reviewers will still go on assessing and gate-keeping articles associated with a journal prior to its online publication, presumably as a quality check prior to access by the 'widest possible readership'.

The *Journal of Digital Information* in which one of Willinsky's arguments is published similarly slides between seeing popularity and seeing expert peer judgement as the appropriate source of assessment for academic work. On the one hand, its website advertises open access and scrutiny as the promise and heart of its new electronic form ('Journals do not have to be slow and exclusive'), and, on the other, its banners seem concerned to show that traditional quality checks and associations with experts are all in place:

> The Journal of Digital Information (JoDI) is supported by the British Computer Society and Oxford University Press.

> The Gold Standard peer-reviewed electronic-only journal for serious research . . .

> [JoDI] shows that electronic journals can do all that the best print journals can do – offering peer-reviewed papers, wide recognition for authors, backed by high-quality editorial standards . . .

In another revealing recent article, three writers who themselves are employed by important electronically accessed archives and dissemination tools, ERIC and TVEE.ORG, discuss online journal usage in relation to issues of academic reputation and rigour (Rudner *et al.* 2002). They are enthusiastic about the potential reach of the new forms, as well as the ability to monitor hits electronically (and demonstrate the 'accounting' form of measuring quality that James and McQueen-Thomson (2002) argue is permeating both publishing and universities). But the implications of the argument they develop, if accepted, would radically shift emphasis from peer assessment of research quality to one of the popularity with which an article is accessed as the main criteria.

In this article on online journal usage, Rudner *et al.* begin by reporting that a typical article in a scientific journal in the USA is read about 900 times, while some electronic journals in education 'appear to be having a far greater impact'. They say, 'It is not uncommon for an article in *Education Policy Analysis Archives (EPAA)* to be *read* more than 10,000 times; [and] several articles have been *viewed* more than 30,000 times' (my italics added: hitting an article that a link throws up is not quite the same as using it). Indeed, the article continues, previous research has shown that most readers are accessing articles for 'restricted' purposes (for example, because it is required for a set essay) or are 'tourists' rather than 'enthusiastic users', and they cite a previous study that suggests that the 'scholarly, peer-reviewed e-journals' were having 'essentially no impact on scholarly communication in their respective fields'. Rudner *et al.*, however, argue that citation analysis may not be fully appropriate here as citation rates in education generally are low (this was one of Tooley's criticisms of the field). They prefer to draw attention to research on links 'using reports from Google' (in other words, researching how many people go to a particular journal article, rather than what they do once they have accessed it).

Rudner *et al.* acknowledge that for academics *journal reputation* is extremely important, and that currently academics fear that tenure committees may undervalue online journals relative to more established print journals. But their recommended strategy in the face of this is to emphasize that online journals 'have a much greater impact in terms of educating readers', and to suggest that academics emphasize this point, that is, bypassing the issue that the traditional role of refereed journals was to provide an adjudication of quality function. In their suggestions to editors and publishers to improve the 'reputation' of their journal, Rudner *et al.* do not talk about refereeing, but rather encourage various strategies for increasing popularity (number of hits), via such means as knowing which topics are more often accessed ('testing' is good apparently, and so are 'portfolios') and strategies for improving journal and article profile in indexes.

Here once more we see the way education research does not have a single and simple marker of how 'quality' is judged. Historically, especially in universities, the institutional tools of peer expertise are important, as are understood hierarchies of institutional and academic status. But education is a field that has an applied object of study and broad relationship to the community. Writers from quite different ends of the political spectrum argue that the broadest community judgement is an *appropriate* source of 'reputation' in this area. But common too in current debates is an unease with straightforwardly leaving judgement to one or other of these courts of appeal (even apart from the fact that they interpenetrate each other, as I discuss in Chapters 1 and 2).

Willinsky as well as Rudner *et al.* are implicitly critical of judgements of quality that stay internal to a relatively restricted group of other researchers – and so, indeed, were the panel that produced the scientifically-based research report in the USA. But most of their arguments do not want to simply equate quality research with market penetration. James and McQueen-Thomson are concerned that what can be easily measured (hits and links regarding particular hot topics) is assuming more importance than why people are accessing articles and what they think of them or do with them when they read them.

Here we can see how different human and technological interests are beginning to shape and change what counts as good work. The ability to count how many times something is accessed compared with the cost of reviewing how something is used, reviewed or critiqued by others; the fact that access itself becomes dominated by certain indexing and searching mechanisms; the costs of different activities (such as unpaid editing and reviewing of articles) and the differential ability of different institutions and different academics to bear these costs, all play some part in the likely future shaping of this field (James and McQueen-Thomson 2002).

The current situation is, therefore, one of considerable movement and debate in relation to peer-reviewed journals, but at present, whether journals are online or not, and whether demonstrating dissemination is becoming of greater importance now that it can be more easily measured, the peer-reviewing mechanisms discussed in this chapter still remain very important in many fields where the quality of research is judged, and particularly in the institutions where most education researchers are still employed (universities) and where many of them still seek funding for their research (competitive research grant schemes).

Who are the judges?

The judges of research in the case of peer-reviewed journals are the editor(s), the members of the editorial board, and the other academics who are used to referee (assess) articles. The editor and editorial board are named on the journal cover or website. In some cases the editor and board remain in place indefinitely, until they wish to resign, and in cases where a particular person has started the journal and been the founding editor, they will normally nominate their successor, or carry weight in this decision. The editorial board is normally selected by the editor(s). In some cases, particularly those journals sponsored by or associated with professional associations, there is a specified period of tenure of an editorial team (for example, three years). In this case, prior to the conclusion of one team's tenure, the association will call for submissions to be Editor of the journal for the next phase, and applicants will submit their credentials and policy which will be adjudicated by the executive of the association, or a sub-committee of that. Articles are normally sent for review (refereeing) to at least two academics with knowledge of the field of the article; and sometimes as many as five or six people will be used (this was the practice of the AERA journal *Review of Education Research* in the period I was on its editorial board as its brief was to produce 'authoritative' overviews of research topics). Often those named as members of the editorial board will be used more regularly than others for the purpose of refereeing; and they will also be used to provide advice about names of others who might referee particular articles.

So referees are drawn from the networks of those named as Editor and as members of the editorial board. In some journals there is an annual acknowledgement and naming of those who act as referees. In others there is no public acknowledgement. Reports sent to writers of articles do not normally name the referees, although some journals do have a policy of doing so and the issue of the anonymity of the referees is often debated by editorial boards. The judgement about acceptance or revision or rejection made on the basis of the referees' reports will be made by the Editor (or the review editor in the case of book reviews and review essays).

The previous paragraphs indicate some of the formal processes through which people come to be selected to pass judgement on research as peers. But *who* are they? In my experience, part or all of three dynamics may be at play in deciding who, from the entire field of those who are academics doing research, will be involved in judging articles for publication as editors or referees.

First, there is an issue of *status*: the rank that the Editor(s) and the members of the editorial board are seen to have in their academic community. The rank of the personnel whose names are attached to a journal is one way that the status of the publication itself is read: it will shape the extent to which researchers of standing will themselves attempt to publish in that forum, and is likely to be a key issue when major professional associations make decisions about an editorial team. A new journal with a relatively less senior Editor may attempt to give itself greater weight by attaching to its board people who are already 'names'.

One way of ascertaining status can be seen by reading the lists of editors and board members of the journals in a field, and noting the ones who are represented on multiple publications (this exercise will also indicate the power of certain people within a particular research community to define what good research is). Similarly, editorship and editorial board membership is seen as a sign of one's status as a researcher, and can be used for this purpose in promotion applications, grant track record applications, and such like.

Secondly, there is an element of *entrepreneurialism*. Younger researchers who wish to gain greater recognition for a particular type of research, or research focus, may approach a publishing house to start a new journal (though they have to be able to make a case that there is some breadth of interest in the field they wish to name). Established as well as newer researchers who are unhappy with the particular orientation of the main journals in their field may deliberately start a new journal with a self-conscious and explicitly proclaimed agenda to represent a different approach to that field (for example *Journal of Feminist Psychology, Journal of Curriculum Theorizing*). In this case, they will be careful to 'seed' the editorial board with the names of those they consider are doing the most interesting and visible work of the kind they wish to promote – the names on the editorial board are as much a way of advertising the agenda of the journal as is their explicit statement of editorial policy. In some cases too, researchers who have a more instrumental or cynical approach to building a 'track record' may deliberately initiate a number of journals and reciprocal board memberships.

Thirdly, editors, editorial board members and anonymous referees are all ultimately chosen from or with regard to *networks*: their associations with and recognition by other academics. How do networks come to be? Through supervisors and fellow students and colleagues at a particular university; through regular attendance at conferences and active participation in professional associations (for example, standing for the executive, taking on tasks such as conference organizing); through making contact with other researchers whose work interests you – by email, in person following a paper, through mutual acquaintances.

In other words, those who come to exercise power in judging good research in this arena are not simply those who themselves have done good research, but are researchers who have also engaged in certain types of activities and associations beyond their own research projects. Those who *are* involved in these networks are likely to have multiple opportunities to build a tacit as well as formal sense of 'what counts' as good research. Conversely, those who are not involved in such networks or roles in professional associations, journals and conferences may find it more difficult to position their research writing in a way that appears to have the required 'voice' for a particular journal – the voice or particular narrative style of an experienced researcher, an insider, or a peer in the research community.

Explicit and implicit criteria

Referee's report

Reference No: **Date:**

Manuscript title:

Name of Referee:

  Overall assessment (please tick ones as appropriate)

(1) Worth publishing as it stands   (   )

(2) Requires minor amendments as specified   (   )

(3) Requires major rewriting along the lines suggested (   )

(4) Should be rejected   (   )

REVIEWER'S COMMENTS (please type)

Dear XXX

We are pleased to inform you that there has been an initially favourable response to the article ..., submitted by you for consideration for publishing in the Journal. Enclosed are copies of the referees' comments. If you are willing to substantially revise according to their requirements and resubmit it, then we will reconsider your article. Can you please let us know your decision as soon as possible?

When referees are sent an article to review, it is accompanied by a pro forma on which they are asked to tick ratings of the quality of the article (sometimes but not always differentiating features of this such as contribution; methodological soundness; quality of writing); to recommend that it be published as is, or published with minor corrections or polishing, or that something more substantial needs attention before it might be accepted for publication, or that it be rejected. They are also asked for an accompanying written report which discusses the strengths of the article and any problems in it. In many ways these criteria mirror those of the thesis examination discussed in Chapter 3. However, pro formas frequently include two additional features that are different from the criterion-based assessment of the thesis. One common additional question asks the reviewer to indicate whether the article is 'suitable for this particular journal' (and sometimes to make suggestions about other journals if it is not). Another requirement is that in each of the main criteria regarding the submitted article (contribution, methodological soundness, quality of writing), referees are often asked to give a comparative rating of quality: does this make a major contribution, or only a medium or marginal one? Does its methodological design indicate research of the highest quality, or just an adequate approach to its issue?

How does the question 'is this research article suitable for this journal?' differ from the question 'is this good research?' First, it is a recognition that journals are set up with different briefs and different scope. Sometimes they are differentiated by a disciplinary designation (sociology, psychology, philosophy); sometimes by an agenda named in the title ('review of education research', 'culture, pedagogy and society', 'journal of early childhood studies', 'studies in continuing education', 'international journal of qualitative studies in education', 'international journal of inclusive education'). Sometimes, in addition to the title, there is a formal 'mission statement' that designates the type of research a particular journal is set up to publish, particularly any designations regarding methodological style. The cover blurbs of the two journals quoted at the beginning of this chapter are examples of statements of the scope and thrust of particular journals. *Discourse*, for example, draws attention to its interest in a 'broadly critical orientation', and claims that it is not tied to a specific disciplinary approach. *EEPA* explicitly nominates some of the broad range of disciplines, theories and types of article ('theory', 'evaluation', 'retrospective') it sees as falling within its scope. Here are some further examples of journals identifying what work falls within their agenda:

> ... articles from throughout the world which contribute to both theory and empirical research in the sociology of education. It attempts to reflect the variety of perspectives current in the field.
>
> (*British Journal of Sociology of Education*)

> The Editors welcome a variety of contributions that focus on gender as a category of analysis in education and that further feminist knowledge, theory, consciousness, action and debate. Education will be interpreted in a broad sense.
>
> (*Gender and Education*)

> The editor invites submissions utilizing all methods of inquiry. Both empirical and theoretical papers are considered, but papers that combine well developed theoretical frameworks with careful empirical work are particularly appreciated.
>
> (*Teachers College Record*)

Statistics. Given the experimental remit of this journal, it is expected that indications of effect size will be included by authors, where possible, so as to allow readers to form a judgement as to the importance of any experimental findings reported.

(Educational Psychology)

The explicit mission statement is one starting point for a neophyte researcher seeking appropriate locations for publication, but it usually reveals only part of the enacted scope of a particular journal: what type of work it tends to publish, what level of relative quality is required to gain publication. Usually, regardless of whether this is explicitly stated by the editors, over time particular journals will tend to carry particular types of work and not others. Despite the *BJSE* statement about reflecting the variety of perspectives in the field, it carries markedly more interpretive and markedly less quantitatively-based research than its US equivalent, for example. It is not uncommon for new journals to be initiated with very similar titles to an existing journal (consider the numerous journals of curriculum studies, or sociology of education, or policy studies) but the range of work they carry – their 'identity' – is not the same as each other. Experienced researchers know that a decision about where an article will be sent needs to be accompanied by attention to the types of work, and discussion or arguments, that that particular journal has carried; and the article will need to be written to connect in some way with that specific body of work. One clue for new researchers as to where their own work should be directed is to take notice of those journals which publish the type of work they routinely draw on themselves.

A second issue that 'appropriate for this journal' invites referees to take into account without baldly stating it, is the issue of hierarchy. Some journals are known to be more prestigious (and selective) than others (because more high-quality work is submitted to them) and it will be more difficult to be published in them. So a reviewer might say that an article is competent, but not making a sufficient contribution for this particular journal, but might be publishable in a 'lesser' journal – one that receives less material and publishes a greater range of quality. Of course, 'quality' here is contextual. It includes issues of voice that will be discussed shortly; and it also includes substantive topic. An article that is about a study of a school innovation in a city in the USA may be published in a journal that is judged as prestigious, while an identical study whose subject matter was geographically based in a small country may be rejected. The difference in this case is not the quality inherent in the research design or the writing, but the degree of relevance accorded to it because of its geographical setting. American journals are known to be more parochial than those of other countries (this does not mean less competitive or lower quality, just that they prefer locally-oriented research), and yet, because of the size of the US higher education system, and because it is the home of many of the most important searching indexes, publication in these journals often counts for more, even for researchers not based in that system.

A third point is that referees are often asked to judge contribution quality on a scale rather than simply as pass/fail because *all* journals are governed by norm-referenced constraints as well as criterion-referenced evaluation. A journal is published in a regular format and frequency. In any given year, an agenda to publish a limited number of issues must restrict to a given quantity the number of articles which, by publishing, it designates as good research. In the case of journals, 'quality' means relative to the quality and quantity of other articles submitted in the same period, and this is ultimately a judgement the Editor makes on the basis of referees' assessments. If the Editor decides to approve a greater number of articles for publication, the delay until they appear will be increased, and this risks authors in the future deciding to publish elsewhere. If the Editor is receiving too few articles of the quality they would like to publish, they may publish articles they consider marginal, or may solicit other articles from well-known researchers in an attempt to disguise their problem. Potentially, e-publishing may change the dynamic that, currently, 'prestige' is often equated with high selectivity and long delay. Such publications need not produce issues on a regular schedule, but simply as they are filled, and as often as needed. But, as with competitive research grants, there is a political economy of status at work here. One of the reasons peer review is taken as a ready marker of quality is precisely because it is competitive, and many articles are rejected. An easing of publication may lead to different mechanisms for designating markers of quality. One such mechanism that is likely to receive increased attention is the extension of citation accounting to record interest in a particular article within a journal. As journals are increasingly accessed electronically, it will be possible to follow more closely the interest in particular authors and articles, and this may affect the practices of ranking journals, and the practices of journal editors (James and McQueen-Thomson 2002).

Voice

Most of the formal criteria on which referees are asked to comment in relation to contribution and methodology are similar to those of thesis examination, and these are well canvassed in research methodology textbooks, and research discussions around particular problematics. But an article is restricted to a fraction of the length of a thesis. There is no room to spell out in similar detail either the literature against which the study is set or the methodological steps and dilemmas that were canvassed in the research design. The editor (and referees) must judge whether the writer has mastery of the literature and of the methodological terrain on the basis of the limited text that is submitted. In terms of the presentation of an article, there is a lot of skill (or at least tacit knowledge) in positioning the writing to show such mastery without being able to spell it all out – a skill of selecting, for example, just which references to cite, or how much detail to give about particular methodological issues, or how to introduce the article to demonstrate its significance.

This is one of the reasons why it is harder for new researchers to get published than it is for researchers later in their career. The longer the researcher is involved in the networks and activities of their research field, the more they absorb conventions of writing and learn how to place or 'stage' the work – how to present the evidence that they are a knowledgeable researcher without being crass or looking naive. The writer here has to appear textually as an equal in the field – a somewhat different voice from the PhD, where the writer has to appear textually as someone who is worthy of being an equal, having successfully completed their apprenticeship, but who is not getting above their station by ignoring or being over-critical or exaggerating their own contribution when they present this contribution to the gate-keepers of their field.

To illustrate, recently, giving comments to a new researcher on a paper where she was drawing on her thesis work, I advised her not to use the heading 'literature review' for a section, but to give it a substantive heading 'analyzing × programs'. 'Literature review' in the context of presenting an article (at least in the part of the education field where this was placed) signals that you are still thinking in the categories of a thesis, rather than incorporating that essential task into a more integrated and succinct account of your own project and argument. Then, instead of introducing the work by saying 'This paper will *look at* how two particular programs have worked with the new research agendas of higher education', I recommended that she set up her article using words such as '*drawn from* early stages of an *ethnographic* research project', '*examining* close-up' . . . For the opening paragraph, speaking as an editor or article reviewer, I felt she needed to indicate more directly and strongly her researcher persona (one who 'examines' rather than 'looks at', one who does 'ethnographic' work), and to signal the type of contribution she was going to make in the article.

In terms of 'staging' the article, I then recommended that, instead of beginning by saying only what she had set out to do, and leaving quite open what her research would find until the end of the article, I suggested that this writer signal some points of interest at the beginning: 'Even this limited exposure shows how the new programs are built on . . . and are not simply a reaction to . . .' This latter sentence is telling the 'informed' reader what this writer has got to say that is likely to differ from, and add to, what they know from previous research in this area. Note that the issues about presentation here are specific to types of work. Not all of these suggestions would be appropriate with other types of research or other journals. But the writing itself does signal something about quality in this context that is quite subtle but nevertheless important when assessors make decisions about appropriateness of the work for publication.

However, language or 'voice', and problems in knowing how to 'stage' the work, are not the only reasons why publication productivity is more difficult for the neophyte researcher. In social science journals, especially in fields like education, normal rejection rates of articles submitted can be around 50–80 per cent. Rejections always hurt, but they are likely to have more impact on new researchers, especially women. Researchers who are just beginning to test out how they are judged are more likely to take a critical response to a submitted article as a sign of their general inadequacy and unworthiness to be a researcher, rather than as part of the normal pattern. Older hands (or new researchers with supervisors or mentors who act as their coaches, advocates and cheer squads) can choose to read and respond to the rejection reviews differently. They can comfort themselves by arguing that the article was sent to the wrong people, people working in different paradigms or with different values who do not appreciate their work. (Totally dismissing critical comments in this way is not a response I would recommend, but it is a strategy used by at least some successful established academics who are prolific publishers.) Or the recipient of a rejection can use the reviews as excellent feedback on further work that needs to be done to turn the current article into a stronger one. They can resubmit the article to a different journal – either in its existing form to an 'inferior' journal, or in a revised form to the same or a similar journal.

What does good research here look like?

1   The language of the article conveys *authority*, particularly in the abstract and in the introduction. In a recent paper, Kamler and Thomson (2002) examined abstracts of papers published across a number of different education journals. Their systematic examination of abstracts used in particular journals found that few abstracts use 'I', even if the article itself is written in the first person. The most dominant starting point is 'aims to . . .'. That is, *an abstract sets up to tell a succinct story of what type of contribution the article makes to the field* (substantive focus as well as specificity of methodology). The abstract is not written in the first person because it is the writer's attempt to treat the article as a thing out there, as a commodity that must be presented second-hand to someone else – to

make explicit the heart of the article's claim to be a contribution of worthy research, rather than simply to make that contribution.

In terms of style, Kamler found that where abstracts were written in the active voice, it was often the article itself which was the agent ('This article aims to investigate ... It demonstrates ...'). Often however, abstracts were written in the passive voice ('In this research, it was found that ...').

2   Authority is conveyed by choices about *what details to include or omit*. For example, Kamler's study of abstracts found that published articles in international contexts invariably included specification of the country in which the study was carried out if the research was based in Australia, sometimes did this for research based in the UK, and rarely did this for research based in the USA. In US research this detail was common only when the article was about race.

Conveying authority is another way of saying 'judging correctly what the editors and referees and readers of that journal want to know, and what they take as shared assumptions about what does not need to be said'. Kamler found some clear differentiation of abstract form in different journals: phonetics articles presented themselves as a report of an experiment; philosophy articles as a proposition and argument; policy articles included contextual information about countries.

Mastery of an area is also conveyed by the *choice of authors* to cite. Commonly in any particular area of research, researchers in different countries are doing some similar work. The writer of an article may have been most influenced or inspired by some research or writing of someone relatively unknown. But they need to connect the work they have done with names that are recognizable to the audience for that journal, names that readers would immediately associate with the type of work being done – even if that is done as a prelude to arguing that the relatively unknown writing is of more value or particular value as a starting point. Some names have global salience (for example, Jerome Bruner, Howard Gardner, or Carol Gilligan); there are national reference points (for example, Dewey in the USA; Halsey in the UK; Connell in Australia); and there are reference points for types of research programmes, often associated with particular journals (for example, Valerie Walkerdine and critical psychology and the *Journal of Critical Psychology*; William Pinar and Madeleine Grumet for reconceptualist curriculum theory and the *Journal of Curriculum Theorizing*). Often particular names begin to be used as a shorthand for a particular area or style of research, for example, Stephen Ball for a particular post-structural and ethnographic approach to education policy research; and Patti Lather for feminist post-structural research methodology.

3   An article will carry the *house style* of the journal in which it appears. This includes not just the formal citation conventions set out in the

Instructions to Authors; but the type of structural form (report of an experiment compared with setting out a proposition and argument), voice (for example, first person, creative or 'objective' language, and so on) and methodology associated with that journal. There will normally be referencing to earlier articles published in that journal; and some convergence of the selection of authors that tend to be cited in a particular journal.

In the table on p. 84, I have tried to set out the particular characteristics of what the writing *looks like* in the case of academic articles, but this is something that readers should also examine more specifically by looking at particular journals. In broad terms, I have said that in the research here:

- The abstract makes a succinct case about the *specific contribution* of the article.
- References to *the literature* are prominent ('good research' is built on and in relation to other recognizable research).
- The voice is that of an *authority*, of one who knows (even in journals where first-person accounts of the messiness of research are appropriate, they are written to elucidate a recognized problematic in that tradition, not simply confessionals), of one who discusses as an equal other work in the field. (It is not normal, for example, to find declarations of how inferior the writer feels to a previous great figure – except occasionally in book reviews or tributes to a recently deceased 'name').
- The article normally *connects the research to other research*; explains design features relative to the tradition it is working in; draws out the contribution.
- The article conveys *a particular journal's interests, style and technical norms*.

Common failings and problems

Articles submitted to journals can be rejected because the research had methodological flaws, or was simply not on an interesting topic for that journal's readers. I now focus on issues that are more artefactual, and more able to be addressed at the point of writing.

1   *Sounds like someone learning the ropes rather than an equal, a student rather than a member of the research community.* This is the issue about voice and about how judgements are made that I have tried to elucidate throughout this chapter, and that are rarely conveyed either in Instructions to Authors or research methodology textbooks. Some of the ways this might appear in a text are that

- The writer seems tentative about what they have to contribute (for example, giving a description of a case study without using words or positioning to show what analytic agendas framed the study or what interpretive importance it has).
- The introduction and abstract do not set up what the article is aiming to do.
- They include inappropriate details (for example, spelling out things that researchers in this field take for granted, such as mentioning that they began by getting ethics clearance from their university; or that 'on the advice of their supervisor they . . .').

2   *Methodological flaws.* Sometimes these relate to genuine problems in the design of the research from the perspective of the referee's research tradition; and sometimes they are an artefact of what details have been included in, or omitted from, the text. In this case, writers are often given an opportunity to revise and resubmit with the appropriate tests, tables, details of sample or of interview questions included. Sometimes the judgement of a flaw here relates to failure to cite important work or important names (as judged by the referee).

3   *Not interesting enough.* Journals are dealing in relativities with regard to articles submitted. An article might be competent, but judged 'minor' – sometimes on the grounds that 'this is a competent example, but we already basically know this stuff'; sometimes because 'the subject matter of the investigation is of limited or local rather than more general interest'; sometimes, in the case of policy or qualitative or post-structural research because the actual writing is not creative enough, does not bring out new ways of seeing, new meanings. In all of these cases, the research writing is as significant as what was done prior to the research writing in terms of how the quality of the research is judged.

So:
What does good research look like in terms of the journal article?

It is research that addresses the agenda of that journal, takes account of what has gone before, and is seen to add to it. The quality of the methodology, contribution and writing will be in ratio to the degree of competition of other researchers trying to publish in that journal. The article abstract extracts key selling points of methodology, focus and findings/contribution for that journal audience. The article itself cites names recognizable to and appearing elsewhere in issues of that journal. Signs that the author is a student or newcomer are avoided.

5

Competitive research grants

The pragmatics: how do competitive research grants work?

Arena	Judges	Explicit criteria	Implicit criteria	What does it look like?	Common failings
National and European competitive research grant schemes (ARC, ESRC, SSHRC, EU, Marsden, NRC, etc.) Large foundation competitive grants (Ford, Spencer, etc.) Internal university competitive grants	Disciplinary panel Research experts/ experts in the field usually combination of insider and outsider to discipline area of applicant	researchers' track record 'significance' of project design and methodology 'national benefit'	researchers' recognition in networks writing well to task set conventional career rewarded 'to those who have shall be given'	headings mirror assessment criteria follows all instructions *precisely* summary written for non-expert reader emphasizes knowledge of field, past achievements, contribution this will make	track record not recognizable not addressing task writing too much for those who already know the theory (jargon) too little detail on what you are actually going to do

In one sense, national and international competitive research funding schemes are the fortune-tellers of the good research world: their judgements about research quality are made prior to the research actually being carried out. Alternatively, they might be seen as the lexicographers and grammarians of this world: to a considerable degree, their processes and decisions define and legislate the answer to the question. Or they might be seen as the trademark authorities of the research world – the 'safety-tested' or Good Housekeeping seal of approval that publicly advertises that this product has been tested and approved and its quality can be trusted. They judge good research before it happens, and their seal of approval is one way that others, particularly in the academic world, judge research quality and researcher quality.

As with the thesis, or the journal article, or the book proposal, judgements about research quality in competitive grant schemes are made on the basis of a single text, here the grant application. But in this case the issue of what is achieved by the particular research project must be a prediction rather than an evaluation of outcomes, findings, unexpected effects, or actual impact. The grant application text is not constructing a best story about what was done and achieved, but a model or ideal scenario about what can be done.

The grant application procedure make certain issues more explicit. Some 'in principle' sense of what good methodology needs to look like (for this purpose), what is 'significant' (for this purpose) is distilled by this process, given that it must be conveyed in a strictly limited number of pages of text, and must be the subject of some agreement among the panel members who decide the outcomes. The applicant does not have the luxury of a book-length account, or a flamboyant multi-media presentation to persuade readers of the quality of their proposed research; and they cannot directly use beneficiaries of the research to lobby for them.

But of course the competitive grant process is not entirely about predicting futures, or about relying on agreed principles of methodological quality to judge between different applications. The process normally places much emphasis on judging the quality of future research by assessing what a particular researcher or research team has achieved in the past. Few other arenas so well embody the mantra, 'to those who have shall be given'. The process of judging what will actually be achieved by a particular researcher or research team quite properly considers evidence of their capacity or likelihood to achieve high-quality results in the project outlined, and past achievement is taken as a prima facie indicator of future potential. So one important issue in *this* arena is how are judgements about *good researchers* made, and how do those judgements interact with judgements about the qualities of particular *projects*?

What are competitive grant schemes?

The form of research funding discussed in this chapter is that where a body of money is made available for which, at specified dates, and in specified formats, individuals or teams of researchers submit applications for funding a proposed project whose aim and dimensions have been developed by the researchers. Most countries have some national government form of this type of funding (for example, in the UK, the ESRC (Education and Social Science Research Council); in Australia, the ARC (Australian Research Council); in Canada the SSHRC (Social Sciences and Humanities Research Council of Canada); in New Zealand, the Marsden Fund; in Norway, the Norwegian Research Council; and so on. In the USA, some very large private education foundations, such as the Spencer Foundation and the Ford Foundation, work in a similar mode to the processes described here; and in many countries, there are smaller schemes for lesser amounts of money that also work on the lines described below (for example, internal university competitive grants; smaller foundations that might specify a broad area of interest, but solicit applications rather than deciding projects and soliciting tenders). In the EU, the cross-national OECD is an important source of research funding.

The schemes discussed in this chapter are sometimes entirely open as to the types of topics that may be submitted, or sometimes specify a more restricted range of broad areas or priorities (for example, 'complex systems', or 'literacy'), but in these cases too, the actual project described in the grant proposal, including specific project aims, is created by the researcher. In this respect, these schemes differ from those I designate as 'consultancy' research and discuss in Chapter 6. There, the research problem and, more particularly, the outcomes of the intended research, and often some aspects of the research design, are identified by the funding body. In consultancy research, applications or tenders are solicited which may vary in their specific methodologies of addressing the problem, but the research agenda itself (and usually some elements of the methodology) is specified by the commissioning body, not by the researchers.

Here is a typical time-line that a researcher may need to work to in relation to a major competitive funding scheme, using the example of the Australian ARC applications whose closing date is in March. (Information about application procedures and deadlines in other schemes such as ESRC and SSHRC can be found on their websites.):

Year 1

6–12 months prior to application deadline: researchers begin working on grant proposal, usually involving a cycle of meetings then drafting and redrafting. May seek small internal university funding to do pilot study. May solicit new partners to strengthen team.

Year 2

One month prior to closing date: researchers circulate draft application for comment from colleagues (for comments on clarity and flaws in methodology, referencing, etc.) and university research office (to check for detailed technical compliance with the scheme).

Mar.: application is submitted by advertised closing data (a strict deadline).

Apr.: executive in ARC check technical features, then with aid of advisory panel distribute applications to reviewers.

May: reviewers return scores and comments to ARC. It distributes comments to applicants for one-page rejoinder.

June: deadline for rejoinder. Now all comments, scores, ranks and rejoinders are distributed to the advisory panel, who review these in detail, especially where sharp divisions of judgement.

Aug.: meeting of the advisory to discuss and approve a final ranked list. Advisory panel checks proposed budgets of successful projects and makes decisions on amount to be allocated.

Oct.–Nov.: decisions on successful applications are made public.

Year 3

Funding for application is made available.

The distinguishing feature of these open funding schemes is that they are competitive, both in practice and in terms of their rationale and significance for the research field. That is, many more applications are received than are funded. In the national schemes, success rates range from around 50 per cent to 20 per cent, and this is from a field of applicants that is itself already selective from the community of education researchers as a whole. So this is *explicitly* an arena which is set up to make judgements about research quality – to designate some projects as better and more worthy of support than others. Indeed this comparative judgement element of this form of research assessment is such that the decisions made here not only have the effect of supporting particular projects, but have further effects in building individual research careers (how one comes to be seen as a good researcher), and in building the status and infrastructure of different institutions and workplaces. Some element of funding of universities in many countries is calculated according to their performance in the competitive research funding arena, and it is often an element in the perceived hierarchy of status of different institutions.

Who are the judges?

The Research Priorities Board is assisted in the commissioning of new research activities by specially constituted expert panels. . . . Typically, a panel will be made up of between 10–15 members and will be chaired by a member of the Research Priorities Board. The other members of the panel will be a multi-disciplinary mix of leading academics and also research users with knowledge of the particular field in which research is being commissioned. The Research Priorities Board approves the final membership of the panel.

(from ESRC (UK) website on research funding)

If I were to put the research contexts considered in Part 2 of this book on a spectrum relating to, at one end, how far issues internal to universities or disciplines (or 'academic expertise') dominate, and, at the other, how much the judgements derive from users or from political concerns, then competitive grant schemes would be solidly located in the university-dominated (or 'expert'-judged) end of the spectrum, but moving towards the middle. They are less confined to straight university-based judgements of research than are doctoral examination or academic journal publication, but their approach to methodology, significance, quality of the researcher, works very much in parallel with the types of judgements made within those university-based arenas.

Competitive research funding schemes show national and international variation in the extent to which they include some non-researchers or political direction in their controlling bodies and briefs of operation. There is also variation as we go up the hierarchy of funding schemes. The more money and publicly-accountable funding involved, the more likely are judges and judgements to move beyond those internal to the academic area of study. Schemes of lower importance and much smaller amounts of money, such as internal university-based funding schemes for new researchers, may operate with entirely academic criteria of importance and significance. In general, however, in competitive research funding bodies, while the majority of 'judges' (referees, assessors, committee members) are normally people who might be designated 'academic experts', these judges are often leavened with at least some others who represent a user or funder perspective in relation to the applications. A 'user' perspective might be a senior person from an industry body such as an education department. A 'funder' perspective might be someone the body appoints to ensure that the processes and judgements are carried out with regard to the broad objectives of the scheme. For example, in Australia, two members of each 'expert advisory committee' of the Australia Research Council, as well as the Chair of that Council, must be people who are not university academics, but people who might be expected to have some general interest in funds having 'national benefit' in the way that the government currently sees this. Similarly, at the time of writing, the UK ESRC Council included the chief economist from the DES, and senior executives from European television, the Bank of Scotland and non-profit organizations. The Canadian SSHRC more tightly uses specialist academic expertise (and, significantly, only releases names of assessment panels retrospectively), but it too includes one or two professional users in its education panels. Non-academics on the panel are there, in part, to represent a view other than that of those who do research themselves, to provide an educated but not specialist opinion from someone who is not themselves a researcher.

(The Australian scheme differs from many other countries in that funding decisions, while they go through a rigorous process of multiple peer review and are produced as a final ranked list by an Expert Advisory Panel, are not finally confirmed until each one is individually signed off by the Minister for Education. In principle at least, a project that looks contentious or frivolous in its title and short summary might be rejected.)

In major schemes that involve public funding, the processes of selecting judges (reviewers and committee members) as well as the procedures for assessing applications and the outcomes of the process each year are all themselves the subject of further monitoring so that the schemes can be said to be 'transparent' or 'accountable'; that they avoid 'conflict of interest'; and that the outcomes cannot be (easily) charged with systematic bias. None of these issues is straightforward, but the meaning in practice tends to be:

1 that the characteristics of those drawn on as 'experts', regardless of what process or personal connection decided their particular nomination, must meet publicly defensible 'track record' criteria – they must have the achievements that are associated with research 'expertise' that I discuss further below;

2 that although there is a peer review element of the judging of applications, there are procedures to avoid those who work closely together, or have institutional connections, from directly assessing and helping each other (the same does not apply to the ability of referees to make hostile judgements of others that are indirectly in their own interest, though some schemes use a form of triangulation which helps limit this, at least in its extreme form); and

3 big government-funded schemes tend to be accompanied by major

data-collection monitoring of outcomes to check patterns of distribution that result from the judgements. In the latter case, the criteria for what will appear to be a bias is, of course, related both to the politics and the general sensibility of the place and times.

For example, currently in Australia, there is monitoring of success rates by institution, state, age, rank and gender of recipients, but these categories are not all taken up and acted on in similar ways. Differences by institution, to take one example (specifically, poor success rates of universities in regional and rural areas), have been taken as grounds for concern and have produced a new designated priority to direct greater funding to rural projects; but they have also been used as arguments that the institutions that get the bulk of the funds are evidently the concentrations of research strength, and that these should in the future be given favoured treatment. The first takes differences in institutional success rates as a sign of some patterned disadvantage that must be redressed; the second takes these differences as indicators of different quality, that the rigorous procedures of grant assessment have made possible to see in an objective form! The monitoring of success patterns by age and rank has led to new quotas to increase funding awarded to new researchers, but nothing for another group who win far less than a normal share of funding, the great bulk of academics who are neither new researchers nor at the senior ranks that get most of the funding. So patterns of outcomes may be monitored, but what is chosen to be monitored and whether patterned success rates are taken as matters for concern and adjustment are not a given but subject to political agendas and debate.

Now let us consider how the judges in the context of these schemes are similar or different from PhD examiners.

What is an 'expert'?

i   *The formal processes*
The PhD examiners, as I argued in Chapter 3, are chosen on the basis that they are licensed masters in the field of the doctoral research: they are people who have themselves passed the PhD, who hold an academic position and who work, at least in some respects, in the specific area of the thesis topic. In the competitive grant arena, the academics who act as reviewers of grant proposals, and the panel members who decide the eventual comparative listing, are also there as experts or masters of their field, but there are some differences. In the case of national competitive grant applications, to be constituted as an appropriate 'expert' an academic needs more than a doctorate and an institutional position; they

need to have demonstrated a profile within their field that constitutes them as a successful researcher and senior member of their field. Some of the ways this might be demonstrated include having a higher than usual success rate in themselves attracting research grants; being frequently cited by others; holding senior roles in professional bodies of their disciplinary field; having senior university positions. In some schemes, these judges are selected solely from textual databases – such as records of previous grant recipients; citation indices – but frequently more direct processes of networking and nomination are also part of the decision. For example, universities or professional associations of researchers are asked to nominate people; or those currently on the committees use their own networks to solicit suggestions of appropriate successors; or there is an explicit process of triangulated checking about potential members.

In this context, the pool of judges may be seen as more select than that of potential PhD examiners (though there is a large overlap). But it is also a different type of pool and a different type of structured role that these judges are engaged in.

One difference is that although the judges in this arena are experts and a more selected group from the broad pool of those holding doctorates and university appointments, in their role here they are also 'peers' of those they are assessing, not masters assessing neophytes as they are in relation to the PhD. They are judges when operating as assessors, but also themselves researchers of the kind being assessed.

Another is that because competitive grant schemes are designed to produce comparative evaluations between *different types* of research project (those that are not tightly addressing the same problematic, or drawing on the same tight disciplinary paradigm), the pool of experts used as judges gives more attention to those considered to have some *broad* (or 'mature') expertise about what good research looks like – that is, expertise that is not tightly specific to their own field of research. And this broad expertise is normally of increasing importance, the higher up the judging hierarchy the decisions being made, and the more power being given to the people exercising the judgement. Most schemes where applications are assessed by expert reviewers include both reviews by those with specific disciplinary expertise in the field of the application, and some judgement by individuals or a panel that is not specific to the area of the research. This is often the case even in the smaller internal competitive schemes that individual universities may offer, as well as in the major and most prestigious funded programmes. (And this matter of judgements being made by non-specialist as well as specialist readers is a highly pertinent one for research applicants, in relation to how, in textual terms, they need to demonstrate that their research is 'good'. This will be discussed further below.)

So on what basis is one deemed to have expertise outside what one has achieved in one's own research? The judgement here is primarily indirect: that the person has served in other roles where they have exposure to or have been selected to judge outside their narrow area (for example, as dean of a faculty, or on university higher degrees and research committees, in professional associations, on other government bodies). Whether negative information on actual performance in such roles (for example, that the person is known to favour and disfavour certain kinds of work) is taken into account varies.

ii   *So who are these experts?*
We have seen that judges are selected because they have been recognized as successful in their field (previous grants, publications, networks, positions); and at the higher level, on criteria that they have the ability to judge good research more broadly than in their own field. Let us consider some of the personal characteristics that might accompany those selected in this way. The following points are not about idiosyncratic personality differences, and not invariant descriptors of those who assess research in these schemes, but some issues about the 'types' of people that might be more likely, given the experiences being looked for in judges, and given the ways they are selected:

- *Successful themselves*: These are likely to be people more attuned to what are the signs and criteria of doing well, than to the problems of those who struggle; more attuned to the experience of the haves than the have nots (and race, gender, ethnic, class differences may well be part of this – for example, committees commonly under-represent women and have less sensitivity to the processes by which women become under-represented).
- *Experience of holding senior position and doing related administrative work (being a dean, chairing committees, and so on)*: These are likely to be people attuned to working with administrative requirements and to judging very quickly any breaches of rules. In demographic terms they are likely to mirror the same demographic characteristics that have been documented in senior ranks of universities: for example, women and ethnic diversity under-represented; in smaller countries, academics originally from UK and USA over-represented – and all this will be reflected in their personal networks and associations and the experiences they bring to the judgement of applications.
- *Senior positions, ongoing achievements in research and in career*: These are likely to be *busy* people, doing many 'important' things other than judging research grants of others: they will have limited time, will be impatient with the lengthy reading involved which is often an extra to their main work, and is often paid only in a token way.

All of these characteristics are relevant to how the criteria and procedures associated with the schemes are enacted in practice. They are relevant to how applications will be read; and they are relevant to how applications need to be written if they are to be successful.

Explicit and implicit criteria

Competitive grant schemes vie with doctoral regulations in the amount of attention they give to specifying in fine detail the requirements of the submission, and the criteria on which decisions will be made. There are often many pages of instructions regarding matters of eligibility and technical requirements of the application itself: page limits of the application overall as well as particular sections of it; detailed definitions of who is eligible to be an applicant; what details must be submitted on the form; the format in which the project itself must be described. Usually there is a specification of what weighting will be given to different parts of the application – particularly to rating of the researcher or research team as compared with the other parts of the application. Sometimes, there is some indication of priority areas of research that will be given some favoured treatment (for example research addressing certain broad areas, such as literacy or new technology; research to be carried out on rural populations; research that involves at least two different institutions, or an industry partner; or research that involves certain combinations of countries, in the case of EU funding). Sometimes, too, there is a very broad indication of what the scheme defines as its agenda for quality: for example research that will be of national significance, or will produce findings that draw international recognition.

But a matter that referees and panel members are normally *not* instructed on in detail is *how* they are to judge the quality of the researchers, and *how* they are to judge the quality of the research project design itself. In part, these judgements are built into the design of the application form itself (for example, what material the research team is asked to supply in terms of their achievements or track record) and into the procedures of assessment and ranking; and in part these judgements are considered to be what the experts doing this work know and can bring to the task.

What 'good research' looks like technically need not be stated explicitly here because it is assumed that experts who have made their way through this system and long been socialized in its norms no longer need to be reminded of the kinds of criteria that universities set out for supervisors and graduate students regarding doctoral work, discussed in Chapter 3: issues such as showing familiarity and sufficient critical appraisal of the relevant literature, using appropriate methods and techniques; providing sufficient justification, demonstrating authority.

Let us then consider some of the elements by which a research project is assessed in these schemes, beginning with one that may seem the most trivial or obvious, but which is most strongly enforced:

Technical eligibility and correctness

The pragmatic situation of most of these important grant schemes is that there is a huge amount of work involved in assessing grants, often being done by busy people with many other important demands on their time, and in a context where many more applications are made than can be funded with the money available. In these contexts, technical breaches are seized on and rigidly enforced – they reduce the workload! Moreover, with schemes operating with public money, the need for transparency and accountability mean that this has to be done, otherwise they could be subject to appeal, legal challenge, or political embarrassment. (The strictness with regard to enforcement of technical rules in these schemes is often more draconian than in judgement of consultancy applications (see Chapter 6), where rules may be bent or further negotiations take place if a particularly promising team or group has neglected to do something.)

Here, drawn from my own experiences and those of colleagues in other countries, are some examples of technical breaches that have led to research applications being ruled ineligible:

- failure to answer every question (in one case, a very senior university researcher forgot to fill in the box as to how many days per month he would work on the project; in another case, the applicants forgot to fill in every existing grant held by the third member of their research team);
- application that exceeds set page length;
- application that failed to apply 'eligibility' instructions correctly (for example, listing an international co-investigator as a 'chief investigator' when in this scheme they could only be a 'partner investigator');
- listing all kinds of publications under track record when instructions asked that only 'refereed' publications be included;
- using a font size smaller than the specified size;
- missing closing time for submission of applications (in a recent case, a submission to an internal university grant scheme was rejected because the advertised closing time of the scheme was Friday 5 p.m., and the submission had been submitted on the following Monday at 8.30 a.m.).

It is (or was!) part of the persona of many academics to pride themselves on their independence and their disdain for regulation and bureaucracy. But today, to gain recognition for one's research and research standing, very fine degrees of compliance with orders are necessary. In relation to competitive grants, a very high level of technical compliance indeed is certainly a necessary, though not sufficient, criterion of what a good research proposal looks like.

Researcher track record

In most schemes, researchers are given specific instruction on what type of evidence they need to furnish about themselves and their own achievements. In some current schemes in which I am involved, the details required include:

1   date PhD awarded (and institution);
2   current institutional position;
3   previous institutional positions;
4   past five years *refereed* publications (and marking publications specifically relevant to current application);
5   list of ten career-best publications;
6   list of grants currently held, and those applied for;
7   highlights of awards, honours, professional positions held;
8   brief statement of the specific contribution made to one's field;
9   (optional): statement of any way career/research productivity has been impeded;
10 (for industry partner schemes only): statement of record of collaboration with industry partner.

Remember that the issue of what good research (potentially) looks like in these schemes gives much weight to judging the quality of the researcher and the likelihood that they will deliver something good, achieve what they promise. In this scheme and in most similar ones, only some of the people involved in judging this will be expected already to know the work of the researcher, and for them the list above may serve as an aide-mémoire in judging the quality of that work. Others who will judge this track record will be making the judgement purely on the text provided, and in this case we might revisit each of these textual items to consider what work it is meant to do in indicating the researcher's quality and ability.

Date and institution PhD awarded

In part, this item will be used to allow a special quota to be reserved for 'new researchers' on this scheme, but more generally it is part of assessing the quantum of what a researcher has achieved. Post PhD, someone who is to gain a good rating as a researcher needs to be steadily accumulating a portfolio of achievement. Allowance is made for those who have been involved for a shorter period than others, and equally, a high level of achievement relative to a short length of time is one sign by which researchers gain a higher score. Once this would have been judged by date of birth. Today, in the wake of legislation that forbids discrimination by age, and in the context of a more fluid academic environment where, especially in professional fields, an individual may spend time working in their professional area before undertaking a doctorate or taking up academic research, the date of a doctoral award serves as a proxy way of measuring the start and length of an academic research career.

Of course, this is an imperfect measure of researcher history. For some academics in education, it may be an advantageous one: since they may have built a track record of publications and other achievements, and have been working as an academic, prior to completing a doctorate. For others who undertook their doctorate but then embarked on a career in teachers' colleges when research was not a high priority, or took extended time out for family reasons and re-entered the academy in a junior position with a heavy teaching load and limited time for research, this may work against them. They appear on this criterion not to be 'new researchers', but they will not have accumulated an impressive array of research achievements, nor appear to be highly productive.

The institution from which one qualified may be significant in countries with a strong hierarchy of universities or a strong 'colonial cringe' (a belief that qualifications from the mother country must be better than local ones). However in professional fields, the general hierarchy of universities may not be identical with that of quality education faculties since many prestigious universities are less committed to this 'lower status' field. (In the UK the research assessment exercise specifically ranks departments, but in many other countries this is not done). Prestige relativities between countries are also rapidly changing. Whether judges take any account of this part of a researcher's profile is likely to reflect their own personal history and prejudices: where they undertook their own degree, what assessment they now make of different faculties in this area, whether they are specialists in the field, and know something about different departments, or whether they are outsiders who make general judgements about particular universities. However, there may well be a halo effect to qualifications from universities with a visible global reputation, such as Harvard or Oxford.

Current institutional position

Sometimes, the word of mouth is that for the important grant schemes, there is no point in applying if you are not already a professor or do not have a team led by a professor. Is this the case?

Firstly, rank achieved can be interpreted by assessors as one way to judge the work of this applicant. If they have been at work a short time and been awarded a Chair, this can be read as indicating that some people who have looked closely at their record, consider them impress-ive. Conversely, if someone was awarded a PhD three decades ago, but has not been promoted, this might be seen as indicating some unim-pressive qualities in their performance. But of course this is not a tight indicator of achievement, especially in professional faculties that have different agendas and pressures regarding the qualities they are looking for and the type of achievement they wish to reward (in recent years, in many education faculties, a strong commitment to research or identity as a researcher, rather than appearing to be someone primarily committed to teaching, may have been a disadvantage for senior appointment). Nor does it allow for the fact that rank achieved is highly related to mobility, and the extent to which an individual is prepared or able to relocate to take up a more senior post. Domestic relationships are a part of this, and this has been traditionally one factor that has indirectly discriminated against women, whose spouses might be less inclined to relinquish their own jobs to accommodate such a move, and who at later stages, when they might be considered for more senior positions, may have respon-sibility for aged parents, or be sole carers for their own children.

The information about position held may also be used more sub-stantively: for example, to judge the extent to which the named researcher is likely to be very actively involved in the project (for example, if they are dean of a major faculty, and this is not their main field of endeavour), or, more positively, as an indicator of specific research expertise if someone's position is as leader of a unit working on projects specifically related to the focus of this application.

Career positions held
A good researcher is usually judged to be one who has a coherent, steady, productive and building repertoire of achievement. Periods not in aca-demic work, long periods without promotion, moves from tenured to untenured work, may all be judged with suspicion. I once read an assessor's comment on an application from an early career researcher which commented unfavourably on the fact that the applicant had chosen to take a year off after their PhD to travel! The assessor said this might throw doubts on whether they would stick at a three-year project if the grant were awarded!

Despite the detailed prescription of what information is to be included in the application, those who read these texts bring their own experi-ences and agendas to the task. Sometimes they may be in sympathy with those experiences and agendas that have shaped the research biographies they read, and sometimes not. This is why the processes of selecting assessors and judges is relevant to what criteria 'mean'. It is also why I think this process favours those whose biography as a researcher fits a conventional pattern – the traditional young male scientist who does a PhD immediately following his undergraduate degree, followed by a post-doc, preferably in another country, followed by an academic position and steady promotion, accompanied by regular and growing publication and grant achievements. The meaning of that pattern of progress and outside recognition is well understood by grant committees and academics across disciplines. The interpretation of variation from the pattern is often not agreed, especially given the types of biographies common among those who have been chosen as 'experts' for this purpose, and is often not able to be well addressed by the applicant in the limited information allowed to be included in the form.

Publication record
Assessors are looking for productivity, coherence of focus, relevance to current proposal and signs of quality. This is more straightforward for reviewers who are inside the field of the application than those who are not. Take productivity, there is a vast difference between the number of articles or books one might expect from a leading philosopher or historian than from someone involved in multi-authored empirical programmes involving big surveys, and generating many articles from a single piece of research. In some parts of education, refereed conference papers are a normal mode of communication and have respected status; in others, a conference paper is not held to be a sign of particular research quality. Experienced assessors will have some knowledge of this, but will still be looking for signs of steady achievement, and publications relating to previous grants.

On take 'quality', in some fields of medicine and science, assessors are in broad agreement about the relative place in the hierarchy of each particular journal. In education too, it is understood that there are differences in prestige between different journals, as discussed in Chapter 4. Some panels and assessors make formal use of journal rankings derived from the Social Science Citation Index Journal Impact list. But the issue of judging quality of publications of an applied field of professional practice is not as straightforward as it is in a straight discipline. If your object of study is a school system in a local context in New Zealand, or Finland, it is conceivable that some of your theoretical or empirical discussions could be framed for a global audience; but, arguably, at least some of your publication activity should be directed to local audiences who would be interested in the local specificity. This is an even stronger issue for researchers in countries where English is not the language spoken. Yet panels may have a prejudice that publication in an international forum represents higher quality work than that which is published locally. Another problem is that assessors outside the specific area may be guessing the significance of journals and articles based on titles, and titles of articles designed for readers within a field may not be the best way of advertising to an assessor the quality of the work. (It is noticeable with the proliferation of journals, and the proliferation of research assessment exercises in different countries, how many journals now include 'international' in their title. Previously, it would not have been considered necessary.)

For applied fields such as education, the making of judgements about research grant applications does highlight a dilemma in terms of some questions I have been considering throughout this book. Is 'good research' that which meets the highest technical standards? If it is, then we encourage researchers to work to contexts and judgements that assess these rigorously: refereed journals, and the top ranks of a perceived hierarchy within journals (usually with international ranked above national, and national above local); and with 'big' areas ranking higher than more limited parts of these (a *British Journal of Sociology* ranking above a *British Journal of Sociology of Education* and that ranking above a *Melbourne Studies in Education*). But this might work against another criterion that says good research most effectively addresses its problem, or impacts on practice, which might encourage researchers to put their efforts into other forms of publication. In relation to grant committees, my experience has been that many assessors outside an area give more weight to publications in non-applied disciplinary journals (psychology, sociology) than in ones that name a professional area (education, nursing) or a topic area within education (curriculum, race, gender, vocational learning); give more weight to those published in international journals, US or British journals; and give more weight to journals that appear to have a wider spread. In a Canadian discussion of the problems in producing an inter-disciplinary network (under the auspices of major SSHRC funding), Gaskell and McLeod found that economists considered they would lose status by publishing in education rather than economics journals, and quote one academic who argued that inter-disciplinary journals tend not to be as well regarded as those that are solely within one discipline (Gaskell and McLeod forthcoming).

In the case of judging track records of education researchers, is the record of someone who has done only consultancy research and acquired a major following in the circles they work in, a sign of strength or weakness? In arenas we will look at later (Chapters 6, 7 and 9), such a track record is taken as a sign of good research – research that is neither 'ivory tower', nor too 'academic'. But in the case of competitive funding schemes, a lack of publication in *refereed* contexts (and preferably in more rigorous and 'scholarly' refereed contexts) would be interpreted as an unwillingness to submit one's work to the technical judgement of one's expert peers. Of course many people who work in education do both, but it is important to recognize that there are different emphases at work in different contexts, and for researchers themselves, they raise real dilemmas as to what type of research to undertake, how to frame it, and even more vividly, how to write about or disseminate the work.

List of grants

'To those who have shall be given.' It is appropriate that judgements to award major funding should consider whether the recipient is going to be able to manage it effectively to produce the research outlined, and one sign of this achievement is that they have been awarded and completed earlier funded research. However, this does begin to imply an interesting criterion into the question of what good research, and good researchers, look like: that good research costs a lot of money; and good researchers can be measured in part by the size of the grants they have received.

I have argued elsewhere (Yates 2001a) that there is now too often a conflation between size of grant and quality of research, without sufficient regard to the fact that different types of research need different amounts of money to do well. I have often been in committees where the project ranked at number 1 received less money than a project lower down the list, because the applicant had applied for less, and it was appropriate to that project. Yet when it comes to track record later, there is not a means by which the person can demonstrate their previous ranking: what they are asked to do is list the gross amounts of money received (and, similarly and regrettably in my opinion, the *number* of publications written, the *number* of citations received). This encourages an implicit criterion of good research in this context: it is big and expensive rather than small-scale and local.

Awards and honours

As with institutional position, refereed publication, and previous grants, this is another way that assessors tap evidence of judgements that have been made by others about this researcher. Some high-level honours have a known currency (for example, election to membership of a national Academy of Social Science or similar body); but in other cases, apparently similar prizes can have very different meanings in different areas. Some fields (for example, mathematics research) and some countries (for example, the USA and AERA compared with Australia and AARE) award many more prizes and honours: 'best paper by a new researcher', 'best article published in this journal in a particular year', and a host of different types of awards to newly published books. Researchers working in some contexts and areas of research can benefit by the practices in those fields. What appear to be attributes of the individual researcher, are, at least in part, constructions of the area in which they work.

Statement of contribution to one's field
Productivity as in quantity of research output is, as we have seen, taken into account in competitive applications, but new researchers sometimes think that quantity of output is the only way a researcher is judged. In practice, most university-based assessments of researcher quality (not just grant applications, but promotions, appointments, and so on) have at least some understanding of how quantity is manipulable, and about its limitations as a simple indicator. They want to understand the *type of contribution* a particular agenda or project of research by this particular researcher has had, as well as what *impact* their work has had. There is a sense that a good researcher is not one who just works on scattered projects, no matter how technically correct the methodologies for each may be, but one who builds a research agenda, programme or profile that has a coherence, that builds on itself. This opportunity for applicants to explain how they see the coherence and contribution of their work is not always part of the application pro forma – but it is frequently one measure by which reviewers and assessors construct a rating for a good researcher: reading the story implicit in the career details, publications list, and past and current funded projects.

In the UK, the ESRC website contains a multi-page guide to 'How to write a good application', and this reiterates many of the points made here, including the need for the application to tell a story. The questions it recommends applicants to keep in mind are:

- what is the story you are telling?
- what is the audience?
- why does it matter?
- why now?
- why you![19]

Opportunity to provide a statement about any ways in which opportunities as a researcher have been impeded
This section is a relatively recent addition to the ARC grant application pro forma. It stems in part from equal opportunity movements and legislation and concerns about how to take account of women who might have had career interruptions due to pregnancy or child-rearing, especially in the crucial early stages of the post-doctoral period. More recently it also serves the interests of researchers who hold senior posts in universities. With the intensification of academic workloads, there is a vast difference in opportunity to demonstrate research productivity for one who is managing a large faculty or other unit within the university than one who is employed solely as a research fellow. Again, the weight that assessors put on any of this is likely to be related to their own careers, and the composition of the assessing panel overall.

Record of collaboration with industry partner
Schemes of the kind discussed in this chapter are subject to changing emphases. Education and other applied professional areas are expected both to measure up to cross-disciplinary traditional academic standards of what a good researcher looks like, but also to be seen to be doing something useful – and evidence of involvement with users of various kinds (governments and policy makers; professional associations of teachers or principals, or subject areas; consultancy work with schools, regions) is taken as prima facie evidence of such applied relevance. But in the competitive grant arena this is not an essential condition for all grants; and even in schemes specifically designed to fund collaborative research, evidence of a strong relationship with the partner is not a condition that overrides the requirement to have publications and career track record that meet academic standards of quality, peer-reviewed achievement.

I have dealt with the explicit criteria and implicit judgements about a good researcher at length in this chapter, because in many competitive grant schemes it is the major factor in deciding whether a project is rated as good research. Usually the assessment of the researcher/research team is weighted at around 40–50 per cent of the final score (and in the Canadian SSHRC it is 60 per cent), and it is usually essential to be highly rated in this category to have some chance of being successful in obtaining a grant. That is, *researcher* quality is a necessary but not sufficient condition of good research in this arena. In terms of the project itself, the assessment normally has two main elements – its 'significance' and its technical (design and methodological) adequacy.

Significance

What is a 'significant' piece of research?
Assessors may be given some broad parameters to work with (for example, that the project should be of 'national or international, not just local significance'), but they are largely left to make this judgement themselves. In parts of the process where assessors are reading applications as specialists in the field, the question of what contribution/difference/impact/alteration to the field the proposed project might achieve 'relative to the state of knowledge in this sub-discipline' is part of their task. Paradigm disputes are a known issue in research of all kinds, and assessment procedures in funding schemes try to walk a fine line, with varying degrees of success. On the one hand, they must try to avoid research being unfairly rejected on the basis of prejudice, for example, because the assessor is a researcher working on a competing theory of how to address the same topic. On the other hand, given that they need

to rank projects working in different paradigms relative to each other, they cannot simply have each application read only by assessors known to be highly sympathetic to the approach taken by the applicant. There is no perfect way to resolve this issue, and it is one felt keenly by applicants for grants, particularly unsuccessful applicants.

In parts of the process where a non-specialist panel is considering evaluations of different types of projects, their task will be a dual one. First, they will be making their own 'lay' assessment of whether work on this particular topic seems important – and the short summary at the beginning of the application is a key element of the basis on which they do this. Secondly, they will be evaluating the applicant's own case about why their project will be a contribution to the existing knowledge in their field, and reading and evaluating what the specialist reviewers said about the same matter. Some issues here are as follows.

Paradigm differences
My own experience on a number of committees has been that, contrary to popular rumour, assessments that are totally unsympathetic to the type of work being proposed do it less harm than the reports of reviewers who appear to understand and work within the area and show some sympathy to and interest in it, but who draw attention to flaws or cast doubt on its quality. In other words, committees normally have some knowledge that there is more than one paradigm of research (although this may turn out to have been a brief historical moment, if the movements discussed in Part 1, to scientifically-based research and to a narrow view of 'evidence', become entrenched and triumphant). This does not mean that paradigm differences play no part in how research is judged, or that there is no historical change in what is favoured as a research approach, or that, in all fields, iconoclastic new approaches do not have to struggle initially to gain recognition, and this will be discussed further in terms of the textual qualities of successful applications.

Originality and conventionality
In terms of the doctorate, I suggested that a 'contribution to knowledge' requires work that is both recognizable to existing conventions and, in some sense, adds to these. This requirement is heightened in the case of research grant applications. Even more than the doctoral researcher, the applicant must demonstrate knowledge, authority, critical insight, mastery about the field as it is. And even more than the doctoral student, they must demonstrate something more than simple mastery, or they will not be competitively successful. That is the theory. Of course, in principle, different schemes at different times are more or less favourable to different types of originality. Some people *do* get funded to do more and more of the same; and some people fail to get funded at one time for

something that is later recognized as an important new direction for research. But, in pragmatic terms, the aim of a grant application is to demonstrate both mastery and something that moves beyond mere repetition.

Can a small-scale piece of research be 'significant'?
In this section, my aim is not to set out my own argument about what is good research, though the value of small-scale and close-up research is an issue that I care and worry about, given current agendas. Here I want only to discuss the issue of qualitative and small-scale work specifically in terms of the pragmatics of grant schemes and the processes of judgement that operate within these. For the first 15 years in which I was working as an academic, I did not apply for a research grant. I was doing research, publishing, gaining promotion, even serving on committees to award research grants, but my own work was essentially unfunded work of individual scholarship. When it became apparent that universities and university departments would essentially be punished if academics did not bring in specific research money (this had previously not been the case in the funding regimes of Australian universities), and that the workload conditions to do 'unfunded' individual scholarship no longer obtained, I began a new type of project that would cost money. The conditions in which we work shape what we do.

In major national research associations, battles between the value of qualitative and case-study work compared with quantitative work seem well behind us, and it is clear from the strong presence of research of all types in national conferences and journals, from the growing volume of research methodology texts on case study, and from the choices doctoral students make that many education researchers are drawn to small-scale and qualitative work as well as to various forms of discourse analysis, as a form of investigation very suited to education questions and interests. We might remember too how much education as a field has been lastingly influenced by figures like Piaget, Dewey and others, whose insights came from work with a few subjects or on their own school. But what comes into play when assessors are asked to read an application for research that has not yet been done, and to judge whether it is 'significant'?

This question struck me forcibly when I moved from doing my own research on a project that was large (over eight years, and some 400 lengthy interviews) but based on only a small number of subjects, to take up a role as an assessor of grant applications. I began to have to read large numbers of different grant applications and score them against each other on criteria which included 'significance' and, separately, 'national benefit'. Although I understood well the limitations of large-scale surveys and have written often to explain the significance of my own funded project (Yates 2001b, 2003), the criterion of significance does bring into play issues of scale: bigger and smaller, major and minor, and so on. National and cross-national schemes are specifically intended to fund research whose importance will extend well beyond the local. Even at the first stage of competitive grant schemes – internal university funds for new researchers – my experience has been that many education researchers who have done a good doctorate around a case study or small-scale investigation find it difficult to present their application for their next project in a way that convinces the committee of its value to others than those who will be involved in the project itself.

The issue of significance is more intriguing than might at first appear, since, in the context of research and theory, and taking the benchmarks of science and medicine, we well understand that major advances are over that produce new concepts or theories. Sometimes these insights and theories are based on large-scale studies (epidemiological studies, for example), but often they stem from finding a way to build on a whole range of existing knowledge and theories by a focused experiment or study of a particular type. There seems to be no 'in principle' reason why a small-scale and close-up study could not advance some aspects of education research or theorizing 'significantly'. And yet, operating as an assessor of applications, even given my own strong belief in the importance of qualitative, interpretive, critical work rather than empiricist work (not to mention feminist arguments about what lies behind obsessions with mine is bigger than yours!), I found that I was thinking about the scale of different applications, and whether they were important enough, much more than I had expected. And I was one of the small minority of people on the panel who did not primarily do large-scale quantitative research. The issues involved I think are these.

First, although 'significance' can mean 'important conceptual breakthrough' as well as 'large-scale', the latter is quickly evident, whereas the former requires more difficult and careful reading and judgement. Another way of putting this is that a proposal involving researchers across a number of countries conducting large-scale investigations of their education systems has a taken-for-granted appearance of being 'major', whereas a study involving only two schools, or a limited number of case studies has to make a case for its importance. In terms of the 'significance' criterion, there is a more extensive writing task to be accomplished in the second case than in the first. Note again that I am not talking about whether this is rationally justifiable; I am saying that this is often the pragmatic case. It stems partly from types of unstated prejudices that cultures carry: teachers who work with older children or adults are worth more than those who work with younger ones; big is better than small. Feminism has been remarkably unsuccessful in changing some of these prejudices.

Secondly, notwithstanding the fondness for medical analogies I discussed earlier in the book, there *is* some shared knowledge among both insider experts and the lay experts who are involved in assessing applications that contexts (countries, states, cities and towns) are not the same as each other, and that teachers and students differ demographically in a number of important ways. In terms of producing insights or claims that are important beyond the local level, there is some concern about whether the empirical basis of the study will be of broader value, or whether even the conceptual insights being produced by the close-up study will have an idiosyncratic specificity, a lack of usefulness. Studies set up to investigate empirically a range of different countries or demographic 'factors' make clear that they will be addressing issues of 'spread'. That does not, of itself, mean that they are significant – choosing a methodology that rules out local specificities may be a mistake in relation to producing better practice – but it has a common-sense appeal, appearing to address contextual variation and to test issues that may be of importance across such variation. Studies that work on a smaller scale must do more writing work to explain convincingly (a) in what way they will produce an advance to knowledge that is important; and (b) how working with a small group is justifiable or useful given our knowledge of variations that may matter.

One of the things I first became aware of when I had the chance to read large numbers of assessments that other assessors had made of different projects was how frequently they raised issues in relation to smaller-scale work about failure to address the selection of the sample. Those working with small numbers will object that this question of 'selection of the sample' is inappropriate to the methodology of this research: no matter how carefully they are chosen, a few people cannot represent a class or gender; two schools cannot represent a class of different types of schools, and so on. The point is that assessors do raise these questions, that the issue of representativeness and idiosyncrasy and scale are part of common understandings of significance, and the justification for projects needs to be written with an understanding that such questions are likely to be asked.

Can research with a critical or deconstructive agenda be 'significant'?
Many of the issues that I have discussed in relation to small-number research apply also with regard to research that is designed around critical, disruptive perspectives rather than those designed to produce an obvious, usable addition to knowledge and applied practice. New approaches (for example, critical psychology; Foucauldian genealogy) face the usual paradigm difference problems, and will have a more difficult time because assessors and panels are more dominated by those working in opposing paradigms. But what I want to consider here

is how the broader issue of 'significance' also affects such approaches.

In the applied social sciences, I think judgements of significance blur 'contribution to the discipline' and 'applied improvement to humanity/ the professional field'. For those interested in a critical or deconstructive agenda, the issue must be to explain to outsiders the sense in which that work makes an important 'contribution to knowledge', and at some level *also to address the issue of why the work matters*. The writing task is to make this case to outsiders who are likely to share neither the values nor the theoretical background of the applicant.

Design and method

The process of competitive funding assessments, like thesis examination and refereed journal reviewing, places high scrutiny on technical propriety of design and methods – more rigorously than other arenas discussed in this book. Successful applicants will be expected to demonstrate that their design meets the highest standards of appropriate methods, given the aims and broad paradigm of the project. Matters such as adequacy of sampling, use of appropriate controls or statistical tests or combination of methods, explanation and justification of how interviews will be conducted and interpreted, adequacy of time in field for ethnographic work, all receive attention. These are issues covered and debated in other books on research methods and in debates within a research problematic. Here I will not attempt to repeat such discussions, but I want to draw attention to two particular additional parameters that may affect the judgement and the writing of methodology within this particular research context.

1. *In most schemes, applications receive both insider specialist expert scrutiny and also some cross-disciplinary scoring. Given that there are paradigm disputes about methods, how is adequacy of design and methods judged by those not working within the particular field of the application?*
Three issues are likely to come into play when judging good research design under these procedures. Firstly, committees will make secondary readings of judgements made by the specialist assessors (including rejoinders if these are part of the process). This is similar to the work that university committees do in reading examiners' reports. If the assessment is convincing about the expertise of the assessor to comment on this area, and the report argues that within the terms of the approach chosen, some steps have been omitted or are inappropriate, then 'non-experts' on the committee will very likely be guided by such a judgement. If, however, the specialist report smacks heavily of paradigm disputes, or if the rejoinder is convincing, then the committee may give it less weight, and more weight to their own judgements. Note that whether a report is read

as an example of the first or of the second will be derived from the *textual* presentation of that report. (However some schemes work simply with scores and not reports.)

Secondly, those not working in the field of the application bring both their own experiences of research, and usually some shared common sense about whether a research design is convincing. The question they are putting to themselves is 'are these steps and participants, and this array of methods convincing as a way to address *this* question?' Here, the points made in discussing significance are equally appropriate. Common sense carries with it a more ready understanding of some approaches to methodological adequacy (for example, large-scale rather than small-scale) than others. Similarly, the choice of people who are appointed to positions of high-level cross-disciplinary judgement in these schemes itself often produces a committee weighted to those who have a certain type of research expertise (hierarchical, managing large teams, 'widely respected' because their approach is well understood in terms of conventional norms) rather than other types (iconoclastic, communitarian, and such like).

Again, I am not intending these comments to be read cynically, or at least over-cynically. Research funding bodies usually do have some genuine interest in funding new and emerging types of research and often struggle to confront their own prejudices. But in terms of a 'pragmatic' reading of how this context operates, applicants need to be aware of the likely composition of the judging panel and the processes that take place. The implication of the points above is not that non-conventional or emerging research or less popular research approaches never receive funding, but that they have a harder task to achieve in their application. They have to explain to those who do not share their own values, experiences, immersion in particular debates, why a particular approach makes sense.

In terms of design and methods, good research here is judged against (changing) disciplinary norms, and (changing) norms of the 'educated common sense'. But equally important is to recognize how much the judgement is made from the *textual* presentation. It is not simply a matter of what elements are included in the methodology of the application, but of whether a successful case is made about the logic and adequacy of those methods. In the case of approaches that are newer, or less conventional, or more contentious, the writer has to take greater care to construct a case about the authoritativeness of their approach, and the sense it makes.

2. *The problem of balancing utopian standards with pragmatics*
Research applications are often subject to multiple scrutiny of the most rigorous kind in terms of their methods, and because these are proposed

methods there would seem to be no excuse for not meeting the highest standards of current understandings about good research. Realistically, however, applicants never have unlimited time and resources to address a problem (though, in my limited experience, Scandinavian and some larger US research funding come closer to adequacy than most other countries). In countries that are less generous with the amounts schemes have to disburse, applicants will often find they face the difficult task of balancing their knowledge about what would be desirable, given unlimited support, with their knowledge of their own known workload constraints, and their knowledge of the types of limitations to funding associated with a particular scheme. The writing task is to attempt to limit the design, or acknowledge pragmatic constraints, without appearing to compromise adequacy.

What does good research *look like* in the case of competitive grant schemes?

In terms of what good research here *looks like* as a text, the implications of my discussion of the judges, criteria and enactments of assessment are summarized in the table at the beginning of this chapter. As a text, the application needs to:

- meet all technical requirements fully and precisely;
- write well to the task set: use headings supplied; if supplied, use scoring weightings for sections as a guide to emphasis and length of different sections;
- have a highly polished short summary that encapsulates for a non-reader why this research matters and the quality of its design;
- have a project description that *makes a case* about the logic of the design, given the aims;
- emphasize the authority and achievements of the applicants to this point, especially emphasizing a continuous record, and recognition by others via refereed publication, awards, previous grants, institutional position;
- demonstrate knowledge of the field and advance to it;
- explain significance in a form that is understandable and convincing to a lay reader, including, preferably, to one who does not share the values of the applicant.

Common failings

In terms of what differentiates successful and unsuccessful research applications, some things are in the immediate control of the applicant as they relate to writing and presentation and some are not.

Track record

In many cases applicants are unsuccessful because they do not score highly enough on research track record. As explained earlier, the grant process often favours a conventional academic track record: an applicant who is steadily productive, is seen to progress in terms of appointments, who has published in 'prestigious' and 'international' contexts, and who amasses an incremental array of grants. Many people's lives do not neatly fit this model, and many people's values and agendas have led them to spend time, even as researchers, doing types of research activities and publications that do not maximize their appearance. If the lack of success in competitive funding is due to track record, possible remedies might include: becoming a member of a team of someone who scores very highly as a researcher; deliberately spending a few years building a better profile by targeting publications to appropriate journals, and applying for lower-level grants; lobbying to increase understanding of reviewers and committee members of non-linear career paths (including lobbying to change the composition of those who do the assessment); or choosing to establish oneself as a prominent researcher by focusing on arenas (discussed in Chapters 6, 7, 8 and 9) that do not put so much emphasis on a similar judgement of the researcher's academic track record.

Writing too much for those who already know the theory

This is particularly a problem if it is done in the short summary, in which it is essential to set up very clearly what, specifically, the research is about, and why it matters. One common problem here is use of jargon and language which is fashionable in a particular area but which is either obscure to others or in some cases serves as a red flag to bring their prejudices to the surface. For this reason, it is highly recommended that applicants for grants try out their short summary on their colleagues, particularly those working in different theoretical traditions. Can the point and main features of an application be presented in a way that makes sense to a non-academic? If not, it is more than likely that the research will not be funded. A less obvious form of this problem of writing to those who already know the theory is where a term that has been the subject of much research discussion ('adult learning', for example) can carry more weight, have a more 'expert' meaning, to those who have been part of the particular research community than to a reader from another field who fails to see what features of originality and significance are shaping the proposed research.

Not addressing the task

Not only are applications immediately ruled out for technical breaches, but applications that fail to address the specific agendas flagged in the scheme and scoring scheme will also be ranked low. It is not enough, for example, to provide the description of a project – there must be attention to why it is significant.

So:
What does good research look like in terms of the competitive grant application?

'Good research' here is, above all, research that a 'good researcher' does (a necessary but not sufficient condition); research that is seen to meet currently recognized quality standards in methodology; research that is building something that matters (partly an academic judgement, partly a socio-political one). The relative degree of the contribution or impact of a project compared with other projects is important in the assessment; and projects that are small-scale or critical or iconoclastic must be embedded in a strong justificatory rationale.

6

Commissioned research

The pragmatics: how does commissioned research work?

Arena	Judges	Explicit criteria	Implicit criteria	What does it look like?	Common failings
Commissioned research and consultancy	bureaucrats, politicians, sometimes academic referees	track record: ability to deliver	judges' personal knowledge of researchers	headings mirror assessment criteria	deemed politically unsympathetic
		cost effectiveness	methodology and details ideologically in harmony with commissioning body	follows all instructions precisely	others are favoured more
	executive members of professional associations and interest groups	proposal and researchers fit brief		de-emphasizes jargon	too much 'pure research' emphasis rather than
		time-line	ideas for methods or publication forms that would be 'sexy' with the public	translates into achievements whose utility is readily understandable by general reader	outcomes that meet partner's needs
	heads and senior staff of institutions; board or council; staff committee	'deliverables'			
				brevity/clarity of key findings ('executive summary')	

When government departments, professional associations, unions, char-
ities, schools or technical colleges commission research, they are not
interested in some abstract ideal form of good research; they want
research that specifically meets their needs. In this chapter I will be
focusing on the textual form that good research proposals, tenders or
reports take in this context, and will not, except in passing, discuss the
research in action. But a key feature that differentiates this arena of
research from those discussed previously is that, even at the application
stage, the text is not necessarily the key to the researcher's success.
Interpersonal relationships, word of mouth, personal preference all play a
more central role (though, as we have seen, they are not entirely absent
from the contexts discussed in previous chapters).

At a conference not long ago, I was asked to speak on a panel about the
future of education, and came up with a 'Top 10' list of things I thought
were unlikely to change. One of these, only slightly exaggerated, was
'Education policy will not be rational, will not be research-based, and will
bear more than a passing resemblance to the prejudices, experiences and
personal history of the Minister of the day'. A form of at least the final part
of this comment could be applied quite broadly to commissioned research,
whether it is with schools, industry or education departments at various
levels. The extent to which research commissioned in such contexts is
genuinely interested in finding out new things as compared with using
research as a vehicle to mount a case that is well in train will vary. And
the extent to which research briefs and agreements are explicit about
values and the end-points to be reached will also vary. But across this
spectrum, the values and connections of those involved in commissioning
the research will remain a key parameter of how the research is judged.

To make this point is not, in itself, something shocking that dismisses
this arena as a context of judging good research. It simply illustrates a
point I argued in Part 1: that education is about purposes and values as
well as empirical testing of current forms, and that such purposes and
values change and are the subject of debate in democratic societies. It also
reflects something that a number of commentators and social theorists
have noted about how policy and social practice (including education
practice) is conducted today: 'the growing role of social research as a
language for advocating, explaining and justifying ideas and decisions'
(Cohen and Barnes 1999: 29).

Consultancy and commissioned research is one way that research users
in education indicate their own definitions of good research (especially
those users responsible for policy or direction of education institutions and
practices. In Chapter 7 I discuss practitioner research, and research judgements by teachers.) It is also, for researchers based in universities, or
research organizations, or trying to make a living as independent
researchers, a very important source of funding. However, researchers

often face a trade-off in choosing to pursue their work in this form. Competitive grant schemes are often more open in the questions researchers can pursue or the approaches they might take, and contribute more directly to certain forms of reputation as a good researcher – but grants in those schemes are often harder to get and less well funded. Consultancy funding can be easier to get (at least in terms of track record, and of the relative amount of work required for a proposal prior to the money being awarded), but at the price of directly having to take a line (topic, parameters, approach) congenial to those commissioning the work. The researcher may also be subject to closer surveillance and sometimes conflicting demands on the research in progress. But from another perspective, consultancy and partnership research is an important form of legitimation of university researchers: a sign to themselves and to others that their research matters to people outside the research community.

What is commissioned research?

> ### NCVER
>
> ### Adult Literacy Research Program
>
> ### Request for expressions of interest
>
> NCVER invites expressions of interest from suitably qualified and experienced researchers to conduct research into issues related to adult literacy, including language, literacy and numeracy. In addition to an Open Category, the following research priorities have been identified by the Adult Literacy Research Program Advisory Group:
>
> * Re-engaging those with literacy needs
> * Adult literacy and training
> * Adult literacy and generic skills
> * Dimensions of Language, literacy and numeracy
> * Languages other than English and the impact on the Australian Qualifications Framework
> * Adult literacy training provision
>
> Applicants are invited to submit brief expressions of interest. Further details are included in the information kit which can be obtained from the NCVER website [...]
>
> **Expressions of interest must be submitted by 5pm on Friday, 23 August.**

(advertisement in *The Australian*, 7 August 2002)

Examples of the kinds of funded research discussed in this chapter include:

- **National projects advertised by government and semi-government bodies that are awarded by tender**:

  Our biggest job is to think about what are the priorities. We go around and talk to stakeholders of all types, we review previous research we have commissioned and look at what has been done overseas; we look at national policy statements. Then we recommend some priorities to the committee that sits over us, and once these are agreed we develop a briefing note that sets the boundaries, and an information kit so that people can see what angles we are interested in, and call for proposals. In our case we don't have a 'preferred tenderer' system (except in some cases that are highly politically sensitive). We prefer open competitive tenders because we are trying to attract new people and people from different backgrounds.[20]

- **Commissions by interest-group organizations to undertake a project that will simultaneously serve some research-gathering purpose and some advertising, lobbying or policy-formation purpose**. Recent examples I have encountered include a charity which commissions research into the relationship between poverty and education retention and effects of its own interventions; a mathematics teachers' association that commissions its own research into the extent to which junior secondary mathematics is being taught by teachers who are not mathematics graduates; a large teachers' union that funds a major inquiry into public education.

- **Commissions by education systems or funded programmes to supplement their in-house research with targeted research projects to feed specific purposes**. For example my local system, although it has a substantial in-house research branch and data-gathering processes, recently commissioned two university researchers to undertake some fresh research into schools' suspension policies and practices across the state.

- **Very small projects, where a single school or technical college, or group of schools, employ a researcher to do a task that will feed a current agenda or problem**. The research might, for example, produce a small literature review or discussion paper setting out the key work and approaches to their problem; spend two or three days in the institution to provide an outsider's brief on key tensions; or do some action research with a group of teachers to improve their ability to work with students with special needs.

In this chapter, I discuss types of research that include some funded support of the research work and which involve outside researchers, as distinct from practitioner-based and in-house research. It is research where the project description is usually initiated by the funding source, which sets up aims and outcomes and general parameters such as methodology, scope, funding limitations, and a time-line of the research to be carried out. A formal agreement or contract is signed prior to the research being carried out, and it is likely to include some conditions as to 'deliverables', intellectual property, and publishing rights. Contract, consultancy, or partnership work of this kind can take the form of major national or international contracts involving many millions of dollars, or a local agreement to do a specific task drawn up by a school or a professional association with a researcher they know.

In the case of large, government-funded projects, several steps (meetings with various parties both of the commissioning/user end, and of the potential researcher end) may be involved prior to the definition of the project, the awarding of the contract, and the signing of agreements. It is also common for large sponsored projects to be required to meet with a reference group at specified intervals; and for a number of personnel and institutional bodies to give approval before a final report is publicly released. With large projects, internal disagreements and ongoing tensions are not uncommon within the committees that award the contract and oversee the project and report; similarly, changes of agenda for the researcher subsequent to the initial advertised brief and even subsequent to signing of a contract.

In one published account, Jane Gaskell (1996) describes the steps involved in commissioning, conducting and reporting from a large national study in Canada, the Exemplary Schools Project. The decision to generate a programme in this area was made in the climate of governmental concern about a range of issues – work demands, drop-outs – and the existence of a division within a government department with a responsibility to frame national research projects on education and school leaving. The first step was to commission three research papers from well-known researchers about an approach to such a national study. Gaskell comments, 'All of them, *not surprisingly given the previous research of their authors,* recommended case studies of schools as an approach' (Gaskell 1996: 198, italics added). Following this, seminars were held with various policy makers, and formal involvement from two government bodies with interests in this area, and the decision was made on an agreed focus for the project. Gaskell notes, 'At the conclusion of this seminar, one ministry official summed up the discussion by saying the study would be good public relations for the schools and should go ahead' (ibid 1996: 198). Decisions were then made about the formal structure of the project, in this case, a complex arrangement involving setting up a research design committee to establish a research design, appoint teams and arrange the carrying out of the research; with 21 different research teams undertaking the research but their work overseen by a national coordinating committee; and with the contract overall held not by individual researchers but by the Canadian Education Association which itself was required to keep another department, Human Resources Development, 'informed about decisions and provide complete financial reporting' (ibid 1996: 198). In addition to these complexities of structure, issues arose about the composition of the coordinating committee (national coverage, linguistic representativeness, First Nations inclusion); the naming of the study (from 'successful' to 'exemplary'); the time-scale ('Policy research is time-sensitive, and department budgets cannot be predicted years into the future'); how the tension between supporting local diversity and producing an overall position could be handled; the 'good news' compared with 'critical edge' hopes of the study; and the politics of what would eventually be circulated as the report of the project.[21]

There is considerable variation in the actual procedures I have outlined. In some cases, the commissioning body directly approaches a particular researcher or research team to do the work; in other cases the project is publicly advertised and tenders called for. In many cases projects formally take the latter 'open tender' form, but informally leaven this with the former procedures, contacting 'preferred researchers'. In the Canadian study described, the commissioning body initially approached three different researchers, but all were known to favour case-study approaches. In other cases, such as NCVER in Australia, the open advertising is intended to attract a broader field and different types of projects – for example, from researchers in management fields not just those working in education research. The forms that the procedures take is shaped in part by the institutional constraints of the funding body: for example, government departments are constrained to have some openness in their tendering procedures, while a union or charity is freer to directly approach researchers known to be favourable to their concerns.

The degree of openness is also shaped by how the commissioning body wishes the research to be seen by outsiders. For example, although government departments often do approach and give inside preference to favoured researchers, they are also concerned that the project appears to have 'objectivity' and 'reliability' so that it can better be used to support later decisions. The use of open tenders and the propensity to award contracts to researchers based in large and prestigious research units or universities both serve these interests. (Note that this is a point about mainstream perceptions and how they are met – I am not arguing here that such institutes *are* more objective, or do not have their own research agendas.) Similar concerns shaped a recent research-based inquiry into public education in New South Wales (Vinson 2002). The inquiry was funded by the NSW Teachers' Federation and the Parents' Association. But because these groups wanted this inquiry to be seen as independent, they appointed as director of the project a prestigious academic from outside education, and set up 'hands off' conditions for its operation, rather than the close monitoring and control of report release normally associated with sponsored work. In this case, the selection of the principal researcher was the key point at which the sponsoring body exercised control and, of course, they selected a person with a high public reputation, whose findings would not easily be dismissed, and who was known for values appropriate to the concerns of teachers and parents about education.

Commissioned or consultancy research is not a clear-cut category

The dividing line between, on the one hand, 'consultancy, commissioned research and funded partnership research' and, on the other, 'competitive grant schemes' is not clear-cut. For example, consultancy and commissioned research projects are not always initiated by the funding body. Sometimes researchers are allowed to pitch a scheme that they think the body may be interested in. In Australia, the 'Evaluations and Investigations Program' of the Department of Education, Science and Training operates this way, as do some aspects of the work of the NCVER national VET Research and Evaluation Program. I would, nevertheless, include these schemes as commissioned research rather than competitive grant schemes in that the decision on funding is made on criteria of what the project will deliver to the funding organization, and that a contract is drawn up that specifies the shape, conduct and deliverables involved.

A more hybrid combination of competitive grants scheme and consultancy is seen in the 'Linkage' projects funded by the Australian Research Council (and similar schemes are found in programmes sponsored by the Canadian SSHRC, the ESRC, and the OECD). This is one of two major streams through which competitive funding is awarded to university researchers. In this stream, applications must include both a university research team and an industry partner. The applications are ranked on researcher track record, significance and methodology in much the same way as discussed in Chapter 5. But in order to develop an application, researchers must also be involved in extended discussion and negotiation with their 'industry partner' to develop a project that also meets the partner's needs. To be successful, projects need to demonstrate that they will produce a 'contribution to knowledge' (that is, do something more than produce for the partner knowledge that is of use only for that partner); but they also need to demonstrate a history of applied collaboration with the partner, and that they are doing work that benefits the partner's own needs. So, in order to have the partnership that enables the team to enter the competitive array, to be judged as 'good research' in a broad research spectrum sense, they have to be successfully involved in some form of consultancy research arrangements, and producing good research in a local and applied needs sense.

Another example of this blurry line between a competitive 'open' scheme for judging research, and a more directed programme, is seen in Lagemann's history of education research in the USA (Lagemann 2000), where she discusses some differences between the research funded by the Carnegie and Rockefeller Foundations in the inter-war period of the twentieth century. These large foundations in many respects operate more like the competitive funding schemes discussed in Chapter 5 than the instrumentally-oriented and prescribed commissions discussed here. But the research these two foundations chose to support represented different agendas in relation to education, and different views about what good education research was in terms of the needs of the country. Carnegie looked favourably on projects concerned with the selection and training of talent and what one might call 'hierarchy'; Rockefeller was prepared to support projects concerned with general education, or the education of disadvantaged groups.

The division between open schemes and commissioned consultancy research is a spectrum rather than an absolute, but it shapes the points at which, and ways in which, researchers are held accountable for their work – particularly in relation to the type of agreement or contract that is signed, the process of doing the grant, and the process of reporting on it.

At the other end of the consultancy spectrum, the small projects commissioned by a single institution, there can also be some blurriness about whether the activity is research and whether it fits the forms I set out to describe in this chapter. In this small-scale work, even if there is some direct funding involved, there may not be a very explicit contract. In some cases the task may be understood by both parties as one where a researcher contributes expertise to a problem that is defined for them by the school (a form of consultancy). Or the parties may have a history of working together, and the idea of the project and the form it takes might be more jointly arrived at (a form of partnership). In yet others, the school may see what is happening as an example of the first case, and the university researcher may enter the task seeing it as an example of the second, and trouble may arise when later issues about publications and expectations of reciprocal contributions reveal different understandings on the part of those involved.

One academic researcher, Sue, told me recently about her experience with a particular group of schools which had approached her because they were interested in the type of research she had been doing. She spent a lot of time meeting with them, briefing them on her past research and its methods, and helping them to design research-related activities that would suit their own purposes. However, when she wanted to write about this work in an academic journal article, the group she had been working with were not happy, and the collaboration began to wither. 'As soon as I started to initiate some more research-oriented activities it stretches the relationship with the schools, and they start to get a bit suspicious and anxious about what I'm doing.'

From Sue's point of view, she had been spending time, unpaid, in a collaboration that was, at least in part, an extension of her ongoing programme of research, and a collaboration that would potentially give some benefit to both parties. But the example illustrates quite clearly some of the ways different research is understood, as well as some of the ethical and procedural issues relevant to the arena discussed in this chapter.

For one thing, Sue's experience illustrates different ways that research is defined in different contexts. In the academic context (at least within contemporary forms of bureaucratic accounting for one's work), there is an important distinction between 'professional development activities' and 'research'. This is not necessarily a distinction that school-based practitioners support and this will be discussed further in Chapter 7. Many academics who work in education also do not support this distinction (Anderson 2002), but my discussion here is directed to the institutional pragmatics of the situation – what can be counted as research for promotion, grant applications and so on, issues that have been discussed in Chapters 3, 4 and 5. If the work with teachers in the case just discussed was seen only as professional development work by the academic, she could not use it in her profile as a researcher for those other purposes that are important in her own workplace context: as evidence from which decisions are made about the promotion of individuals, ranking of departments and universities, and funding of universities and individuals. An activity gets to be counted as 'research' if it is published in a refereed journal, or, sometimes, if there is a formal contract with significant funding (provided the title of this contract appears to be commissioning some form of research or consultancy service rather than some form of training service – again, often a blurry distinction for education researchers).

Sue's example also shows the way in which relationships between schools or colleges and particular researchers often develop – a relationship that emerges rather than involving a clear-cut approach and agreement at the initial contact. But it illustrates the problems that emerge if there is no reasonably clear and, preferably, written agreement as to what is being contributed by both parties, and what both parties are entitled to expect from the collaboration. This is something that frequently happens with newer researchers: they find they have done a lot of work for a particular group or body, but do not have a contract that allows them to receive appropriate recognition, and are hurt when they find that ways they want to use their work, that in their own context are unexceptional, are not understood or approved of by those with whom they are working.

This discussion about commissioned research has emphasized some different interests that may be at work between commissioning bodies and an academic who enters a contract with them, but the situation is neither static nor (always) as clearly binary in form as that might imply. Scheeres and Solomon (2000a, 2000b), for example, discuss how a demand for collaboration has simultaneously been penetrating the workplace practices of all three of the partners (government, industry and university) involved in contracted research in the vocational training area. They argue that the critique from the Left that accuses academics engaged in commissioned research of 'selling out' to the economic rationalist agenda ignores the way that academics are pulled into such agendas in their own workplace, and that the very tensions that colla- borative researchers encounter are central to important problems education researchers today should address, that is, are a site of good research rather than an impediment to it.

Who are the judges?

> We're not just funding things because they look intellectually interest- ing. Our question is, in what way will it make a difference? . . . and of course, we look for value for money.
> (Research director of a government-funded education body)

The type of research context being discussed in this chapter covers a large variation in institutional context, political orientation and scale. In some cases it involves research funding of many millions of dollars and deci- sion making by very senior bureaucrats and politicians and committees involving many people; in others, funding is small-scale and can be committed by one or two people for a particular purpose in their school or organization. But I will begin by talking about what judges in this arena of consultancy research have in common. This is most readily seen by a focus on what they are not, in particular, how judges in this context differ from those who decide the quality of theses, or refereed research articles, or competitive grants.

What these judges are not

Judges in this context are not insiders of the academic research com- munity in the way that examiners and journal referees and competitive grant committees are. They do not bring the same training; they work with different reference points and pressures from those who are university-based; they are located within a different set of institutional agendas and priorities.

Technical expertise

Usually, the person or committees commissioning, judging and over-seeing research of this kind do not themselves have doctorates or extensive experience as a researcher. Major funding committees will be likely to include, but not be dominated by, some members selected for their research expertise. But regardless of how much technical expertise about research methodology is present in the awarding body, judgements about the technical qualities of good research (methodology) will not be located as directly in state of the art debates drawn from the academic literature or research conferences. Their technical expertise is nearer to that of the educated lay person, or to the institutional common sense that characterizes their institution than to the form of peer expertise that the scientists discussed in Chapter 1 are familiar with (that what makes research 'scientific' is not guaranteed by the techniques used but by the *peer scrutiny* that takes place by the members of *the research community in that field*). The technical expertise of commissioning bodies or individuals will be shaped much more by experience about what has worked or not worked previously than by theoretical arguments about methodology.

Points of reference

The motives, agendas and forms of accountability of those involved in deciding and overseeing consultancy research are not governed by some abstract commitment to quality research. In Chapters 3, 4 and 5 I discussed how assessors generally have been selected for their research expertise, and their accountability in formal terms is one of *process*: of having operated fairly in terms of such expertise, and of not letting that be overridden by personal connections, conflict of interest, and such like. In the area of consultancy and commissioned research, decision makers will be held accountable for many *substantive* aspects of the decision beyond the process of ranking different applications: the shape of the project to be funded; the characteristics of the research team to which the work is awarded; and the outcomes of the research, both content and form. Judgements and accountability here will be governed not by comparisons between different research projects, but by comparisions between the use of funding for that particular research purpose, rather than for other purposes within the organization. In other words, the motives and judgements of those assessing good research will give much higher priority to the issue of how the research project and its findings might potentially be used by themselves and how it might potentially be used by others. In the first case, 'good research' will be research that serves well the internal agendas of the body commissioning it (or the personal career agendas of the person who holds power in the decision making). In terms of potential uses by others, 'good' research is framed or conducted so as not to produce material embarrassing to or critical of the body that commissions it.

In the Canadian 'exemplary schools' project, for example, Jane Gaskell discusses how the decision about naming some way into the project (using 'exemplary' rather than 'excellent' or other terms) was helpful in gaining the involvement of schools in the project, but also constrained ways in which the actual research could be shaped, since the term 'exemplary' implied a selection principle and design approach that 'risked losing a critical edge' (Gaskell 1996: 200).

Politics and power struggles

Consultancy research judges are institutionally situated to place more emphasis on instrumental agendas, value for money, and end-point uses of the research than contexts discussed in earlier chapters. This context is also one where internal debates and power struggles about what is important are frequently explicit, especially in large-scale projects in which a number of government departments or institutions are involved in the management committee. Prior to the designation of the project to be funded, there will usually be meetings and negotiations between groups and individuals with slightly or greatly different agendas as to what will be given emphasis.

Experts on grant committees, university doctoral committees or editorial boards also do not necessarily agree about what research is best, but they do work in institutional contexts that have some agreed parameters for judging (on a grant committee, for example, it is formally expected that a member who personally favours only quantitative studies will be amenable to the possibility of high quality occurring in a qualitative application). In the case of commissioned research, this may not be so, and meetings about the project to be tendered or the report that is required may be used as vehicles for struggles about relative power in the organization.

Institutional and personal agendas

On an individual level, judges will be concerned about how this research (cost, personnel, format) will appear to their superiors in the organization: does it address what they are known to value? If not, how can it be framed to appeal to them? Individuals will also demonstrate variation, or personality differences, in what they want the research to show. Some will give high priority to research being 'safe', not doing anything or using any methods which pose any risk of controversy or criticism. Others will be concerned to demonstrate their own ability to take initiatives, to be creative, and to promote new ideas and directions.

So, whether or not they have extensive research experience, judges will not primarily be judging research as a researcher themselves, but rather as a manager or interest group representative. Their interest is what the research achieves, both as an event (the commissioning of *this* type of project to *this* group of researchers) and as an outcome (what the researchers produce as findings or report). They are people who bring expertise relating to day-to-day experiences and concerns about costs, and about decision making between competing agendas. In relation to any particular project, points of relevance for the researcher hopeful of winning a contract include: what hierarchies, reference groups, pressures and points of reference is this source of funding working with?

Explicit and implicit criteria

REQUEST FOR TENDER (RFT) PRN03197

Making Education and Career Decisions:

School Students' Aspirations, Attitudes and Influences

The Department of Education, Science and Training invites organisations with appropriate expertise and experience to conduct focus groups with students, parents, and career guidance officers to address the following issues:

- how are the study choices and career aspirations and decisions of 15-year-olds formed, how and by whom are their views and attitudes influenced and at what points;
- how important are the influences impacting on student choices and decisions, and how does the relative importance of these influences change as the students move through their schooling;
- how do the key influences form their own opinions and preferences, and how do their influences impact on the students' decision making processes;
- whether, how and why student aspirations change by the end of year 12; what is the role and influence in this process of career guidance teachers and career information in secondary schools;
- how is VET in Schools perceived by secondary school students, including its status with those who take the subjects and those who do not, and the reasons why the students take or do not take VET in Schools;
- what are secondary students' attitudes to the traditional trades as a career option; and
- what are the attitudes to teaching as a career among senior high school students, especially among male students.

Information from this project will inform education and training policy and further work in this area.[22]

Many of the conditions set out over many pages of legal detail in an 'invitation to tender' or a tender contract are also implicit in less formal negotiations to do contract research. Normally, the agendas specified are outcomes (deliverables, or what is to be produced); costs; time-line; evidence of research team's standing and capacity to do this particular research project; some parameters of the procedural constraints regarding methodology and time-line; rights regarding intellectual property. In broad terms, these explicit criteria cover the same basic considerations of 'what is good research?' that students in my classes give (see Chapter 1), and that the more formal academic judgements discussed in previous chapters also encompass: that the researcher is good (well qualified, good track record); that the research meets good technical standards; and that good research achieves something that matters. But the contextual emphases here are different: different aspects of what makes good research are emphasized, and some different issues come into play in defining what a good track record or methodology or research outcome looks like.

Background criteria

The act of committing money to a specified research purpose and/or the potential outcomes of such research must serve some purpose for the commissioning body. (The act of committing money can serve a purpose distinct from any concerns about what the research is to achieve.) Judgements and accountability here will be governed not by comparisons between different research projects, but between the use of funding for that research purpose compared with for other purposes within the organization. The purpose might be to find out something they need to know, or to evaluate a direction, or to get some evidence-based input as to new policy directions. But it might also be to elicit data to support a current policy direction, or to demonstrate visible commitment to an external accountability requirement (for example, commissioning research on the views of indigenous participants in a particular programme).

What counts as good research can change overnight. A few years ago I did a project examining databases on gender equity, commissioned through a body representing state ministers of education. Unfortunately, after the report had been completed by the research team and just as it was about to be published, an election was called and the federal government changed, and as a result the work was effectively buried by being delayed for a year, and then published without proper proof-reading or distribution. In this case, it was not even a problem of the work being considered politically off-side – it was simply that this was no longer a priority issue. Another case involves the Queensland

Longitudinal School Reform Study – a major and very expensive project involving a team of high-powered university researchers, conducting work that was intended to provide a foundation for reform of a state education system (Lingard *et al.* 2001). When the work had been underway for a year, the government that had commissioned the study was defeated at election and a party of a different political persuasion was elected. Researchers spent some months of delicate negotiation with the new government to persuade them that the research should continue and could feed the platforms on which that government had been elected.

The different orientation and flavour of commissioned research compared with an open competitive grant application can be seen by considering the tender for conducting focus-group-based research on school students' aspirations, attitudes and influences quoted at the beginning of this section. Many researchers are interested in the big questions indicated as part of this project brief, and indeed many books, journal articles and theses have been written on the topics it identifies. The major research question 'how important are the influences impacting on student choices and decisions, and how does the relative importance of these influences change as the students move through their schooling?' was only one of seven similar big questions listed in this project description. A researcher undertaking a thesis or applying for a grant would be likely to narrow or refine the specific aspect of the issues they could investigate with a particular approach, and to develop a project that they would pursue over several years. But in the tender quoted, the time-line given is as follows:

- 24 May 2003, project is first advertised nationally;
- 29 May 2003 (5 days later!), an information session to be held in Canberra;
- 10 June 2003, closing date for tenders;
- 20 June 2003, date by which contract is to be signed;
- 19 September 2003, date by which final report is to be delivered.

In this brief time span, the research team will have to design a new project; clear some space to work on it; organize ethics clearance both with universities and different education departments; find schools and students who agree to participate; carry out (or sub-contract) focus-group interviews across a big country; and analyse and report on the findings. The purpose of the project is to contribute to and meet a time-line driven by policy concerns with VET (Vocational Education and Training) in schools, and it is being conducted alongside other initiatives, including a parliamentary committee of inquiry into the matter. Good research in this case is research that will look respectable and that can deliver something in the time requested.

Now consider some of the explicit criteria commonly sought in tender documentation, and how they are defined in this particular context:

Track record

> **8 Related research**
> Please provide brief details of related research conducted by you and your organisation within the previous three years. Research proposals must not duplicate existing or current research conducted by the proponent or others.
>
> **11 Researcher(s) expertise/experience**
> This should contain details about the organisation(s)/researcher(s) submitting the proposal and should provide evidence of their suitability to conduct the research project proposed.

(from 'Guidelines for Proposals' NCVER National VET Research and Evaluation Program Information Kit, February 2003)

For this kind of research, the research team needs to demonstrate a track record that fits the purposes of the funding organization; and there is a strong track record emphasis on efficiency and reliability.

Clearly, a teachers' union is not going to award a research contract to researchers known for an anti-union position; or a charity concerned with disadvantage to award a contract to researchers whose main profile is developing selective mechanisms to identify a hierarchy of talent. And it is common after a change of government to see a new regime of researchers winning the research contracts. In most cases, researchers who have been publicly critical of a government or organization will not be given consultancy research money by them, though such researchers may continue to win funding via the government-funded competitive grant schemes. The university department in which a researcher is located, or an institute or think tank to which they belong, may have a known political profile that will single them out as preferred candidates for some governments and rule them out with others.

But the issue of what type of track record fits the purposes is not just about political values apparent in previous work, though these are often what is most visible to researchers who are missing out on contracts at a particular time. Fit or acceptability can also be about methodology, status and networks. Those who are known for action research will be sought out by bodies seeking this type of work; those whose expertise is in national surveys will be sought for that. In a substantive area (classroom discipline for example, vocational education, or gender and education) commissioning bodies will often do a quick check to see what names keep coming up as leaders in that area. Often, too, it is not so much about formal publications, but about what researchers can demonstrate about previous similar research engagements – and the direct experience or word-of-mouth experience of those making the decisions about those researchers. Interpersonal relationships and networks and a portfolio of previous similar types of consultancies will be important in building the persona of a good researcher in this arena.

The other track-record issue that is given greater prominence in this context than in the arenas we have looked at previously is *efficiency and reliability*: a record of delivering work to order and in the time-scale required. In one previous experience in which I had tendered for a government contract with a team of university researchers, the department told us that although ours was the favoured proposal, some members of the committee preferred to award the project to a particular research organization that existed solely to do contract research. Because that body depended entirely on tenders such as this, they had an excellent track record of reliability, ability to follow orders and to deliver research on time and in the form required. University researchers typically are involved in building their own individual research careers. Less cynically, they prize their independence and know that their reputation is built on the things they write or are known to stand for. They are often working as academics because they believe in research activity as something other than delivering agreed public relations outcomes. They may then be uneasy about and attempt to reshape some of the methodological and outcomes agendas built into the consultancy brief; or they may simultaneously be pressured by other demands of their workplace, and find themselves unable to give the tender the priority they had intended, or to deliver precisely on time.

(In the case I was involved in, the commissioning department wanted us to consider modifying our proposal to include some role for the research organization that some members of the committee had favoured, and we agreed. It is very common in awarding of big contracts for some further negotiation of teams and agendas to occur between the initial tender document and selection of short-listed applications and the final contract.)

In another case, Jane Gaskell discusses a Canadian scheme that is more like the hybrid grants/industry-linkage Australian scheme I described earlier. Difficulties arose in getting the network to produce the work to which they were contracted because many of the individuals involved in the university teams 'remained accountable to their primary worksites, and were only loosely accountable to the network' (Gaskell and McLeod forthcoming).

Process, approach, methodology

At the negotiation and contract stage, the commissioning body often sets out in detail the parameters of the budget, the time-line, the main components of the methodology (for example, major questions to be addressed, and major components of methods – such as specifying a national survey and a number of case studies including both rural and urban examples) as well as the composition of the management committee and interim steps to be met during the project. The parameters of methodology are not necessarily decided on grounds of what the research technically needs to do to produce answers on its key questions; they may be included because it is important that certain interests be seen to be represented (for example, inclusion of particular states in a national project or particular countries in a European project, because too much previous research has been awarded to other states or countries).

Some specific issues that come into play in relation to project proposals are:

'Expertise' relates to demonstrated knowledge of context

> **1 Background**
>
> Provide a brief summary of issues relevant to the area of investigation. This section should provide evidence of researchers' extent and breadth of knowledge of the priority area requiring investigation.

(From 'Guidelines for Proposals' NCVER National VET Research and Evaluation
Program Information Kit, February 2003)

When I asked the research director of an organization that commissions many tenders what would signal to her committee that researchers have (or lack) appropriate expertise to carry out the work, she placed as much emphasis on what was said in the background section of the proposal as what was furnished in terms of CVs and track records. Applicants are expected to know and to mention key contextual issues that the commissioning body sees as important – relevant national policies, understanding of the institutional structure and arrangements and processes of the body being investigated, knowledge of research that has been done previously or is available from other sources. Academics assessing theses or research grant applications or journal articles similarly make judgements about whether the research shows knowledge of its subject matter and of previous research, but the substantive assessments they make about what is relevant will not be identical (though they will overlap). In academic publications, there is much more attention to judging accurately the state of a developing *research* programme (for example, via a literature review); in commissioned research there is much more attention to judging the contextual parameters (legal and policy contexts, relevant interest groups, as well as non-redundancy of research effort) to which this research is expected to speak and to be accountable.

Request for tender 2414

For Consultants to Undertake the Review of Independent Indigenous Vocational Education and Training Providers

Tenders are invited from consultants to undertake a review of independent Indigenous vocational education and training providers. [...]

The purpose of the review is to examine funding or Independent Indigenous vocational education and training providers, what services they provide, how they might be improved and to compare the outcomes of this sector with the vocational education and training sector as a whole.

The successful tenderer will be expected to have a good knowledge of Indigenous vocational education and training issues.

The successful tenderer will be expected to have a demonstrated working knowledge of Indigenous education issues and peak Indigenous organisations

- a demonstrated ability to effectively communicate and interact with Indigenous Australians;
- a thorough knowledge and understanding of recent national education and training initiatives and related policy and programme considerations; and
- experience analysing and developing financial/funding formulae.

As part of the project, the consultant will be expected to consult with vocational education and training institutions, Indigenous people and communities, and other stakeholders. It is anticipated that the scope of the consultancy will be a total of 20 working days.

(From *The Weekend Australian*, 3–4 August 2002)

Methodology attends to 'transparency', impact and 'value for money'

---

4 Methodology

Describe the methodology proposed for the research project. This section of the proposal is crucial and is the area that is weak in most proposals that are not supported. The methodology must identify each stage of the project. The template provides structured stages that should be used as a guide. Please ensure you clearly indicate the following:

data gathering method(s)
key people/organisations who will be targeted as sources of information how the data will be analysed

5 Timetable

Describe the project stages, milestones and timeline including dates and number of weeks required. ... The following milestones should be included:

Interim report one
Draft final report (including executive summary)
Final report

Note: NCVER will organise for external reviews of interim and draft reports. This process can take up to four weeks.[23]

The 'Guidelines for Proposals' from which I have been quoting not only require sections setting out the methodology, timetable, deliverables and key research questions; they also require specific detailed sections on staff allocation within the project; a detailed budget set out according to a template; a statement of quality assurance processes; and a 'Risk Management Plan'. Surveillance, control, due process, accountability for process and money all assume high visibility in project design.

In the case of a tender, once the general explicit criteria are set out in the guidelines, what differentiates between potential applicants? Two main implicit criteria come into play when such proposals are judged. One is the relative quality with which proposals make a case about their *ability to do what is required*. Different projects will offer different things in terms of the named personnel and their track records; their decisions about how to allocate funding for different parts of the project; with what astuteness they appear to identify the further methodological issues or problems that will need to be negotiated for the work to be carried out.

The second criterion that differentiates applicants at the proposal stage is *what new or value added components* they add to the original brief. For example, before such things became common, proposals to set up an interactive website; or to produce multiple forms of reporting back for different stakeholders would positively differentiate one proposal from another that aimed to produce only the standard form of report and executive summary.

In process, a good consultancy research project is expected to achieve what it promised at the agreed intervals. One problem here is that the management committee for a project is very likely to encompass different interests and agendas within it, or, as a result of other outside pressures, to change its own emphases in the course of the project – leaving the researcher to negotiate how they reconcile changing demands with the original agreement or contract.

What do good commissioned research proposals and reports look like?

The proposal or tender stage

For a specified brief, a tender should address each heading *exactly* as specified in the brief. The researcher track record emphasizes achievements in similar types of research and in similar types of consultancy; and (where appropriate) reliability, quality and status of the institutional base from which the researcher works. Language is businesslike and written in the third person. A detailed (and realistic) budget for different components of the work is important. The document shows how the aims of the brief will be realized, what will be studied, for what reason, and in what way. It seeks ways to inject creative additions to deliverables.

Scheeres and Solomon describe how they wrote a successful submission for a project involving workplace ethnographies to develop training packages on communication skills by ensuring that the submission presents the project in a 'linear and procedural' form rather than in ways that ethnographies might be proposed and justified for a thesis or a research grant application. The methodology, as reflected in the submission, provided a linear procedural description of tasks:

1 collection of data . . .;
2 collation and analysis of findings;
3 identification of oral communication competencies and strategies . . .;
4 development of 'Train the Trainer' modules;
5 trialling and revision of modules;
6 production of modules;
7 Delivery of modules in food industry enterprises around Australia.

(Scheeres and Solomon 2000b: 122)

They comment that, even though their own ongoing interests as researchers are in the complexities of workplace knowledge and practices, the construction of worker identities, the challenging of certain contemporary taken-for-granteds, the way in which a submission for funding of this type must be presented necessarily embeds a different type of research rationality:

> This list describes certain kinds of research practices that resonate with a 'positivist' approach, emphasising determinacy, rationality, impersonality and prediction, using the natural sciences as the model [. . .] It is, therefore, the perfect match for the required outcome, that is, a rational, linear description of the communication skills needed for productive and efficient work and the kind of training that would lead to these outcomes.
>
> (Scheeres and Solomon 2000b: 122)

For a proposal without a specified brief, a proposal document sets out succinctly (usually only 1–2 pages at first stage) what would be done and why this would be of value to the organization. It sets out in summary form a proposed time-line, the qualities of the researcher/research team, and an indicative budget. Outputs and achievability are emphasized.

The reporting stages

Consultancy forms of research can require a range of reporting tasks. Sometimes direct reporting is in the form of a findings statement and brief for the commissioning body, who themselves decide what further form of more public report is produced. Sometimes, the output required includes a report or materials for wider circulation. Often initial interim reports may require more detailed accounting of the research in progress, to ensure that the work is being done as agreed and is on track. Specific 'findings' reports may be required at specified stages.

For a management committee, and especially for a committee that sits over the one that actually supervised the work, what will be required is a succinct and easily readable statement of

- what steps have been done in the research;
- what are the findings (or achievements);
- implications for action.

In terms of reports for wider circulation, the form of outcome report(s) will attempt to fit the purposes and institutional pressures discussed in earlier sections of this chapter. Usually the funding body will closely scrutinize this final reporting, and will exercise editorial control over contentious wordings or sections. If public perception is important, for example, the research should produce an account which is clear and readable in a form appropriate to this audience. It should also reliable and authoritative, enhancing the purposes of the commissioning body rather than inviting a critique of them. In the Canadian Exemplary Schools project, the purposes of the national body that held the contract were served by funding the release only of an official (approved version) national report in both French and English, in video and print form. They did not give priority to releasing individual school reports, whose emphasis might differ from the main message: 'The CEA's emphasis on the national report as opposed to the school reports was a sore point with researchers, who had worked hard to make their reports publishable, and with schools who anticipated having copies of the reports for their own purposes' (Gaskell 1996: 205).

For research that is commissioned to make a difference, a presentation of the implications may be more important than the statement of 'findings'.

> We are increasingly trying to shape the final report to be succinct and analytic, leaving the findings in an appendix, and up front an analytic account of what was the key message coming out of those ... Of course along the way we would have required interim and draft reports to check that the research was doing what it should have been doing ... Sometimes, as the final reporting or outcome stage we bring the researchers together with key stakeholders and have a meeting or conference; sometimes we produce a glossy brochure, synthesizing the findings; sometimes we produce briefings for policy-makers; we put things on our website. The research report is just the beginning.
> (from interview with research director of a government body)

In the context of commissioned research, the act of having the research done is itself of importance, not just the issue of what is 'found'. At the reporting stage the commissioning body will want an outcome that demonstrates that the money was well spent, the work was done well, the outcomes are impressive or relevant. Different interests among relevant parties will also shape final reporting. It is common for reporting to take multiple forms to accommodate different interests and be appropriate to different stakeholders. It is also common that there will be some conflicts of interest among researchers, contracting body and stakeholders, and some power struggles over what will be released, in what form, and to whom.

Common failings

Researchers who apply for and miss out on research contracts in this arena may be failing on grounds that are internal to the application, or on grounds that are beyond their control. Some examples of characteristics of unsuccessful applications are:

- Applicants do not have a profile for this type of work.
- Applicants are from a state/city/institution that has already had a lot of contracts and the national body needs to award this one to a different source.
- Applicants fail to demonstrate knowledge of the specific context (for example current policy, or institutional hierarchies).
- Regardless of what is in the application, the known profile of the researcher or research institution is politically less attractive than that from another source (that is, the problem is who they are and what they have done previously, rather than what they are offering on this occasion). It is probably less common here that particular researchers are ruled out on political grounds, than that they lose to other researchers who are ruled in or given an inside running, because they are seen as particularly in tune with the purposes of the commissioning body.
- The application does not address all elements of the project brief.
- The design of the approach does not appear convincing in its ability to address the objectives and/or appear to a general reader as 'reliable' (for example, proposing a case-study approach to a project in which a survey would normally be used) and/or able to be properly carried out within the specified budget.
- The application reads like 'academic' work: writing that is more about intellectual concerns than the 'real world'.
- The application is not well presented: sloppy, unbusinesslike.

So:
In the case of commissioned research, what does good research look like?

'Good' research here will fit the purposes and values of the commissioning body. 'Good researchers' will be those known to the decision makers directly or by reputation for their previous similar work. Good research will meet businesslike standards in terms of contracts, process and outcomes delivered on budget and on time. Ability to follow orders is important in research design, and ability to avoid any embarrassment for the commissioning body is important in research methods and reporting. Good researchers here will be skilled at negotiating conflicting agendas and demands. Being seen to deliver reliably may be as important as the substantive quality of what is delivered.

Good research here is research that is not too academic; that emphasizes its systems of delivering cost-effective results on time; that is likely to come up with the answers the commissioning body wants; and that has ideas for producing these answers in ways that will enhance the commissioning body's profile.

7

Schools, teachers and other practitioner users

The pragmatics: how do practitioner users of research work?

Arena	Judges	Explicit criteria	Implicit criteria	What does it look like?	Common failings
Schools	teachers	applied potential	well promoted, high visibility	reader-friendly	conditions for take-up not available
Vocational colleges	principals		supporting resources or	key idea important	
	department	not too complicated	conditions		research not
Education support officers	head	works as guide or	accompany	how-to-do-it kit	conducted from implementation perspective
	education department	manual *or*	issue has high public profile	video	
Community	advisers and professional	inspirational	with parents *or*	catchy title and cover,	looks 'academic'
	development consultants	addresses issue that it is	promotes individual	best-seller	not disseminated via proper channels
		required to	career advance,	*small* book	
	teacher professional	address *or* addresses	*or* advances	often conveyed	researcher not good public
	associations and networks	issue of felt concern	school profile	by word of mouth rather	performer
	instructors	authorized or mandated by	specificity to user (e.g.	than print	
	individual parents and	central body *and/or* speaks	primary rather than secondary	digests of research	
	organized parent groups	to new problem or zeitgeist	examples)	if print, uses illustrations and guidelines lavishly	
				is published or presented in professional contexts	

In previous chapters, the arenas we have considered have had relatively clear boundaries and forms. There is a clear point at which decisions are being made, and a form of paperwork that accompanies the decision making about better or worse research, or acceptable or unacceptable research. This chapter is concerned with a more fluid issue: what characterizes research that gets picked up and used (or is undertaken) by education practitioners, professionals or involved community users, such as parents? End-point users of education research of course include policy makers, curriculum consultants and education administrators of various types, not just teachers and instructors. But in many cases the former groups are also involved in commissioning research, and those issues have been discussed in Chapter 6. This chapter is about the more grass-roots context of 'usefulness', an image that often lurks in the public debates about the lack of usefulness of much education research.

My problem is that it is much harder to bring the arena of this chapter together with my purposes in this part of the book – to define the territory in a descriptive way, and then offer an initial pragmatic and empirical account of how judgements are made. In the case of schools, teachers, practitioner users and parents, the question of what type of phenomenon we are trying to understand here is itself the subject of vast and contending bodies of the education literature. What even counts as research here? And where do we look to see what it means for a teacher to judge education research as 'good' research? What *is* the theory/practice relationship – is it application of one to the other? dialogical? reflective practice? theory in action? Are we talking about people's self-conscious knowledge of what research they have taken up, or is this something that we should judge from their actions rather than their opinions? Are we talking about short term or longer term? direct or mediated? Are we assuming that researchers are people other than the practitioners, or are we including practitioners' own research activities?

Because my emphasis is on the networks, texts and pragmatics of making assessments about research, and because I am directing my discussion more to those who identify as education researchers in a primary way, this chapter will effectively be limiting its discussion to only some aspects of what makes good research for teachers, practitioners and parents. It will be more concerned with conscious and direct take-up (including practitioner-research activity) than indirect (such as reflective practice); more interested in research as a commodity than as a formative strand in framing education and cultural discourse and common sense. But this emphasis does need to be understood as only part of the story. A recent investigation of research impact, for example, discussed cases where ideas found initially in research contexts (the idea of individual differences in learning styles, for example) were almost universally held by teachers, without there necessarily being any self-consciousness about this as a *research* idea or finding, and without particular researchers or pieces of research being seen as the source of this way of seeing (Australia. Research Evaluation Programme. Higher Education Division 2000: 31).

The 'grass-roots' education practitioner arena: some issues in defining the territory

Where do we look to see what judgements teachers make about research? A recent weighty report on research 'impact'[24] commissioned a number of different teams to investigate impact, and three of them take rather different starting points to understanding what teachers do in relation to education research, and very different methodologies to showing what research impact looks like.

One chapter (Holbrook *et al.* 2000) undertook a major mapping exercise, using databases of various kinds and surveys of various interest groups to identify where education research was happening. This chapter produced a rather different picture of the practitioner than the one that often springs to mind in discussions that use binaries about teachers on the one hand and researchers on the other. The largest single group doing education research in Australia, according to this analysis, are in fact postgraduate students; and a high proportion of those students are students in a part-time capacity only, and employed full-time as practising teachers and administrators. From this perspective, many practitioners are simultaneously engaged in formal academic research. The survey indicated that the major motivation of these postgraduate researchers was 'intellectual challenge and personal interest', but also that they saw this intellectual work in most cases as closely related to their roles in the workplace. Both they and school principals saw these teacher/ postgraduates as an important source of useful research for schools and other teachers.

In another chapter (McMeniman *et al.* 2000), McMeniman and colleagues viewed teachers as active mediators and transformers of knowledge, so they undertook case studies that used video-simulated recall supplemented by concept-mapping and interviews, to ask teachers about research influences on significant teaching decisions or events. They produce a picture of teachers not as actors who make a single decision about a particular research issue or approach at a particular point in time or in isolation, but as an ongoing 'reflective practitioner', one who is 'an intuitive, idiosyncratic self-starter who is able to navigate a pathway through this labyrinth of complexity' (p. 495). That is, a teacher is someone who is producing research *in* action, and who is taking in and processing a whole range of research and experience in a way that is different from focusing on a particular piece of research and assessing it in turn. This study showed that teachers participate in and relate to research in a number of different ways: they directly access research; they participate in research studies designed by others; they do formal research as part of their studies; they do formal teacher–researcher activities outside accredited study; and they actively experiment in their own classrooms (p. 496).

Taking another approach again, a third team (Figgis *et al.* 2000) took four different education issues for practitioners (boys in schools; new technologies; students at risk; and early literacy) and backtracked the ways in which teachers, or schools, or policy makers had built up their approach to the issue in question: looking at the web of initiatives, personal contacts, formal events and literature they drew on. Like the previous study, this builds up a picture of the different and varied contexts in which teachers 'access research':

- conferences and workshops;
- personal development activities;
- taskforces and reference groups;
- formal meetings;
- chat over tea or sandwiches at the above gatherings;
- articles about the research in publications of professional associations;
- short reports published by the researchers;
- internet sites;
- media coverage;
- research-based products for use by teachers;
- postgraduate studies;
- collaborative research (practitioners with researchers);
- commissioned research.

(Figgis *et al.* 2000: 347–8)

This account also identifies many different mechanisms through which practitioners actively pursue research knowledge about a particular issue:

- turns to 'expert' colleague;
- colleague introduces the practitioner into a network;
- accesses formal information;
- has active exchange with information source;
- participates in research.

(Figgis *et al.* 2000: 348)

The analyses above were made by studies in one country at one particular period. The ways in which teachers engage in research or use research will be different in contexts where there is considerable devolution of curriculum and assessment from those where decisions are centralized and greater uniformity is expected; in states where extended higher education qualifications are required compared with places where teachers are not required to do this; in situations that mandate certain directions as important and provide sanctions or incentives to seek further education in those areas than those where teachers have a freer choice of further direction to meeting their needs. Berge and Ve, for example, discuss how changes in the form of the schooling system produce certain new conditions for research in schools in Sweden:

> Over the past three decades school policies have shifted from a centralized system, including regulated national curricula, towards decentralization, including goal-oriented national curricula. ... The arguments for the shift have focused on overcoming the negative aspects of too much state regulation of teachers' work and delegating more professional power to teachers. With the new goal-oriented national curricula, with less regulated timetables, schools can differ more than before. From now on teachers in each school can choose what they regard as the best ways to reach national goals in their classrooms. The debate has also focused on how to make schools more effective in reaching the aims of compulsory schooling and on how to 'measure' efficiency. National steering and control of compulsory schooling presupposes that, although schools have the same goals to achieve, they will have to perform different kinds of evaluations and follow-ups.
>
> (Berge and Ve 2000: 5–6)

To take another example, in technical and further education, research about competencies or pedagogy has been more often directed to and disseminated by system-level decision making than seen as a matter of judgement for practitioners. At some periods and places, the broader field of adult education has been decentralized and allows for considerable individual input on its form, and at other places and times (such as the present), it is being increasingly made accountable in a more corporate form. Again, the differences here shape what research and what kind of research is seen as relevant (Coats 1996).

In the following sections, I restrict my discussion to conscious uses and assessments of particular research projects and research publications in comparison to the broader questions of long-term and indirect research influence, or of the teacher as a reflective practitioner doing research in action rather than as a more specific, bounded project.

Who are the judges?

i *Practitioner–users*

> Does the research show that single-sex schools are better for girls?
>
> (teacher at a public forum)

We want ideas, not answers . . .
> (teacher quoted in 'impact study' of Figgis *et al.* 2000)

Teachers feel there is too much exhortation, too much research is at the exemplar level.
> (from interview with school-based 'professional development' teacher)

Thank God someone's talking about gender in relation to *primary*.
> (from interview: researcher reporting on teachers' reactions)

Throughout the project, the teachers, pupils and researchers experienced both a desire for and a fear of change.
> (Berge and Ve 2000: 5)

The model appeared to be contextualised in what appeared to me to be a deficit approach. The SRLS research was used to advocate that teachers were not currently using many of the productive pedagogies. While this may have been the legitimate SRLS finding, the teachers at that professional development responded to this suggestion by questioning the representativeness of the sample groups in the study.
> ('Critical friend' reporting on teachers' response to a major research project, Hill 2002)

It needs to be something I can use.
> (from interview with teacher)

In this section it would be as easy to tell a story of diversity as of commonality: some teachers (and schools and school leaders) actively develop new intellectual and political concerns and seek out as well as undertake forms of research that build these; others look for work that offers practical assistance in their day-to-day tasks. Some resent and distrust any research that is not derived from practitioners or classroom-based studies; others are impressed by 'experts', statistics, and international gurus. But let us consider some of the characteristics of these judges relative to the types of issues we have discussed in other contexts.

Positioning and points of reference

Teachers don't have a shared language of what research constitutes.
> (interview comment by an ex-teacher who was employed for a number of years as an in-school professional development director)

Some questioned the use of the word 'pedagogy' suggesting it was academic speak and not the language of their professional discussions.
> (Hill 2002)

At a minimum, practitioner–users have in common that they are involved in some task other than the peer or insider assessment of formal academic research: they work as teachers, instructors or administrators, and their relationship to research is from a position situated in those practices, not from an abstract set of criteria or, rather, the situated practices of the university committee or journal reviewer. At a micro level, different interests are at play for those who work in a context where promotion and rewards accrue on grounds other than formal publication lists and research grants achieved. Like those involved in awarding consultancies, their interest tips towards the issue of what a piece of research *achieves* as compared with technical (methodological) quality issues.

This orientation can be seen in a number of forms. In the gender area, while academic researchers might be debating the adequacy of each other's theories, there is much formal and anecdotal evidence that practitioners themselves draw as much on 'popularist' literature and authors as on researchers who have the kind of track record approved by promotion committees and grants committees. In this case, what matters are the ideas and how they connect with practitioners' concerns, and what matters less is the carefulness with which evidence or theory is built. Teachers and principals involved in the study 'backtracking' their uses of research in relation to new technology made a similar point: they were looking as much for inspirational ways of thinking about this issue as for narrowly focused controlled formal studies of small aspects of the work (Figgis *et al.* 2000). And a researcher involved in a major, structured, longitudinal study of schools commented that while policy makers wanted the findings, teachers and schools were more interested in the tools they were working with – the structured observation schedules and the ideas guiding the project. They wanted to use and discuss these themselves, rather than waiting for the academic researchers' big formal findings.

Another example is the popularity of action research for practitioners compared with conventional academic studies that might be seen directed to the same issue (for example, the comparative value of two alternative pedagogical strategies). One way of seeing this is that a criterion of good research for practitioners is not research that proves something 'in general' or 'with high statistical probability', but research that works in this particular classroom, school or neighbourhood centre ('there needs to be a space for me' is how one school-based practitioner reported it). Another way of seeing it is that, for the teacher, instructor or principal practitioner, it may be much more important in career terms to be seen to have engaged in research than to have produced a particular written report from it – that is, the reverse of the normal university ways of judging achievement in the research arena.

At the agent (human subject) level, the positioning of practitioner users is less uniform than that of judges discussed in earlier chapters: research plays a less uniform role in their life-path agendas than in contexts where people have in common a career interest in research or as a researcher. What they *are* likely to have in common is that research and research interests are something to be squeezed in among other elements of a busy working week. This shapes the type of research writing and communication and directions that are of value to them.

Related to this, the judgements that practitioners make about research are shaped by the extent to which their system or institution supports them (time, resources, opportunities for engagement and advice).

Experience and training

> Teachers are highly localized tribes: they hold quite dearly to specificity.
> (interview comment by school-based professional
> development coordinator)

The training, workplace culture and daily tasks of teachers produce some different ways of judging relevance than might be seen by academics when they nominate a 'relevant' expert to judge a particular piece of research. In the academic context, what is often foregrounded in the classification of the research is the education process it addresses (for example, discipline, gender, assessment or individual differences in learning), or the bodies of theory or methodology it is working with. For a teacher interested in those areas, the research may be seen as relevant only if it is done specifically in the area of the system that is the same as the teacher's own institutional location. This applies particularly to historical differentiations of training and culture between early childhood, primary or elementary, secondary and adult and technical sectors which are often given greater weight in assessing the relevance of research than national context: for instance, an Australian primary teacher may pick up work that was done in British primary schools but may not be prepared to look at work that was done in Australian secondary schools or vocational training institutions.

Differences in training and background are also evident in the choices that individuals make about engaging in research, and in the directions a particular field of practice takes up. For example, secondary teachers who initially undertook undergraduate degrees in the humanities, especially English literature, may be drawn to further study that is less at the applied pedagogical end and most marked by the 'academic' intellectual interests of their subject field. Early childhood teachers and adult education teachers both have a field history (and a gendered and class history) of being positioned outside the mainstream of teacher training and structures of institutionalized employment, and those fields have often developed areas of interest and favoured theorists and politicized use of research that is different from secondary teachers, for example.

ii   *Institutions and associations*

Schools and other education settings (technical colleges, adult learning centres, pre-schools); collective professional associations (unions, subject associations, curriculum associations), and teacher networks of various kinds are significant in the judging of research in the practitioner context. They operate both as collective expressions of certain judgements, and as filters and gate-keepers on the research that is circulated.

Schools' attention to particular types of research or directions of research will be constrained by the formal directives and budget of the system and by informal 'community' and especially parental concerns that highlight particular issues at particular times (see too the discussion of the media in Chapter 8). More broadly, these institutions (and education departments) will be strongly concerned with what is *not* good research in terms of their interests: research that has potential to appear critical of that institution or system. Again, there is a potential conflict of criteria here between what grant committees judge to be worthwhile, and what institutions that allow or disallow access for research purposes, may judge to be worthwhile. In the former case, research that is structured only to tell 'feel good' stories is likely to be seen as poor research, as research that is not sufficiently rigorous in its methodology, and not sufficiently producing 'new knowledge'. In the latter case, research that produces a critical perspective on the institution or school may be seen as poor research in that its negative effects on the functioning of the institution may be a more important outcome of the research than any new 'contribution to knowledge' that is gained. These are not unresolvable issues, but they are certainly constraints felt by many university researchers and postgraduate students as they negotiate ethics committees, permissions of various kinds and day-to-day research practice.

In some cases and contexts, the pressure for research to be effectively an arm of marketing can become extreme, and be felt as a pressure by the teachers and the researchers.

'Teachers are pressured to do research that makes the school look good.'

'They were interested in controlling how they were talked about publicly.'

These two comments were made in interview discussions I had in the course of writing this book. They are comments by two different people, working in different cities. One was speaking of her experiences in a private (fee-paying) school; the other of her experiences with a group of designated disadvantaged schools. Pressures are likely to be felt in private schools which are competing for students, and concerned about their image; but are also increasingly felt in state systems where schools are being positioned in the same way as part of the rhetoric of market choice (Kenway 1991; Ball, Bowe and Gerwitz 1996).

iii   *Parents*

I have attempted in Part 1 to discuss some of the changing agendas that can be seen operating in education research when this is investigated over time or across national settings, but it is not the purpose of this book to develop or pursue theories of cultural change and education. Here I want to touch on the issue of parents and community only briefly and pragmatically: in terms of their role as consumer-users of research. For parents, this may be in terms of direct choices they need (are now required) to make about their own child's schooling: private or public? selective or comprehensive? 'progressive' or highly disciplined? single sex or co-education? Is it important to buy a computer? Or it may be about decisions they make as part of a parents' association, or school council, or in choosing between different policies.

As user-judges of education research, parents share some characteristics with teachers. They too have an engaged or positioned interest in what research might contribute, not only some general commitment to research as an enterprise; they too do not spend their days mainly on activities internal to the research community. Like teachers, they read research from a frame heavily shaped by their own experiences of education: in this case, often their memories of their own schooldays, and their own experiences of their child. But because they are engaged from a different perspective to that of the teacher, parents may be more prepared either to defer to the expert conclusions of the researcher, or, conversely, to reject particular research out of hand because it does not reflect the parents' own values (for example, their religious convictions).

Explicit and implicit criteria

As there is no single point or context of judgement of research in this arena, I will just offer some comments on issues, types of scenarios and the explicit and implicit processes that come into play.

Visibility

Research cannot be judged (taken up, used, approved, initiated) by practitioners as good research if the practitioner or practitioner community has not heard of it. Action research and self-research are self-evidently visible. Research solely disseminated in academic journals is unlikely to be so, except to the minority of practitioners undertaking research degrees. Even education departments with a research division, or schools that actively seek out research carried out on a particular problem, will normally access academic research indirectly, for example through user-friendly reviews of the literature or through intermediaries – by using existing contacts with universities or researchers to get direction on what is available. Conversely, if a researcher is a major self-promoter, preferably a visitor from another country with a media-friendly manner and a few key points to sell, then their work will be highly visible. Researcher visibility is increased by: putting out popular versions of work; holding workshops and addressing teacher conferences on the work; writing a regular column or reporting one's research in publications for teachers such as *Education News, Rethinking Schools, Our Schools/Ourselves*; having an ongoing relationship with a school or group of schools or subject association; being a university supervisor of people in key positions in schools and education departments.

In this arena then, the equivalent of *researcher track record* discussed previously is that they are known to the practitioners: either directly (through practitioners' own studies and research involvements; or attendance at workshops and professional conferences), or at a distance. Institutional position and rank can be helpful in establishing 'expertise'; and international status can be helpful in establishing expertise and glamour. But these are not as important as the practitioners' direct and indirect experiences of the researcher and the type of work they do. Researchers who in other contexts would be ranked poorly on research quality may flourish, especially if they are good presenters, and vice versa. Indeed, to some extent, the structural demands (including time on task demands) of different workplaces make it difficult for researchers to be regarded equally well in university and school contexts: being highly engaged in school-based activities works against being highly productive in the form that counts for university promotions.

An alternative form of visibility is achieved via the *institutional source* of the research. Research done or mandated by the bodies that pay the practitioners is likely to be disseminated with visibility to those practitioners (and often, also, via the press to the general community). Certain other organizations too have in place established mechanisms of dissemination: for example unions or subject associations which distribute newsletters and support materials to teachers; or major non-university education research organizations such as NZCER, ACER, NFER, who gain money by marketing tests, digests and other types of reports that can achieve the larger sales available in the school market compared with the smaller university sector of education. These digests, disseminated to practitioners, will primarily make visible the outcomes or end-points of the study, its implications and possibly its scale and broad form. What will rarely be visible will be the specific methodological assumptions built into such things as the framing of a survey or the approach to interviews and focus groups.

Usability

Research cannot be judged by practitioners as good research if they cannot decipher it, or if it seems so boring that they lose the thread of what it is showing. To make an obvious point, what is decipherable to a thesis examiner or, possibly, to a grant committee in terms of jargon and technical or even very formal language, is not necessarily readable to practitioner assessors of research. But readability is not a stable criterion even within the practitioner community. For practitioners who are actively engaged in new directions or who are politically engaged, research that is provocative, case-study based, overtly political, introducing new concepts, or requires more work to be understood, may work well. For those who seek research to help them in their daily grind, the readability/usability benchmark may be drawn further down the scale.

Usability takes different forms. From the perspective of administrators looking for directions that can be mandated in a variety of sites, the emphasis is likely to be on studies that have been larger scale, and appear well tested, and that can guide resource allocation, applications of rewards and sanctions, support mechanisms, and so on. The perspective of an individual practitioner is in terms of what something means or its applicability in a particular situation. In both cases, usability *may* take the form of the research generating steps or a model or a handbook of 'what to do' – but it may also take the form of providing a 'way of seeing' that allows the practitioners themselves to build a new approach to the issue in question. Issues of gender and new technology are two areas which have provided many examples of research of both types being drawn on by teachers and schools. By contrast, in the discipline and classroom management area, the more recent preference has been for kit or manual types of usability, although this was not always the case (Yates 1999b).

Even though at some points new ideas and agendas can be of more importance than tightly designed 'how to do it' studies, there is frequently resistance to research that is seen as too pure in its framing: 'I found that teachers were very critical of research that had "too much exhortation", that seemed to be "too much at the exemplar level"' (from interview with former in-school director of professional development). Yet teachers can be equally critical of research presentations that assume they are only interested in and/or capable of dealing with 'how to do it' questions, research that seems to patronize them.

'Usability' of research is increased by kits and workshops; but it is above all promoted by forms of practitioner-based action research.

This chapter began with some reference to academic doctoral study as one way in which practitioners make choices about research, engage in it, communicate it to other colleagues and their school. But this does not mean that the criteria governing the two arenas are identical. A recent discussion of doctoral education in the USA commented: 'dissertations that might have been powerful analytical narratives of practice ... become schizophrenic exercises in pleasing doctoral committees who provide guidelines that often do not fit the reality of the students' research' (Anderson 2002: 24). Anderson was commenting here on the heavier emphasis in dissertation examination on technical qualities of methodology and research design, contrasting this with the value for practitioners of a more fluid engagement in which their positioning as practitioners allows them to make judgements about what is of value.

In this arena then, the equivalent of the scrutiny of *methodology and design quality* discussed previously takes a number of forms. Sometimes it is of virtually no importance: the message and the ideas or ways of seeing are valued, not how that point was reached. Sometimes it is assessed quite categorically, on grounds of appropriateness (administrators may have no interest in work that takes a case-study or interpretive form or is not 'objective'; teachers may reject out of hand research that conflicts with their own experience, for example of class size having no effect). When research is being used for ends that teachers do not approve (for example, high stakes testing, or when they sniff a deficit framework), they may avidly read details of methodology and scrutinize these for flaws.

Addresses something that matters

In each chapter, we have seen how research 'significance' is assessed in somewhat different ways, although this does not mean that some research is not widely valued across different contexts. In the case of practitioners and grass-roots users, 'something that matters' may be politically dictated from above ('all teachers will now become teachers of literacy'); may be a problem felt within the practitioner's field of practice (children who are dropping out, or obviously bored); may reflect social changes (how should we operate given new technologies? what are the required characteristics of the 'new worker' and how can these be produced ?); or may reflect waves of community or media interest (co-ed or single sex? selective or comprehensive? how do we provide for gifted/ADHD/cultural differences? and so on).

Sometimes the conditions for assessing good research are set outside the individual practitioner: it must produce demonstrated improvement in student outcomes, for example. Sometimes, what matters may be idiosyncratic to the individual practitioner, or to their area. Sometimes a new sense of 'what matters' is driven by teachers initiating and seeking out certain types of conferences and ideas, is generated from teachers to researchers rather than by researchers to teachers.[25] Even when a particular research direction is mandated from outside a school or by the hierarchy in a school, a teacher's judgement and use of research may represent a pragmatic bringing together of that externally mandated judgement with their own ongoing purposes and concerns: they will look for research that meets the former conditions but which can be used or adapted for the latter ones.

What does good research here look like?

> In this school, I introduced teachers to research on gender that was specifically about primary schools. I also negotiated conditions for support that gave teachers time to do case studies of their own classes. These were so good that I wanted to get it out there. First of all, I arranged for teachers to do presentations at a conference for other teachers. Then I wanted them to do the same at a bigger conference of education researchers. To persuade the principal to allow us time to do this, it was necessary to put a very strong case that this was an important marketing opportunity for the school. In terms of publications, I think it has been important to spread it around. First, we published a report on the project in a publication that circulates to teachers in a form that will look good for the school. Then we produced a conference paper for two education research conferences, again highlighting things of value for the school image. These papers in turn were published in an edited book, and in an education research journal, gaining academic credibility and circulation to the research. Finally (now that I am working in a university), I have also published in international research journals. In the initial presentations and publications, the school is named, and the research is discussed in the context of this school as a leader in education innovation and professional development. The most recent articles for the academic research community does not name the school and discusses the research in terms of more general issues about practitioner research, feminist theory and gender inclusive curriculum.
>
> (Evelyn Johnson, who has worked as a teacher, then academic, then school research coordinator, and now academic, speaking of publications for different audiences such as Johnson 1999, 2000, 2002a, 2002b, 2003)

The textual form of good research in the practitioner arena takes a number of forms: it can be produced in different genres, and its internal characteristics are related to those genres.

Research produced outside the practitioner context:

The provocative best-sellers
These are best-selling books that sweep around the globe and are widely discussed in the press and on media talk-shows as well as in the staff

room and at professional conferences (Freire's *Pedagogy of the Oppressed*; Illich's *Deschooling Society*; Tannen's *You Just Don't Understand*; Hirsch's *Cultural Literacy*; Belenky *et al.*'s *Women's Ways of Knowing*; Biddulph's *Raising Boys* are a few examples). Successful research here normally

1 takes up a social issue or issue of technological or economic change that is widely experienced and problematic;
2 takes a strong position, and one that explicitly opposes some existing approaches to this problem;
3 offers an answer and a new way of going about things;
4 is usually short, direct, clear rather than long and turgid.

Another form of this genre is the prominent press article or, even more, the regular column in a paper read by teachers.

Research digests and research translated into user-friendly forms
Sometimes good research here, research that is accepted or built on, takes the form of digests of key points that are distributed in workshops or in publications for teachers. This may take the form of kits in which the emphasis is on actions arising from the research. In this case an academic researcher may rewrite their original research in a form for a practitioner audience: reducing jargon, eliminating as far as possible extraneous details about research design, expanding research implications (for example, Rigby, *Bullying in Schools and What to Do About It*, 1996). Successful texts are usually framed as a partnership with the practitioners: in which actions and activities to be done by them will work in combination with the starting points here to make the research meaningful.

The evidence-based practice movement also aims to disseminate practitioner-friendly digests of 'rigorously evaluated' research findings on education processes, using bodies such as the What Works Clearinghouse discussed in Chapter 1. Organizations such as the Curriculum Corporation and ACSA in Australia, and publications branches of national research organizations such as ACER and NFER all aim to disseminate to practitioners in appropriate forms, as well as initiate or commission particular types of research and more formal research reports.

Practitioner research

While it is in process, good research here is research that is do-able and that is producing results or insights that are of value. Or, if the practitioner is cooperating in a larger study in which they are not the designer, and which is not designed to produce immediate outcome, 'good research' is that which looks important (where the researcher or institution or funding context are important), that appears to be conducted professionally, and where the researcher-practitioner's role is well-briefed and well-acknowledged on an ongoing basis.

In terms of publication/dissemination, good practitioner research (what was done, what was its point, what was its outcome) will be conveyable informally (staff rooms, casual conversations with colleagues, professional meetings) as well as formally. Written reports will include low-tech dot-point in-house publications, glossier print and IT-based presentations to audiences outside the school and, occasionally, articles in academic journals, or in books.

What will be highlighted will be: contextual details about the school/institution setting, and about how the project came into existence (whose initiative, sources of support), major elements of the study, and outcomes.

Common failings

Research is likely to be taken up or appreciated if it can fit with the system arrangements of the practitioners, and if it is accessible and appropriate to the agendas that the system or institution or individual are pursuing. Research may fail because

- it does not address a priority issue for this group;
- the research is not framed to address action or implementation questions;
- the form of writing or genre of publication/dissemination is too academic (seems too remote or unconnected to everyday realities);
- there is a lack of personal contacts and relationships between researchers and practitioners.

Conditions in the field may not allow room for practitioners to become involved, either because of overall workload; or because system arrangements and priorities and constraints change. For example, a shift to a more vocational emphasis in further education (Coats 1996) meant that programmes and research initiatives for women in further education had to demonstrate their value on vocational and economic criteria rather than, as earlier, on humanistic or feminist criteria. Similarly, in the 'backtracking' study of three teachers and principals who had been involved in developing work around boys' issues, the researcher commented that the story very clearly 'highlights what can happen when the interplay of research, policy and changing practice successfully come together, and, conversely what happens when this falls apart' (Figgis *et al.* 2000: 296).

So:
What does good research look like for practitioner-users?

It is research that provides a 'way of seeing' *or* an approach to, *or* a guide to action on, *or* answers about 'something that matters'. Something that matters may be defined politically or at the system level; it may be Zeitgeist or media-generated; or it may be generated by individual or collective practitioner interests in developing their work towards particular ends, or in addressing problems of that work. For some practitioners good research will be provocative and politically aligned, for others it will be research that is valued as having weight and objectivity. Clarity, brevity and innovativeness of presentation will be valued. The methodology and range of what is counted as good research will be relative to the structural arrangements (decision-making form, workload, time, support structure) of the system in which researchers are engaged.

8

Book publishing

The pragmatics: how does book publishing work?

Arena	Judges	Explicit criteria	Implicit criteria	What does it look like?	Common failings
Academic book	Commissioning editor (publisher, commercial)	sufficient readership	potential sales	preface and cover calls up the identified readership	being Norwegian/ Finnish/ Australian/New Zealander, etc.
		adds/fills gap	location of author		
	Series editor (academic)	academic quality	track record of author	more varied formats than thesis and journal articles	writing about Norway/ Finland/ Australia/New Zealand, etc.
	Referees (academic)	literary quality	timeliness or fashion		
				specific citations reduced, but bibliography remains	at end of cycle on that subject
	Publishing board (commercial)	appropriate for that publisher/ series			
					clash between author's and publisher's vision of readership

Books are one of the most visible ways in which education research is selectively taken up and disseminated. What is done in this arena touches on all of the other contexts discussed in Part 2. One sign of high-quality thesis achievement is taken to be its suitability for publication in book form, and examiners are sometimes explicitly asked to judge the thesis in these terms. Academic journals review books and commission essays about important books, and book reviews are among the most widely read features of academic journals. And articles in academic journals combined into a book form are expected to circulate to a wider audience than the journal format. Grant committees are interested in what researchers have produced from their research, how this has been judged by others, and to whom it has circulated; and books are one important means of demonstrating this track-record productivity. For those commissioning research and for practitioners, a researcher who has published in book form has more visibility and a more understandable record for a lay audience than has a researcher whose work appears only in academic journals. In terms of the press and media, book publishers work hard to have their publications reviewed and discussed in the press, and this is one of the ways that education research filters to the notice of the press.

Book publishing, then, is an important arena for the assessment of education research because of its connection with the other areas in which the research is circulated and judged. It is a context which draws from and speaks to both the academic 'insider' about quality in research, and the broader field of engaged community/institutional purposes and questions, areas whose emphasis is more on what research has produced than on how well or reliably that came to be.

As in the contexts already discussed, judgement of good research by commissioning editors for book publishers involves some attention to the qualities of the researcher, the significance of their work, the technical quality of their work, and the qualities and appropriateness of the texts they produce. However, these criteria are, once again, given a particular interpretation here. They are approached from a quite specific set of agendas and interests that do not simply replicate judgements of research quality by an academic thesis examiner or academic journal editor.

For education researchers, the book publishing arena is taken as some measure of the status of their work. For example, in the Australian system of funding universities according to research achievement, publication of a research monograph with a recognized commercial(!) press scores 6 points as compared with an article in a refereed journal or a book chapter that scores 1 point (but a textbook or a research report published in-house by a university department scores zero). Nevertheless, the extent to which such publication is a measure of the research quality of the work as compared with a measure of the saleability of the work is less clear. Not all publishing houses have the same history or mission.

Some background on publishing houses

Historically, many university presses were set up to disseminate high-quality research, and as an associated public relations exercise for that university, and the issue of commercial return was not such an important one. Being selective about the research that is published is one way of advertising the status of the institution, and, reciprocally, being published by a press with such a reputation is a way of advertising the status of the researcher. Commercial publishing houses did always need to be concerned with markets and return on their publishing enterprises, but they too took diverse decisions as to what form of publishing they would be known for: whether textbooks or research monographs, controversies or encyclopedias, whether the works they would publish would have a particular political flavour, what topic areas they would specialize in. Some would take decisions to cross-subsidize high-quality but low-selling research monographs that gave a quality image to the press or that would establish them as the 'publisher of choice' for that particular topic area, using profits from other books such as continually reprinted textbooks or tests. The 'mission' of different publishing houses, the procedures they require for publishing proposals, and the ways in which publishing proposals are assessed, are now usually clearly set out on publishers' websites.

> [Our mission is] To publish high quality and competitive products and services for the learning needs of students, academics and professionals in the social sciences.

(Open University Press website)

> Cambridge University Press is the printing and publishing house of the University of Cambridge. It is an integral part of the University and has similar charitable objectives in advancing knowledge, education, learning and research. ... For millions of people around the globe, the publications of the Press represent their only real link with the University of Cambridge.[...]
>
> Cambridge is one of the world's largest and most prestigious academic publishers in the humanities and social sciences, publishing in the region of 1,000 new publications annually. This massive output encompasses a vast range of publishing from the successful Canto paperback imprint, aimed at both students and general readers, through undergraduate textbooks and a large range of upper-level academic paperbacks, to highly specialised monographic works of primary research.

> The press also publishes a range of academic reference books, exemplified by the famous *Cambridge Histories* begun back in 1902 and still hugely successful today. In recent years the balance of Cambridge publishing has begun to change significantly as the academic world has itself changed, and new formats, such as *Cambridge Companions*, have arisen in response to the needs of the higher educational community.

(Cambridge University Press website)

In recent decades, education research has been significantly affected by two developments that have reduced the diversity of publishing outlets available to researchers. One is associated with globalization and a series of mergers of previously separate organizations into a smaller number of major conglomerates (in the course of preparing this book, Open University Press, an independent publishing house based in the UK, was bought by McGraw-Hill, a major US-based company). These changes can bring others with them, particularly increased attention to general management accounting practices.

> [C]ontrol of the publishing industry by a shrinking group of multinational media conglomerates results in the application of generalized management standards that are less responsive to the specific needs of publishing. In other words, the managerial orthodoxies of the entertainment industry are increasingly being employed in the publication of literary works and academic research. For instance, a former Disney Corporation executive was made head of Penguin Books. Pantheon books, formerly a quality publisher of Nobel-prize winners and acclaimed authors such as Noam Chomsky and Michel Foucault, installed as its head a former banker known for his lack of interest in books. On being shown less-than-blockbusting print runs for books of some these acclaimed authors, he suggested the company should be 'ashamed to be publishing such books'.
>
> (James and McQueen-Thomson 2002)

A second development, more marked in some countries than others, has seen major changing patterns in the funding of universities so that they receive less direct public funding for their operations, and are required to earn more through direct activities such as fee-paying courses, international marketing, associated commercial ventures. In Australia, this has seen the demise of many university presses, since they were not bringing commercial returns to their host university, but had traditionally received some university subsidy for their operation. This imperative to be independently commercially viable has also reshaped the operations of the university presses that do remain, with much more attention to commercial viability in their publishing decisions, including seeking subsidies from authors for publication of some works that are seen as high quality but have a limited market. UNSW Press now opens its website section for potential authors by foregrounding its success as a production and marketing entity:

> We welcome new authors. The publishing team of UNSW Press holds a successful track record in both production and marketing.

(http://www.unswpress.com.au/aguide.htm)

And when the Cambridge University Press website moves on from its own opening story of its glorious history and connections with the university to the (specifically) Education section, it talks of 'finding new international markets', 'extensive market research', 'customer care and support'.

Taking up education research in relation to the arena of book publishing does bring us back to some debates I discuss in Part 1. For one thing, it raises the question what sort of a 'thing' is education research? Books published in the field of education include research-based studies, collections of research reports and debates, polemics, and textbooks. But these are not clear-cut categories: your 'polemic' might be my 'writing as a researcher'. What the publisher hopes will be a widely selling textbook might be your dearly cherished and highly polished final account of your research project. And how the university promotion committee will see what you have produced is another matter. The form of writing that is allowable in this particular context may hide rather than reveal some aspects of the research acts that preceded it (methodology, for example, or links to the research literature), and this will be discussed further below.

> Scholarly publishers are positioning themselves not as the carriers of arcane or deep research, but as potential conduits for academics to write differently for a more general market. . . . By 1999, general readers were the largest fraction of the total sales of university presses, overtaking libraries and institutions, and college sales.
> (James and McQueen-Thomson 2002)

In the case of book publishing generally there is a strong dialogue between quality and commercial interests, and my assessment of the education market is that the commercial interests dominate. In other words, it is more likely that you will get published if you are writing about something that a lot of people are interested in, no matter that you do it poorly, than if you write a very good book for which there is a very limited readership.

> The sales and marketing division are increasingly not at the service of publishing; it's the reverse.
> (from interview with Australian publisher of books in education)

Who are the judges?

Judgements about publication of research in the form of a book are normally made in two stages: first at a proposal stage where the book is judged on the basis of its author(s), its outline, the case made as to its potential readership, and its outline of content and sample chapters; and later at the stage when the full manuscript is submitted and assessed. (Sometimes the full manuscript is submitted at the initial stage, but today this is less common. Sometimes a book or project is solicited by the publisher from an author, but similar criteria will be at work to those I will discuss here.)

A number of people will be involved in the decision making about the book: the commissioning Editor (sometimes called publisher) or editorial specialist in that area; if it is part of a series, the academic series Editor(s); other academic referees to whom the proposal and sometimes the manuscript is sent; and other committees and boards of the press, which attend to marketing interests and profile interests for that publisher, make broad decisions about the directions in which that particular press is heading, and who oversee and have the power to reverse decisions made by editors. Those who will have the most direct contact with the researcher will be the commissioning Editor and series Editor, and they will be the judges who most directly assess the substantive quality of the work along with academic referees. Powerful, indirect judgements will be made about the publishing possibility for particular research by the commercial and sometimes (if it is a university press) academic members of the board of the company, or the sub-board that deals with its list in this area.

The specialist editors are key people here, in that they not only make direct decisions about particular proposals or the shape of their list, but they also decide on series editors, select reviewers for the proposal or manuscript, and represent the claims of this particular book in other internal committee decision making within the company. In terms of their own background, people who fill these roles come to them through varied paths. Most will have taken a degree, but frequently not in the field of research they are now overseeing; and most will have some training in publishing. Many have started in quite junior positions in a company, and had experience in a range of roles and editorial fields. Some are disenchanted academics who have retrained. Many are young. They will be in their position because of the skill they have demonstrated in their former publishing career, rather than on any other basis.

Specialist commissioning editors bring to their judgements of research and researchers their own sense of the field; their sense of good and appropriate writing; and their knowledge of readerships, markets and marketing. Theirs is not the perspective of an academic who has been socialized through a PhD apprenticeship in the area in which they work, through other colleagues who are also academics or researchers, and through university administrative structures that reward certain types of research production. Their perspective is not based on an apprenticeship built in a particular, often narrow, agenda of research, one that generates particular disciplinary commitments and allegiances in terms of what constitutes good research. The editors build up their own sense of the field of education research and what it is doing as an intimate watcher rather than as an inmate. They give particular attention to understanding and using the networks of the field; and have a nose for new issues that are emerging and topics that are declining in interest. They go to conferences, and read programmes and listen to the gossip about different types of work and the people who are creating interest. They form their own networks of informants, often people they use as series editors; they read the general trade press (both of education and of publishing) and the daily press and media; keeping an eye on how their counterparts in other publishing houses are themselves reading the field. From this they gather information about topics and researchers who matter: what is important and who is important.

The other skills and knowledge that these editors bring are their own trade skills: their understanding of good (appropriate) writing – what kind of presentation, especially its naming and structure, is attractive to readers and book buyers; and their understanding of markets and marketing – knowing who are the potential buyers for this particular type of research, and what would appeal to them.

People in these roles are judged by their commercial achievements (how well the books they commission sell) and also by how the list of authors and books they build is seen by others (including the critical reception given to books in reviews, the awarding of prizes, and the word of mouth and gossip at conference book stalls about whether books look interesting or dated; and the in-house comparisons between those working in the same field for different publishers). They want to be seen to be publishing those who others also think are important or interesting; and to make the right decisions in choosing accounts that will be commercially viable. Their reference groups are in publishing, not the research community; though the reception of their books by the research community and other education book buyers is part of this scene.

Series editors are academics who have themselves established some reputation in a particular area, and to whom the publisher sub-contracts the seeking out of appropriate work within a designated agenda. They take an active role in soliciting manuscripts for the series, either approaching researchers who are well known for doing interesting work in that area, or using their own knowledge and networks (for example as thesis supervisor and examiner, or at conferences) to approach new potential talent. The designation of Series Editors works not only as a means of sub-contracting certain editorial tasks (soliciting and assessing proposals); but as a way of attracting proposals and advertising what a particular publishing house stands for – their own reputation is intended to help indicate to potential authors what type of work is of interest. The aim of a series editor will be to attract 'good' authors (ones that their field will currently or subsequently see as important) to 'their' series, and to shape a body of work that says something to the field. For academics who take on the role of series editors, it is part of not only building their own career profile, but also of proactively helping to shape what counts in the broad field. Developing a new book series can be one way of advertising, establishing or consolidating a particular direction of education research.

Reviewers or readers are academics working in the area of the proposed manuscript, to whom a proposal (particularly an unsolicited proposal) and the finished manuscript is sent for assessment and critique (in the case of book series, the finished manuscript assessment is usually the responsibility of the series editor rather than an outside reader). The higher the academic reputation of the press, the more rigorous will be this stage of the process. Usually at the first stage (the proposal) a number of readers are selected in order to give the editor triangulated assessments of how the book might be judged or might appeal to different markets – for example in different countries, or disciplines or types of courses. At the proposal stage, the task of the academic reviewer has some similarity to referees of grant applications or journal articles: to say, on the basis of their own knowledge of this area, whether the application, and writer, in question are reputable, and whether their work is making a worthwhile addition to existing work in the area. But in the case of book proposals, the issue of potential sales is explicitly part of the picture. Reviewers are asked what other books already exist in this area, and to assess who its readership might be, as well as how much and where it might be used. The readers may be academic competitors of the researcher in question, and personal prejudices may enter the judgements made at this point. A bigger problem, however, is that it may be difficult to find readers prepared to do this task, or to do it at all carefully. Normally they receive only a small token payment for the task; and it does not have the reciprocal visibility that preparedness to serve on grant committees or to referee journal articles may have.

Those involved in *committees or boards* that oversee the commissioning editors' decisions will be there to make decisions about the profile and commercial interests of that press. They will be guided by the education list editor's track record of previous judgements and their outcomes, but may intervene if they are attempting to improve the 'bottom line' of the publishing house, or to reposition its profile.

Explicit and implicit criteria

The websites of publishing houses set out instructions for proposal submissions, and these signal certain explicit categories of interest. The Open University Press proposal guidelines ask for a case to be made in terms of:

- *Readership*: For whom is the book intended? What would be the main market? Lay readership? Overseas potential?
- *Level*: What level of ability is assumed of the reader? To what level does the book take the reader?
- *Courses*: Is the book intended as a main text, supplementary text, reference only, general trade book? On which taught courses would you hope to see it recommended as any of these?
- *Existing books in the area*: Which are closest to this and how does this compare?
- *Coverage and organization*: Description and reasons for this particular approach.
- *Background*: Was this plan developed from teaching/research/other? If based on your own courses, please specify.
- *Features*: What aspects of this proposal would you emphasize as being of most importance? Deliberate omissions? Any other features you would like taken into account.
- *Outline*: Provisional list of contents and working title. Chapter headings and sub-headings, plus brief chapter synopsis.
- *Author(s)*: Brief details of other posts, degrees, relevant qualifications. Publications – if books, please specify. Nationality.

These headings point to some of the criteria on which research will be judged in this particular context. Good research will have a substantial readership, and can be presented in the form of writing that is appropriate for the intended readership (level, courses). It is research (or research writing) that adds something not already well covered in existing books, and that can persuade editors and readers of its quality of coverage or contribution relative to its topic (coverage and organization, outline). Assessment will involve an interplay of attention to market possibilities; to writing quality/creativity of presentation; and to the quality and qualities of the topic, research contribution and author. The cost of producing a particular book (because of artwork or tables, or because of reproducing materials for which fees must be paid) also enters the calculations of publishing viability.

Weighing the elements of this interplay has some parallel to the various components by which grant applications are assessed, discussed in Chapter 5. If the researcher is the major figure in their field, that may outweigh (or at least heavily tip the balance of) all other criteria regarding their proposals, both for grant committees, and for publishers.

Track record of success in winning previous grants counts a lot for grant committees; and track record of producing books that many people buy counts a lot for book publishers. As with films and their stars, a 'name' can sell books.

Another element of track record likely to be assessed here, from informal sources rather than the proposal itself, is reliability: the writer's record of delivering on time and in appropriate form. Publishers have to manage production schedules, and researchers who are unreliable in meeting a contracted delivery date are less likely to find ready outlet for their work.

In the case of books, good research is topical and, to some extent, culturally specific. It reflects what the community or other education researchers are interested in reading (or teaching) at this particular time. Whole areas rise and fall in interest and these take both global forms and national variation. For example, in relation to my own longitudinal study discussed earlier, we discussed publication possibilities with publishers in different countries. An Australian editor said she would be interested provided we presented it as a story of what different schools do to students from different backgrounds (as she put it, '*Making the Difference* twenty years on' – referring to a previous education best-seller in the Australian market). She would not be interested, she said, if we foregrounded our interest in gender and feminism, since the market for these had disappeared. A US publisher, however, said there was a strong market for books on subjectivity and gender, but we would have to be careful about how we discussed our interest in class, since this was not well accepted in the US market, and it would also be important to downplay the specificities of the Australian schooling system.

For academic journal articles, I noted earlier that 'good research' was norm referenced, not just criterion referenced. It was assessed relative to the quantity and quality of other material being submitted. In the case of books, similar implicit criteria apply to the topic areas that are published. Editors who sense that a certain area is or is becoming topical, but who lack current books in the area, actively look for new books that will 'fill a gap'. Conversely, the story of declining sales in a particular topic area, or the editor's belief that the area is already well covered by books already on publisher's lists, can result in a lack of interest, no matter how highly its 'quality' might be judged by academic reviewers.

Certain themes that have been points at issue for education research in many of the previous chapters often affect researchers in how they position their work for publishers and readers. The first is the issue of demonstrating specialist expertise versus the need to work in ways that can be widely understood, and 'transparent' to non-researcher judges in the field. This is not a simple binary. My discussion in Chapter 1 of the committees set up to establish guidelines for 'scientifically-based' research shows that although they emphasize the need for performance in terms of the 'specialist expertise', *peer* judgement modes that are common in science and medical research, they also frequently appeal to broad *general* opinion ('reputation') of the quality or lack of quality of education research. Researchers seeking grants are judged primarily and explicitly in terms of their publications directed at academic audiences, but indirectly the judgements of significance are also influenced by a climate of opinion, and books that circulate to non-specialist audiences are one part of how a climate develops. Increasingly too, issues of impact and dissemination to professional audiences are also taken into formal account by grant bodies and promotion committees.

In writing their research, education researchers are commonly engaged in considering how to address both specialists in their field and more general audiences. Developing a programme of research by interchange with peers (publication to a specialist audience) might involve, for example, attention to specialist concepts that appear initially as jargon, and to points at issue in relation to methodology, and to microspecificities of the topic. Reaching a non-specialist audience might require minimizing jargon and discussions of methodology and selectively emphasizing only certain components of the wider study.

Book publishers want to sell their books as widely as they can, but the pressure to write to a particular level of readership will be markedly different with different publishers and different national locations. In a country with a very large higher education system (as the USA), or with a topic that may be of interest across large numbers of university students (say, currently, anything by or on Foucault), a more 'academic' presentation in relation to jargon, details of methodology, referencing may be acceptable. In a country with small total numbers of higher education students (say, New Zealand or Australia), or a small population for books in the native language (say, Norway or Sweden or Finland), research will need to be either accessible to a very general readership in that country, or of interest to a specialist readership around the world, or be subsidized for book publication that would not otherwise be commercially viable. Countries such as Norway and Canada do have publication subsidy funds that recognize and help to address the problem of producing research that is of specific interest for an inherently small market.

This brings us back to another issue that recurs in the debates about good research, even within the evidence-based movements canvassed earlier: the tension between seeing good research as something that speaks universally, and seeing it as being something that speaks locally, with contextual specificity. It is, broadly, true that very 'important' theories and arguments will tend to circulate globally (though that may be a tautological statement). It is also, broadly, true that readers would prefer to read about research based on their own education system and referring to their own policy context than about others. Of course, people have some appetite for comparative examples, but, generally, readers like recognizable illustration of findings about some aspects of education process, and can dismiss out of hand books that are evidently based in a different country. National differences of terminology ('primary' or 'elementary' school; 'FE' or 'TAFE'), differences in widely used acronyms (of which all education systems seem to have large numbers) are all potentially irritating to readers. Again, the political economy of publishing means that there is a more ready means of publication for the local specificities of large market countries (USA, UK) than of smaller ones. In addition, those large markets that are well-supplied with material adjusted to their own local specificities of acronym, policy, structure, have readerships that are less amenable to research from alien systems than smaller markets whose readers are accustomed from their initial higher education studies to the necessity of reading from outside their own location.

What does good research look like?

The hope of many thesis writers, after labouring for years to produce their magnum opus, is that it will next be published to a wider audience as a book. But publishers do not want to see the thesis itself as the book or book proposal, and some now say that they will not accept proposals based on theses. Of course many thesis writers have managed to publish their work or some aspects of it as a book, but it is important to see why there is some problem in assuming that the two forms are interchangeable. The thesis requires attention to the finest detail, demonstrated knowledge of 'the literature', high levels of attention to and justification of methodology. Often the topic itself is a relatively limited one, designed to focus on one particular aspect of a problem, and limited precisely because of its fine detail and thorough coverage. Examiners of theses are a captive audience: the writing has to convey authority rather than find ways to attract a reader and hold their attention (though it doesn't hurt if they can manage this).

The thesis is written for academic specialists in the area. The book, however, is required to make a case to a wider readership: to take up things they are likely to be interested in, to minimize attention to less interesting aspects, even if these matter a lot to the researcher. Literature reviews are a good example where there are some different agendas at work in the two contexts. In the thesis, they are there to show mastery of the field as well as to set up a case about the value of the particular research approach of the thesis. With the book, they are only relevant in so far as they are part of the story of the case the writer is making. It is not important to demonstrate knowledge of everything that has been written on the topic, or to refer to large numbers of other authors. In the case of books that are about a particular empirical project, it is more common that the discussion of existing research will pay attention only to a few major, widely known writers, and use these as a means of orienting the reader to the work.

Methodology too is rarely covered in the specificity or with the prominence it may have in a thesis, or journal article or grant application. It will be discussed in the body of the text if it is important to the claims, particularly in controversial areas (for example, Rutter *et al.*'s (1979) *Fifteen Thousand Hours*, or Neville Bennett's earlier work, *Teaching Styles and Pupil Progress* (1976), that sparked the widespread debate about progressive and conventional approaches to primary school teaching), or if it is developing a new approach to research and analysis (Henriques *et al.* 1984; Steedman, Urwin and Walkerdine 1985; Ball 1994). But often, the presentation of methodology will be relegated to an appendix and severely truncated.

The extent to which jargon is allowable, and the density of referencing will vary according to the intended level and spread of readership, as well as to the nature of the subject matter and debate in a particular field.

Even a very scholarly book must sell itself to potential readers and buyers. Some of the ways this is accomplished are:

- by the book title and chapter titles. These need to be informative and enticing.
- by the cover blurb and abstract of contents that is circulated in flyers and advertising material. These aim to show the significance of the topic, the importance of the author, and to quote other significant people (widely-selling authors themselves) as to the quality and interest-level of the book's contents. These blurbs also name (call up) the categories of readers to whom the book is addressed;
- by a preface or foreword from someone other than the author (series editor in the case of a series) whose name is expected to carry some weight and who attests to the quality and specific interest and type of contribution the book is making. The more important the person writing the foreword, the better;
- by the author's introduction, that usually sets up how this work came to be done, and sells, in the form of a succinct overview, what the book, and specific chapters, aim to accomplish.

One common way researchers represent their work in a book form is to borrow techniques from journalism or fiction. For example, they may begin by telling the story of two or three individuals, or may tell a personal anecdote that provides a 'grab' to the reader, or they may refer in some way to a concrete representation of themes and issues that more analytic sections of the text will take up. The opening paragraphs of the book are particularly important for the purposes of drawing the reader into the topic at issue. Here are some ways authors have done this:

Chapter 1 Vicki and Thanh

Statistically speaking, the best advice we can give to a poor child, keen to get ahead through education, is to choose richer parents (Connell, 1995, p. 6)

Imagine two children about to start school. They are both five years old and are eagerly anticipating their first day. Imagine that each brings with them to school a virtual schoolbag full of things they have already learned at home, with their friends, and in and from the world in which they live.

(Thomson 2002: 1)

This is an introduction to a book by Pat Thomson on Australian schooling, *Schooling the Rustbelt Kids*. Through the opening quotation it signals its major theme of inequalities, and at the same time links this book to probably the best-selling book on Australian education, written 20 years earlier, *Making the Difference* (Connell *et al.* 1982). That connection is also established by the sub-title of this book ('making the difference in changing times'). The cited passage is a particularly striking aphorism, one that hits the reader and compels them into the problem. The chapter then begins with the two stories of Vicki and Thanh, the types of stories one might find as colour pieces in newspapers or magazines. These stories give concrete and highly readable form to some of the issues Pat Thomson goes on to discuss in terms of other wide-ranging types of research evidence, drawing on sometimes difficult bodies of theory to develop her argument and approach. But the opening sentence to the reader starts differently and more invitingly: '*Imagine* two children...'

Here is another example of a recent book by Nancy Lesko using similar concrete visualizing as its opening grab. The opening deliberately sets up something very familiar and very accessible as a way of easing the reader into a text that is going to propose some very unfamiliar ways of thinking about this phenomenon:

Consider for a moment some familiar public spaces: your local mall, a cineplex, the outside seating of fast food restaurants, a bowling alley, skate-boarding sites, video arcades, or buses around 3 p.m. any Monday through Friday. Ubiquitous in all of those spaces are teenagers – almost always in groups and sporting hair, clothes, piercings, and attitudes that mark them as belonging to 'another tribe'.

(Lesko 2001: 1)

And here is an example of an opening sentence from a book by Richard Teese which draws heavily on some traditional and 'dry' forms of evidence, on large-scale quantitative surveys and analyses of collected statistical data, as well as on some theoretical frameworks associated with the French theorist Pierre Bourdieu. The book is a research-based account of inequalities being repeated in the processes of schooling, a story that, told as a straightforward 'research report' might be quite dry. But the book begins thus

> There is a striking parallel between the poverty experienced by many workers denied opportunities to work, but kept in the workforce, and the failure experienced by many students denied opportunities to achieve, but kept on at school.

(Teese 2000: 1)

In all these cases, the opening of the book has a very different form from that of a thesis, journal article, or grant proposal. All of those genres, in different ways, are about 'what I set out to do, and why'. The opening of the book, however, is more about what the researcher, having done the work, now has to say. He or she attempts to sum this up in the most striking way, to encourage the reader to find out more about what makes the researcher able to make such claims, to encourage them to read more about what else they have to say. Qualification, hesitation, modesty are not normally part of this opening grab.

Common failings

One common failing would be to treat the book as if it were a thesis: to assume that having something important to say (in the writer's estimation, or their examiners' estimation, or even in terms of their academic field's and journal referees' estimation) is all that matters, and to underestimate the significance of having a topic and form of presentation that sufficient numbers of people will be prepared to buy.

Another is a failure to match the type of research/analysis/presentation with the right publishing house or book series. For example, as I discussed earlier, it is not usually possible today, except where heavy subsidies are available, to publish a book that is both very specific to a small national market and also aiming at a restricted group of readers (for example, other researchers and graduate students). In this case, the researcher will normally be required to modify their presentation to reach a wider range of readers in the local market (undergraduate students, general readers, readers in other faculties); or to reach an academic readership beyond the local market. Similarly, some publishers primarily sell scholarly reference books to libraries; others primarily rely on sales as textbooks. Attempts to propose a book that is very scholarly in form to a publisher who wants to market widely will not be successful.

Sometimes the failing is one of presentation (failure to present the topic and book outline in an inviting way that suggests its interest to potential buyers); but sometimes it is a failure of topic and timing. Commissioning editors may read their sales figures and decide that the cycle of interest in a particular topic has peaked. In this case, researchers will need to consider whether it is worthwhile approaching a different publisher; or if they can emphasize differently some elements of their research so that it connects with topics seen to be of interest.

So:
What does good research look like for a book publisher?

Good research is research that many people want to read about or that many libraries want to stock, or that many courses want to have students buy (and on this criteria the best research speaks widely to American college students or to global undergraduates). It is research written by a big name author, or one with a track record of popularity (previous sales success), or research that addresses a subject of highly topical interest. It is research writing where having something striking, useful or controversial to say is more important than having a detailed justification of approach and methodology (except where this *is* the controversy at issue). Creativity and skill in writing matters. Naming of the research area (book and chapter titles) assumes high importance. Testimony from important (big names) or salient others (university teachers) as to the contribution and significance of the research is important.

9

The press

The pragmatics: how does the press work?

Arena	Judges	Explicit criteria	Implicit criteria	What does it look like?	Common failings
the press the media	individual journalist editor chief of staff	timeliness important because of source or implications of study will be of interest to readers strong position by researcher researcher has established profile as commentator	researcher on databank or previous contact with journalist available when called will take position journalist looking for (if seeking debate) likes big studies 'colourful' – lends itself to photographs or colour story	short, sharp summary version ('magic message') catchy, sensational highlights controversy removes qualification and tends to exaggerate 'factual' or incontestible status of finding/ claim implications highlighted	researcher's findings too 'middle of road' researcher can't speak succinctly to general audience too complex not interesting for 'general reader'

The commercial mass media are advertisements which carry news, features and entertainment in order to capture audiences for the advertisers.

(McQueen 1997: 10)

Some years ago, when I read Humphrey McQueen's book on the politics of the press, I felt his formulation was a little crude, a trifle over-stated. But when I sat down to talk to Maralyn Parker, the Education Editor of the *Daily Telegraph* in Sydney, about this book, she began by reminding me of the same point (or at least a similar point): 'You've got to remember that basically the Editor is trying to sell newspapers.' Of course the press covers quite a spectrum in terms of the politics of different papers (and journalists), and the extent to which education is covered. But it is salutary to begin by remembering that in this context, *whatever* the politics of the newspaper (or television or radio programme), an important consideration will be not whether the research is technically good, and not even whether the research is useful or relevant to practitioners. The question will be, 'is this research *of interest* for the readers/viewers/listeners and potential readers/viewers/listeners of *this* publication?' Will it be something that gets them talking and writing letters to the editor? On this matter at least, the differences between tabloid and broadsheet newspapers, or commercial and quality television programmes, or talkback shock-jocks and serious radio, are matters of degree rather than category differences of genre. Blandness is always a problem; complexity and qualification of the argument are likely to be a problem; and the packaging of 'the talent' and the message is a key issue.

However, the spectrum of media and press outlets in a particular country is also a factor in what counts as good research copy. In countries with large potential readership, able to support specialist education papers such as the *Times Education Supplement*, and *Times Higher Education Supplement* in the UK, and *Education News* in the USA, there will be scope for a wider range of research interests to be discussed, and even for there to be some relationship to debates taking place in academic journals or arenas discussed in previous chapters. Newspapers that have a regular supplement, or employ an education columnist or education editor will more actively be looking for stories than those that do not, though the types of stories they seek may be strongly circumscribed by the advertising market of that supplement of the paper.

Who are the judges?

The judges here are journalists and their editors and chiefs of staff. Journalists may initiate story ideas and pitch these to their chief of staff, or may be assigned a story by the chief of staff. Editors make decisions about how much of a report finally appears. The person who has the most immediate contact with the researcher or research report, and who makes decisions in relation to the interpretation of the research and its status, is the journalist. They, along with other editorial staff, are making judgements about the interest level of the research relative to other happenings inside and outside education.

Except in very rare cases (in specialist education papers), none of the judges here will be insiders to the world of education research. Their training and socialization is as journalists; and their commitments are to good journalism rather than to advancing the cause of good education research. If they are specialist education reporters or editors or columnists, they may build a wide knowledge of education developments, but their perspective is one that is shaped by broad movements and issues of the education field (political claims and policy changes, community issues), or personal interests and contacts, and research outcomes and claims and positions relative to those matters – rather than in what is being built by particular researchers or the technical quality of what was done. Indeed, in many cases, education *research* is less important to education journalists than other stories about education.

Journalists are trained to look for and to present a good story (see Hartley 1982; Granato 1991; Oakham 1997). This book is not the place for an extensive examination of what assumptions and political values are at work here, but Maclure (2003, chapter 2) and Gill (1994) provide two interesting analyses of how issues relating to the English curriculum have been specifically and selectively taken up in press coverage – what is foregrounded, what is appealed to, what is ridiculed; and Apple (2000) discusses in more general terms the politics of the common sense found in contemporary press treatments. Different newspapers are known for different political flavours, though Maclure's analysis shows that there is more commonality in certain cultural responses to some aspects of education than that common sense about the diversity of the press implies.

Simply as a starting point and working at a pragmatic and empirical level, the concepts journalists are likely to be consciously working with (and that are conveyed in textbooks in journalism courses such as Granato (1991) and Oakham (1997)) include 'newsworthiness', timeliness; 'good colour' (lends itself to interesting illustration); ability to spark debates; shock or surprising findings; something likely to have impact on the readership or broad community. In terms of making judgements (about the range of research, or different types of research) within the research field or research community, journalists are likely to be seeking advice from researchers or bureaucrats they already know rather than judging this directly: phoning contacts, triangulating sources to find which researchers are mentioned most often, and so on. So the network of particular contacts which the journalist builds up is important in terms of which research is emphasized, and which researchers are quoted or given a profile as experts (but that profile in turn can indirectly feed back into arenas discussed previously).

Within the context of their own workplace and their own career agendas, journalists will be competing for column inches. They will be looking for stories that have strong or evident appeal, rather than those that are of less widespread interest and that an editor might cut. This cause is particularly advanced if they can develop a story where there will be a debate, with strong cases on both sides, and continuing interest and letters from readers. Particular journalists, especially those with a regular column, will be attempting to build their own particular profile of the types of stories and approach to stories they are known for, and this will have some bearing on which researchers and types of research are considered important. Some journalists will actively seek out a way to develop a new discussion in relation to education; others will rely on press releases and pre-packaged digests or contacts that are immediately to hand; some will build a following for a particular approach to education (for example, 'back to the basics') and will look to research that feeds that line, including research that takes a contrary line that can be attacked for its jargon or other weaknesses.

In terms of relationships with researchers, journalists will be involved in similar types of agendas as the judges discussed in relation to grant committees – looking for signs of who is considered important and being influenced by those they happen to have been in contact with – but the journalist's network will be built in a different and less regular fashion than the academic community networks, and will be open to proactive moves on the part of the researcher. The personal contact plays a much more important part in this network. Sometimes this relationship is initiated by researchers (and increasingly by their universities or organization with their public relations offices, and their neatly packaged, conveniently indexed databases of experts prepared to be contacted), or is promoted by how researchers respond when first contacted by a journalist. Sometimes it is sought by the journalist, particularly with researchers who are associated with high-profile investigations, especially important government enquiries; or who repeatedly appear when the journalists trawl the internet in relation to topics they are pursuing.

Explicit and implicit criteria

> Right now quality of teaching has become a new focus. Previously it was leadership and structural reform . . . If you're in someone's contact book,

you've got it made... To me, it would be along the lines of 'this is going to be interesting to my readers ...' anything that is catchy as far as teachers or parents are concerned. The parochial dailies (suburban and provincial papers) will pick up research if you write it nicely in about 250 words, especially with a picture. If it has a local connection you are definitely in.

(comments made by metropolitan
education journalist, from interview)

The press treatment of the standard English question was in one sense, therefore, part of a specific policy struggle ... Yet standard English also *transcends* the specificity of particular times and policy trends. Its hold upon people's imaginations – as a sacred vessel of national identity, an engine of economic expansion, or a kind of societal super-glue – goes back a long way [...] The demand for 'proper' English also connects [...] with deeper psychic anxieties about the threat of 'Others'.

(Maclure 2003: 23)

Criteria relating to significance: what are they looking for?

In Chapter 1, I noted that when most people produce examples of good research, they tend to talk about three types of criteria: that it was technically good, that it made a contribution to knowledge, that it was doing something that mattered. For the press, the third of these criteria overwhelms and almost obliterates the other two. And it has its own distinctive ways of deciding 'what matters'.

How do journalistic judgements differ from the decision making about significance made by grant committees and academic journal editors, or the decisions about what matters made by practitioners or policy makers and institutions involved in commissioning research? In the former case (discussed in Chapters 4 and 5), there is a major emphasis on what the research is adding to existing academic research and theory in its area, with a sub-emphasis on how this research will affect the broad field of practice to which it relates. In the latter cases, there is a major emphasis on how the shape and outcomes of research will link to or affect practices or situations of concern to the institution or the practitioner. In the case of the press and media, the central criteria are newsworthiness and interest to the readers or audience. There is some crossover of criteria and judgements across these different contexts: issues such as the status of the researcher within in their community; and whether a study is doing something that will have wide-ranging impact across the country. But the starting points are distinct. In the case of the press, some issues that filter the decision making will be:

Timeliness
This can be as elusive as global zeitgeist or as specific as a new political
initiative or election debate. It can refer to substantive topics and the
sense in which they are (or are not) felt as issues by a non-researcher
community at a particular time. And it can refer to the internal dynamics
of the press discussion itself – the extent to which a certain slant on an
issue has already been canvassed; and the search for a fresh way to take
this up.

These issues are not self-contained – it is at least arguable that the shift
towards boys and men, rather than girls and women, as topics that matter
in the press bears signs of all three (Yates 1997a). Maralyn Parker's[26]
comment about the shift she is observing (and contributing to) in Australia, in terms of a move from an interest in leadership and structural
reform to one interested in quality of teaching, is another. Writing in the
UK, Maggie Maclure notes that despite the deep psychic and cultural
veins that the issue of standard English taps, it is not always a 'hot' topic
for the press: it was in the 1980s and 1990s in the wake of some specific
reforms of the national curriculum; whereas at the turn of the century,
the new 'National Literacy Strategy' and the types of debates discussed
earlier have become stronger subjects of press attention (Maclure 2003:
44). Researchers and research projects, funding decisions, and bureaucratic focus all play some part in deciding what interest is timely, and it is
often hard to distinguish what is leading and following the changing
developments. What, for example, led to the shifts of accounting and
values that led to education faculties around the world suddenly dis-
covering huge debts in the 1990s, and, conversely, to the more recent
emergence of education as an issue that governments want to say is
important, and to contribute funding towards? My purpose in this book is
not to theorize about the sources of particular shifts, but to draw attention
to the fact that what journalists see as timely and newsworthy does
change. Researchers themselves might well be continuing to do good
research in a particular area across several decades, but may experience
quite different press receptiveness towards it at different points. They
need to have some sense of how their particular research needs to be
presented or named to connect with that particular sense of timeliness.

Another more direct link between research and timeliness occurs with
the release of new policies, or with the emergence of a particular community or teachers' union issue. For example, changes to the senior
curriculum, or to school funding formulae or the release of a new government report on some aspect of education commonly lead to a search
by journalists for researchers who can provide different perspectives on
the issue.

Controversy or surprise

> The most important news value may well be **conflict**.
>
> (Granato 1991: 31)

Research that contributes to a debating point, or that challenges widely held assumptions is 'good'. In terms of controversy, researchers who take strong positions on new technologies (that they will make teachers and schools obsolete or unrecognizable; or that they should be banned from schools) will be seized on with delight. Research that has a more differentiated account of gains and losses will be harder to present. In terms of surprise, research that can sell its findings around headings that conflict with what might be expected are popular: 'Big study shows no SES effect on school outcomes' or 'School bullying policies don't work'. Others promise to reveal something that has not previously been made public: 'No job, no uni for one in 10'; 'VCE Secrets Revealed'. However, some columnists in 'quality' papers develop a profile for specifically providing some perspective that is different from the binary presentations that generally find favour, and may find a differentiated and more complex account of gains and losses from a particular development to be the kind of 'news' they are interested in.

Linked to impact and consequence

> An event that affects a large number of people ... is obviously news-worthy. ... News coverage will vary according to the level of impact in the locality.
>
> (Granato 1991: 31–2)

For education, studies that have been commissioned by important bodies and foreshadow likely changes to the structure or conditions of institutions are important. It is likely, for example, that the advertised research tender to conduct focus groups of student attitudes to career choice discussed in Chapter 6 will be reported, since it is linked to a parliamentary inquiry and to foreshadowed policy changes in the area of VET in schools.

Bigness or prominence

Any major international study that ranks the national education establishment in some way is guaranteed attention, particularly if it relates to mathematics, science or literacy. If a study has received very large amounts of support, or involved very large numbers of people, that in itself is likely to make it of some interest – though the coverage will be proportional to the extent to which it meets other criteria.

Colour

Research that generates a nice story about a particular person or school or group, preferably with photographs, will be attractive to newspapers, and current affairs media. For local and provincial papers, anything with a local connection will be popular. For papers with a specialist readership, such as *Sydney's Child*, relevance to parents and child-care workers and readability will be important. Where education supplements become reliant on a particular form of advertising (for example, from private schools, coaching colleges, or for higher education employment), this is highly likely to shape the editorial content regarding the selection of stories, and what research is considered important.

My experience with my longitudinal 12 to 18 Project helps to illustrate some of the dynamics. This was a large and complex study, continuing over 7 or 8 years, but it was qualitative, rather than survey-based. The first press story on the project – in its first year, well before it had 'found' anything – appeared in the regional newspaper, where part of the study was located. The story highlighted the ideas that: (1) important university researchers were doing research in this town; (2) a local school was involved; and (3) this was accompanied by a photograph showing researchers and students being interviewed together with our video camera set up. Later stories on the project included two reports in suburban newspapers where the university where I was based was located (picking up a story first published in that university's own monthly public relations bulletin, which it circulated freely to the press for just this purpose) – so the local connection in this case was simply the university which was the source of the project. Other press interest included radio interviews by youth radio stations: here the connection was that this was a study about the target age-group of the station. Another was a story in a national newspaper, generated by an initial contact where the researcher had been following some new policy debates about gender and education, heard about the project in passing as I provided some background information on the policy issue, and decided to do a later story specifically on the project.

Another way of illustrating the dynamics of press treatment can be found in Maclure's and Gill's analyses of how the issue of the English curriculum and related research is represented. In the UK, Maclure (2003) suggests that newspapers reflect a pervasive scepticism towards both educationists and academic writing. The criterion of what is good research is that which most resembles conservative 'non-expert' opinion. Researchers are particularly cited if they not only speak with such a voice, but can be quoted criticizing avante-garde research, and can be associated with elite institutions, and descriptors drawn from the common sense about science (rigorous, painstaking) (Maclure 2003). Gill's (1994) analysis of a similar set of proposed changes to the senior English curriculum in Australia argued that the research that was actually commissioned to evaluate the changes was dismissed as a 'whitewash' because it was broadly favourable to the 'progressive' reforms (in this sense, supporting Maclure's argument). Gill showed how the headlines of the many articles on this education research clearly reflect the media's interest in portraying controversy and extreme versions rather than the more moderate and differentiated results of that report. Headlines included

> Liberals Slam VCE Report 'Whitewash'
> VCE: 'Socialist'
> VCE: Social Goals v. Education
> The VCE is Making Guinea Pigs of Students
> Academic Attacks New 'VCE Eduspeak'
> University shuns the VCE Brand of English
> VCE Subjects Raise Visions of Monty Python 'Mickey Mouse Marxism' Fears

(Gill 1994: 99)

Criteria relating to visibility and access: how does research become known to journalists?

In the case of theses and research grant applications, to be eligible for consideration, research must follow instructions and be submitted on time. In the case of the press and media, given that there is no formal process of submission, the research must in some way enter the journalist's field of vision. Here are some of the ways this occurs:

- The researcher is an important person (heading an important institution or body or inquiry, for example) and doing important work (as seen by the source of funding or commissioning, for example). They have previously come to the notice of the press, or are readily thrown up by search engines on the web (usually only works if linked to 3).
- The researcher cultivates the journalist by approaching them at functions or in their workplace (usually only works if there is sufficient link to some form of the 'what matters' criteria discussed above).
- The researcher is in the journalist's contact book because they have responded well to a request for information in relation to a previous story.
- The research/er is known and mentioned by the small circle of academics that the journalist uses as key informants.
- Publicity material is sent by publishers, universities and research organizations to the newspaper or radio or television station (but personal contact can be more effective).
- Public relations departments of universities and other research organ-

izations produce easily accessed lists of researchers cross-linked by areas of expertise.

In other words, networks are of central importance in terms of what is visible; and the most academic forums in which good research is judged (formal academic publications, competitive grant arenas) are relatively unimportant as direct sources for uncovering good or important research here (although universities and national research bodies now have their own publicity machines to attempt to remedy this). Where research is interacting strongly with education policy making or is being widely discussed in a global research arena, it is also likely to be noted by the press; but for other types of research, what is visible is a more idiosyncratic and pull–push process, through the overtures journalists make to find people and areas of expertise; and through the overtures and artefacts researchers and their institutional bases make to attract the attention of journalists.

> It is essential to be available when called. Usually I'm working to a deadline that day – don't phone me back in the evening with your glass of wine in your hand.
>
> (working journalist, from interview)

The researchers that get quoted are not only visible to the journalist, but available and amenable. They are prepared to spend time explaining something even where they are not themselves going to get direct kudos. They are prepared to have a strong position on the issue at hand. Not only does this again require choices by the researcher as to how they allocate their time between the different contexts I discuss, but what the journalists are looking for may well run counter to the criteria that a PhD examiner would look for in judging quality: the quality to be self-critical, to understand the limitations of particular lines of work. My own national research body, AARE (Australian Association for Research in Education), has a Code of Ethics which includes the following planks:

> [on research methods] Researchers should recognise the uncertainty of all claims to knowledge, and in particular should recognise that justifications for research methodologies depend upon epistemological views which are disputed and uncertain. Where research results are presented in a context where this is not well understood, researchers should beware of presenting them as though they are infallible. They should declare the existence of alternative professional opinions to their own ...

> [on reports] Reports of research should draw attention to the limitations of the results, both in reliability and in applicability. Researchers should avoid and if necessary act to correct misuse of research and misunderstanding of its scope and limitations. They should not exaggerate the significance of their results, nor misrepresent the practical or policy

implications. This is particularly important where the results are for widespread public consumption.[27]

Any researcher who takes this literally is unlikely to be approached more than once by a journalist. Being ethical in this particular way is likely to mean not being good research 'talent' when it comes to the press and media.

I have been emphasizing the networks through which researchers and their work can become a subject for journalists. But researchers can also attempt to be more direct and proactive in publicizing their work via the press. They can directly submit short articles for publication in the 'op ed' sections of newspapers, or they can circulate accounts of their work already digested into a journalistic form, one that demands little further writing work from journalists.

Criteria relating to technical features of the research design and research writing

> *LY:* Do you take account of any features of research design or methodology?
> *Journalist:* Big is good.

In many cases, the nature of the research project design is of little interest: what the journalist is interested in is what were its findings and what are the implications of these. Being a known researcher or 'name', having a strong position, and having some clear things to say are all more important than the design and activities that produced those things that are now said. Much of the time, the journalist is not even reading a summary of the study itself; they are seeking in written or verbal form a more directed story of the project that focuses on outcomes/message/implications. They do not usually set out to make technical judgements about different types of research. Nevertheless, there are ways in which issues of design and methodology affect what gets taken up as important in this particular arena.

Controversies where the 'sides' are criticizing each other on methodological grounds

Where there are major debates around an issue that is very visible to ordinary readers – for example, the issue of producing league tables of school rankings; the class-size debate; debates around who should get 'disadvantaged' funding; the processes of scaling of results in the final school certificate to produce a common tertiary entrance score across different subject areas – then accessing the controversy by talking to experts on different sides is likely to mean that the journalist has to at least touch on issues of design and methodology. In these cases, the discussion of technical matters more likely takes the form of an explanation of different paradigms or design issues, different 'sides' of a debate, than assessments that rank research of better and poorer quality. The politics of the implications of taking one or other approach is likely to be given considerable attention.

Research design mediates judgements of what is 'important' or newsworthy
The media (at least in my part of the world) are rarely interested in research as a topic in its own right. They are interested in it in so far as it affects more visible things: potential new treatments, judgements about where we are falling down in terms of school outcomes and potential political debates that may flow from that; parents' interest in how to bring up their sons and daughters. For newspapers, the scale of a study (the international studies by IEA and UNESCO; the ongoing data-collection by national bureaux of statistics) is one indicator of whether a study might have some impact on politicians or policy. Alternatively, especially for television, studies that are local and that have an action or evaluative component are important: stories of schools that have trialled single-sex classes; or lunchtime fitness programmes; studies about bullying or self-esteem that can use photographs and stories about individuals or can answer talk-back radio listener queries about individuals.

Methodology, transparency, common sense
In relation to research methodology, the press tends to work with 'common-sense' assumptions about research and reliable knowledge; to follow well behind changes in this field in the academic community or even the user community. Two assumptions about what methodologically good research looks like are widespread:

1 it is 'big' (or, that getting answers from a lot of the target population is better than a small study); or
2 it involves experiment or controlled comparison.

The assumptions of interpretive researchers, that this form of research is producing knowledge that is different from being simply a poor man's version of a survey, and that it is not simply about being 'descriptive', are generally not well understood. Even with small number studies, reporters want to focus on 'how many' and want findings that take the general form 'young people today are x' or 'schools today are y'. (They often want to present the findings to readers by telling individual stories, but that is not the same as their understanding of what the researcher themselves should have done.) They do not readily accept that knowledge of education processes might be contextual, far less ideas of discursive construction. They commonly work with a perspective that casts research (and researchers) as *either* objective *or* biased; not one that sees all research questions and designs as shaped by particular interests and perspectives. The Tooley debate and the moves to evidence-based studies discussed in Chapter 1 work well within this widespread common sense of what research looks like. The media understand and present individual stories as 'colour' that illustrates something general, something in which research base was a survey or experiment, not as something that itself can generate knowledge.

In recent years there has been some minor change in this, led by the work of advertising agencies and polling companies for political parties, which have both turned more and more to focus groups to see some of the way opinions hang together that they are not able to access by survey. But the questions about differential methodological quality within such approaches have not yet entered the common sense in the ways that asking-a-lot-of-people-some-questions-and-reporting-their-answers and giving-a-treatment-to-one-group-and-not-to-a-similar-group have done.

These issues apply even more strongly to forms of research or theory that are most avante-garde, that are mounting new concepts or ways of seeing, using new technical language, challenging common sense.

The point I am trying to draw attention to here is similar to that discussed earlier in relation to short summaries on grant applications that will be read by an inter-disciplinary committee. In terms of research design, researchers not working with large surveys or with experimental methods or with common-sense concepts will have to do more work to provide a bridge to common-sense logics about the value of their approach. In the case of grant committees, they must justify in some way the value of their design. In the case of the press, this is not necessarily required provided they have strong, clear and not over-complicated outcomes and implications to report.

The flip-side of the criteria I have been discussing here is that good research in this sphere is not necessarily ground-breaking research, or the newest contribution to a research agenda. Because research is reported in contexts that are topic driven, and found through networks and contacts, a researcher who is reported on a particular topic may, in the context of the peer researcher environment, be marginal rather than central to the research being done in that topic (but be an all-round 'key informant'), or may take up research perspectives that the field itself has moved on from. Just as the media have an annual cycle of education events whose stories are essentially repeated each year (children going to school for the first time; annual final school examinations begin; examination results are released), so research issues can be revived every few years as if they had never been discussed before – class size, co-education versus single-sex, selective versus comprehensive schools are all examples of this, and often draw on particular research studies quite idiosyncratically – quite differently, that is, from the weight studies would be given relative to each other in a formal literature review.

In other words, 'timely and newsworthy' does not necessarily mean that the research itself must be new or making a new contribution. The latter is a stronger requirement for academic contexts than for non-academic ones. Indeed, in the case of the press, repeating a particular research message over and over is likely to attract more attention to the research than is having a lot of different things to report.

What does good research look like for the press and media?

1 *It is presented very succinctly, has some strong key points, and is clearly linked to implications.*

   In a thesis, a researcher may have 100,000 words to present their work; in an academic article, they may have 6000 words; a journalist (or op ed piece for a newspaper) may well have less than 200 words. There needs to be something to make a reader want to read this column among all the others – some headline point or some attention-drawing photograph. A key point that is controversial or linked to an important change or practice will be helpful.

2 *It uses 'everyday' terms rather than academic jargon, and highlights the key point for the reader/listener.*

   Politicians have now learnt the lesson of the 'magic message'. They decide on the key point they wish to make and repeat it over and over so that it is captured in the news sound bite, is the main point remembered from a longer interview, and becomes the focus of the news story. Researchers who follow a similar strategy have similar media impact.

3 *It highlights controversy – or it targets particular journalists and presents itself as a balanced and expert rejoinder to controversy.*

   Generally the press and the media work in binaries and emphasize conflict. They prefer different researchers to represent each side of the binary, rather than to report a single researcher who sees both sides. They look for extreme representatives of positions in the field rather than moderate ones, unless the middle ones are the ones driving policy. Some writers however, particularly columnists in 'quality' outlets, look for an expert rejoinder to cut through the pack mentality represented in 'lesser' accounts.

4 *It makes strong claims, not qualified ones.*

5 *It lends itself to photograph opportunities, or, in the case of the electronic media, the researcher is good 'talent'.*

   In the case of television, both the appearance of the researcher, and their ability to talk in clear media 'bites' will be important. Being certain rather than hesitant is desirable.

6 *It comes from an 'important' source; or it comes with a personal introduction.* Research commissioned by governments or UNESCO; or research commissioned by bodies such as a teachers' union or principals' association which might link that research to further action, especially in the form of a press release or press conference that presents the research to meet points 1–5 above, will usually get some attention. Universities and research organizations and individual researchers are less guaranteed of such attention, and their press releases will be noted only where their topics are particularly sensational or timely or colourful. But researchers and public relations staff who develop personal relationships with the journalist will be able to provide verbal explanations of why the research matters.

Common problems or failings

Research can fail in terms of media attention on three main grounds: its topic, its form, and the characteristics of and choices made by the researcher.

Topic

The research fails to demonstrate adequately why it matters or why it is interesting to non-researchers. Failing to have such a link is not an inherent quality of the topic, but is a matter of how it is represented in *this* context. At different times, and for different audiences, different representations of what the research was about and why it matters are required.

Form

The research is academic, wordy, middle of the road, too qualified, too complex, too arcane, precious. An academic research project may need to have many of these qualities in order to attract funding or academic publication, but for media purposes, it needs a re-presentation. It is not enough to present a summary or abstract of the project; the new story needs to highlight its outcomes and implications outside the research world.

The researcher

Researchers who are not available to journalists, or who insist on attempting to tightly control how their work is represented in the press, are likely to receive less attention from the press. Researchers who are long-winded, introverted, boring will be avoided. Researchers who are hesitant and given to self-doubt (and gender and class patterns that associate with this) will be unattractive as talent.

So:
What does good research look like for the press and media?

It is research that is timely because it connects to an event, policy, social change, or to an issue that is being debated in the community. Or it is research that helps feed an agenda being promoted by the journalist or their paper or programme. It offers colourful, sensational or surprising claims that will interest non-researcher viewers or readers. It has clear, simple and strong messages, and clear links to implications. It reflects a positivist view of research methodology, and a binary view of research topics. It is research done by an important person or body; or by a researcher or institution who proactively cultivates media interest. 'Big' studies, local studies and human interest studies are favoured over research that is technically-oriented, or moves too far and too rapidly from past understandings. Examples selected as good research need not be the most recent research on a topic or judged most important by the research community.

Situating research practices

Assessing how particular research genres and contexts work is not the same task as deciding what research to do and how to go about it. Understanding how political decisions and policy interplays shape the arena does not make redundant the need for individual researchers or university departments or research organizations to work through what particular agendas they will pursue, what theories and purposes they will take up, and what will be adequate or appropriate methodology for a particular project or type of concern. The earlier chapters of this book attempt to draw attention to some of the likely effects and effectivity of pursuing research in particular ways in particular times and contexts. But researchers themselves contribute to the construction of who they are, and to the construction of 'what is good research?' by what they do, and by the way they take up the positionings available to them. In this final chapter, more final thoughts than a conclusion, I draw attention to some ways of using, locating, and thinking about what is missing in the type of discussion I have embarked on in the previous chapters.

Positioning research agendas and research careers

> I am not a conventional academic, in a traditional sense. But I do suggest that I am a contemporary academic, that is, an academic whose writing is exemplary of the kind of work that is emerging within the current conditions of the academy.
>
> (Solomon 2000: 2)

Researchers in the field of education are diverse in their career paths. Some take a conventional disciplinary apprenticeship route. Indeed, they may continue to work in the discipline and department in which they began their apprenticeship (economics, for example, or psychology) and to do research that impacts powerfully on education by remaining relatively pure in their concern with the narrowly bounded problems, focused criteria, methodologies and theories of that discipline, rather than entering some of the messier interplay of issues and agendas to be found in education faculties and circles. Other people may not identify with a traditional discipline at all. They may work for substantial periods in other professional roles in education before they formally identify as researchers or embark on certification as researchers via doctoral education. But increasingly the conditions of work of researchers in education are not those of the archetypal scientist devoting themselves to the pursuit of a particular problem (and indeed nor are the conditions of real-life scientists). Universities, research organizations, governments require that a range of different forms of research work be done by the same individual (Gibbons *et al.* 1994; Scheeres and Solomon 2000a).

In the thesis from which I quoted above, itself a new form of doctorate by publication and indicative of some of the new modes, Nicky Solomon discusses the way in which she came to take on different types of work in the course of her own career in education. Solomon examines the different forms of research and writing she has engaged with in her work, and the manner in which the researcher too is being written as a subject in the course of doing such work. It is not just that sometimes people in academic or other education jobs are also expected to do commissioned evaluations of programmes, or to produce instructional materials; that they are required to seek and carry out consultancy contracts and produce the 'hybrid' texts related to these, and that sometimes they are required to do the type of research and writing that certifies academic respectability ('disciplined' texts). It is that these different enterprises are not neatly self-contained. Work in one permeates the other, or is even the condition for producing the other, though what is required in each does not take the same form. 'Each group of my publications (instructional texts, hybrid texts, disciplined texts) is a realisation of the relationship between programs of government, institutional locations and the position (and positioning) of the writer' (Solomon 2000: 16; see also Scheeres and Solomon 2000a, 2000b).

One rationale for writing this book is that education researchers *are* hybrid workers. Research training requires some attention to the different arenas I have discussed in different chapters, some sensitivity to differentiation of genres and contexts. But discussions about good research also require some attention to the movements and relationships *between* these genres and contexts. In the argument above, Solomon discusses these relationships in terms of governmentality and 'technologies of the self'. One way of reflecting further on the various scenarios I have discussed in the various chapters is to look at how they do work to 'inscribe' the subject, the researcher – how they draw them, as Solomon argues, to align their own wishes, their own conduct, with certain socio-political objectives of contemporary times.

Another way the discussion and tables in these different chapters might be used is to quite straightforward and strategic ends. Often doctoral students who are mature and experienced professionals read the methodology textbooks, but still, in some way, find it hard to write in the academic mode. Often too new researchers are puzzled and upset by the unexpected rejections, whether from journals, or teacher-collaborators, or publishers. Understanding that the very qualities that are prized highly in one arena (self-critique in the doctoral thesis, for example) are counter-productive in terms of success in another arena (winning a tender, for example) is helpful for researchers who work in universities, given that those institutions want them not only to exhibit success in the first arena, but in the second as well. Pursuing some of the points of tension between contexts might also be helpful in building a better discussion or ability to negotiate with each context. For example, the concerns of schools and practitioners for certain kinds of research do not necessarily fit smoothly with technical requirements about methodology favoured by major grant schemes. Researchers themselves can work with these differences and reconstruct their work for each task, or they can choose to focus their efforts self-consciously on one type of work rather than another, or they can lobby for greater recognition in schools of the conditions of academic work, and in grant schemes for better recognition of the conditions of education researchers, particularly the need to work with professional and not just academic audiences, and to acknowledge that expanding expectations in this way is not a time-free obligation for the researcher.

The 'rules of the game' type of discussion could then be read from a 'how to succeed in business' perspective of the careerist individual, and I do not disown this as one purpose of this book. I hope that new players do find it useful. But the understanding of contexts and rules of the game is equally important to researchers attempting to pursue broader purposes, to work for better forms of education, fairer social arrangements, through the work they do. Reformist and politically engaged researchers like any other researchers have to actively construct their work relative to the different arenas and times and national, political and historical backgrounds I have discussed here.

As an illustration, take two important projects concerned with inequalities, schools and curriculum in Australia, the project associated with *Making the Difference* (Connell *et al.* 1982[28]), and the project associated with 'new basics', 'rich tasks', 'productive pedagogies' and the Queensland Longitudinal School Reform Study (QLSRS).[29] These two projects have taken different approaches to doing good research and to bringing about change, but both have been important (have made some impact) because, at least in part, they *have* attended to the issues of different constituencies for education research discussed in Part 2.

In the early 1980s, *Making the Difference*, a study of schools, families and inequalities, became one of the best-known and most widely discussed works about education in Australia. The research team constructed the study in relation to then current academic sociological work in the area and they published forms of the work in international academic journals, but they also spoke to many community and school meetings; published in teachers' journals; worked on and wrote reports for government departments. Two decades later, the QLSRS is also making a broad impact (including its associated work on 'new basics', 'productive pedagogies', 'rich tasks', and its central contribution to its state government's current corporate school reform strategy). This project too has a team of researchers who are careful to engage many different arenas of the education field: the academic journals and conferences, the bureau-cracies, the press, the teachers and administrators of schools.

But methodologically and in terms of 'research as writing' the two projects take quite different approaches to their concerns with inequality, disadvantage, empowerment, and better learning. *Making the Difference* used qualitative methodologies, and was unambiguously political in its approach to research ('In the most basic sense, the process of education and the process of liberation are the same . . . Teachers too have to decide whose side they are on' (Connell *et al.* 1982: 208)). The researchers sought to persuade teachers, parents and administrators by using por-traits and narratives, letting them *see* how lives and experiences were different in the relations between working-class families and their schools and ruling-class families and their schools. The study was care-fully structured in terms of the design and selection of student and parent interviewees that underpinned the comparison, and it was led by researchers with well-established track records (as well as newer ones). But the heart of its methodology was a tool of imaginative recognition.

By contrast, the QLSRS works with a different rhetoric, that of 'new times', that is not avowedly political in the everyday sense of taking sides. It too has a team which includes some very well-known and well-respected researchers as well as newer researchers, but its main tools are structured observation studies, statistical data and discursive arguments about the literacy needs of the contemporary world. The researchers here take on some comparable contexts for research as the earlier inequality study (schools, parents, community, government departments, the press, book publication). However, much more than the earlier study, these researchers seek to produce change by working within the system, with key researchers moving between academic and corporate, policy-making roles; as well as working directly with schools.

These two major projects are examples of education research that attend to different genres and contexts and constituencies. Each consists not simply of a single investigation and report, but of a programme of work designed to operate in more than one register. The differences in approach taken by the two projects two decades apart is also instructive of a sensitivity to the socio-political context and changing times that I discussed earlier. The differences between the two projects reflect some movements of research and theory over those two decades (from reproduction theory to effectiveness studies), and some changing politics of different eras – for example, that appeal to confrontational opposed interests between classes was more acceptable in the 1970s and 1980s than in the 'third way' era of the turn of the century (Yates 2002).

In earlier chapters I mention other examples of researchers who have worked across different arenas and written about the tensions and problems of doing good work as they do so: Johnson (2002a and b, 2003) in Chapter 7, identifying with teachers and talking about the problems of working as a researcher inside and outside employment in schools; Tsolidis (2001) in Chapter 2, negotiating issues of the engaged researcher ('being feminist and being different'), working not only across the different support environments for research in different policy eras, but also constructing research agendas in relation to an expanding and developing set of theoretical concerns; and Scheeres and Solomon (2000a, b) in Chapter 6, working in commissioned projects on workplace training and discussing how collaborative research agendas speak back to researchers across their different settings. Many other examples of such discussions could be found.

What I am trying to illustrate here is the salience for research design of the contextual issues I have discussed in this book, and also that those issues themselves neither determine nor foreclose the creative acts and normative decision making that researchers necessarily engage in. A consideration of these projects or others (the 'effective schools' movement, or the 'self-governing school', or projects concerned with showing how race, ethnicity, gender works in schools) adds something to the discussion of good research set out in earlier chapters, and also to discussion of technical methodology issues. It is why I prefer in teaching research courses to begin with substantive education issues and accounts of attempts to research these, rather than with texts whose main starting point is the discussion of methodology (Yates 1997b). Earlier chapters in this book often focus on the characteristics of a single, bounded project or application or piece of writing. But what constitutes the 'piece' of research, or the 'research project' is not unambiguous, either temporally or in the arenas or genres it encompasses.

What is good education research?

This book has been more about 'What is "good" education research?' (how is good research *designated*?) than about my own answer to the question 'What is good education research?', and to say that is not simply playing with words or playing with punctuation marks. It is a reminder that the question needs to be pursued in more than one way. The focus of this book, how 'good' education research gets enacted, judged, defined, and constructed in particular contexts, is important in any discussion of education research methodology, and in any discussion about education research quality. We need to discuss the conditions we work in, and to recognize that judgements are not free-floating abstract things, but practices performed in particular contexts, with particular histories and relationships, and using particular materials, frequently specifically textual materials. One of the major thrusts of this book has been to draw attention to the multiplicity of these judgement contexts for education researchers, and to the difficult and often unclear ways they are interwoven across contexts. Today, more than ever, lack of self-consciousness and lack of reflexivity about the genres they must work in is likely to work to the disadvantage of the neophyte researcher. Discussion about the form of different arenas, policies, institutions and institutionalized judgements is important in education research training and also in academic and professional bodies of researchers, in funding contexts, and in the broader community politics of the education field.

In terms of these politics, one theme that runs through many chapters of this book is the intricate dance between popular judgement and expert assessment as the criteria by which 'what is good education research' is designated. Even in an Academy of Sciences attempt to explain what scientific research is, in the case of education research, these experts introduce the issue of popular reputation to mitigate judgements that their normal bottom-line belief in 'peer review' might otherwise have supported. Here and in many of the debates about what type of research is good research, and in debates about the quality of education research as a whole, there is suspicion of anything that does not sit easily with common sense, 'experience', or existing widely-used language concepts. At the same time, such debates are permeated with hopes that education research might be sharpened up or transformed so that it takes us well beyond what we know and have been doing in the past. Utopian yearnings that if only the right research was done, education as we know it would be transformed, and everyone would learn perfectly, have the best outcomes, get the best jobs, are not the least of the conditions that make life difficult for people who work as researchers in education.

Much of the second part of this book has been concerned with quite banal particulars. It is not a highly theoretical argument, it does not pursue the discussion of power in any systematic way or in relation to particular theories. But overall, in addition to wanting these chapters to be helpful, to offer some starting points and guidance, I do think I am advancing an argument about education research, even if it is not all that I would want to say about that subject. The chapters set out some beginnings for looking quite specifically at who is judging research in particular areas, how they came to be there, what might be influencing them, what signs are they going on when they make their judgements. My argument is that the banalities and the messiness evident when we try to do this are not some peripherals to the more substantial questions about good research, they are inseparable from what education research means and looks like as a set of practices.

In this book I have not discussed at any length technical issues of methodology, either within or across paradigms. What makes research of a particular type superior to other research of the same type, and what makes research inadequate in terms of its own approach? The fact that I have not discussed this does not mean that I do not think these things matter. Of the contexts I discuss here, more of my own work is in the academic world, and I spend quite a lot of time dwelling on, teaching about, writing about, the minutiae of methodology, and I do think these matter. But that was not my subject here. My aim was to discuss the conditions we work in.

My own answer to the question 'what is good education research?' would be, at least as a starting point, the same one I hear from many different people to whom I have asked the question. I too think that good research needs to be technically good (to have methodological integrity or logic), to be making a contribution to knowledge (to be something distinct from public relations or propaganda), and to be doing something that matters (to be framing questions that contribute to better and fairer education experiences, outcomes, social arrangements rather than punitive, deficit-oriented, anachronistic ones). But the substantive enactment of these concerns is necessarily situated, and learning to read the fields in which education research *is* situated is, I would suggest, a useful thing to do.

Notes

1 For anyone worried about this hyperbole, can I make clear that I do not think finding a cure for cancer is easy; I do not think education researchers are superior to medical or scientific researchers; and I have immense respect for the research and achievements of researchers who work in those other fields. My point is that although in the world as we know it, I can conceive of researchers finding a cure for cancer, I cannot conceive of education research that achieves a similar level of general acclaim that education problems are now solved. The reasons why and how this is the case are the subject of this and the following chapter.

2 Dr Geoff Masters, *ACER Newsletter* No 94, 1999, p. 1

3 The descriptions here are taken from the information and publicity materials produced by the organizations mentioned, both on websites and in hard copy, and distributed freely at conferences such as the American Education Research Association conference. See http://www.ed.gov/offices/IES and http://www.wwcinfo@w-w-c.org (What Works Clearinghouse).

4 See, for example, the websites at http://eppi.ioe.ac.uk and http://www.dfes/gov.uk/research.

5 There is of course a large literature about this topic (such as Latour and Woolgar 1979; Kuhn 1996); but I have restricted my discussion to an examination of current debates as they are evident in education.

6 I am indebted to the journalist Maralyn Parker for drawing this to my attention.

7 In BERA panel presentation at the AARE annual conference in Brisbane, December 2002.

8 My approach began by taking particular substantive issues of education research inquiry, and considering the different ways in which these are taken up, both over time and between paradigms. I also thought it important that students engage with some of the discussions in history and philosophy of science and social science and that they be exposed to viewpoints other than my own. The rationale and outline of this approach is discussed in Yates 1997b.

9 These guidelines are from the University of Melbourne regulations, available at http://www.gradstudies.unimelb.edu.au/pgstudy/phd/handbk/hdbk_g.htm. A comparable set of quite detailed (and similar) criteria, advice and guidelines is set out on the University of London Institute of Education website: http://www.ioe.ac.uk/doctoralschool/info-viva.htm. Most universities now make their doctoral guidelines and criteria available through their websites.

10 From University of London Institute of Education guidelines 'Preparing for the oral examination of your thesis', http://www.ioe.ac.uk/doctoralschool/info-viva.htm.

11 From examiners reports of theses submitted by university departments for the AARE Exemplary Thesis Award, 2001.

12 University of Melbourne guidelines, http://www.gradstudies.unimelb.edu.au/pgstudy/phd/handbk/hdbk_g.htm.

13 From Collard (2000), Figures and Landscapes: male and female principals in Victorian schools, PhD thesis, University of Melbourne, Faculty of Education.

14 From Dillon (2001), The Student as Maker: an examination of the meaning of music to students in a school and the ways in which we give access to meaningful music education, PhD thesis, La Trobe University.

15 These sentences are taken from the PhD of Elody Rathgen (1996), On good authority: towards feminist pedagogies. University of Canterbury, New Zealand. A more extensive published discussion of the writing form and tasks of a 'feminist post-structural thesis' is Rhedding-Jones (1997).

16 When I attended the Univerity of Melbourne in the late 1960s, it did not have a sociology department, preferring to stick to disciplines like the classics, history and English. Since then, boundaries have been breached. English has transmuted into Cultural Studies, an anthropologist was appointed to a prestigious Chair of History, and the sky has not fallen in.

17 University of London, Institute of Education: http://www.ioe.ac.uk/doctoralschool/info-viva.htm

18 http://www.pkp.ubc.ca./ojs, see also Willinsky (2002, 2003).

19 ESRC 'How to Write a Good Application': http://www.esrc.ac.uk/ESRCC...chfunding/grant_application_guidance.asp

20 From interview with a research director of a national education organization.

21 The article by Gaskell that I have drawn on here (Gaskell 1996) is a later discussion of aspects of the project, published in an academic journal (another interesting example is Scheeres and Solomon 2000b). Gaskell's account is a relatively rare example of a detailed published account of the steps and tensions of a major study of this kind, though it is of course a story written by one of the participants who had a particular role in the project, and, no doubt, other stories could also be written. More commonly there is an official report that is the agreed and cleaned-up story of what a project entailed; and many oral insider accounts of just what pressures were brought to bear.

22 From Australian Government (DEST) advertisement in *The Australian*, 24 May 2003.

23 From 'Guidelines for Proposals' NCVER National VET Research and Evaluation Program Information Kit, February 2003.

24 Commissioned and published by the Higher Education Division of the Aus-

tralian Department of Education, Science and Technology. See Australia Research Evaluation Programme. Higher Education Division, 2000.

25 In my own PhD, for example, on *Curriculum Theory and Non-Sexist Education*, I found that in the 1970s there was more new activity, and a greater number of conferences taking place among schools and teachers on this issue, than among formal academic education researchers, though it was being taken up in other areas of academic inquiry.

26 Journalist and education editor of the *Daily Telegraph* in Sydney.

27 On AARE website: http://www.aare.edu.au/ethics, and in print form included in Bibby (1997).

28 There is retrospective discussion of this project from the perspective of 20 years on in *Discourse* 23 (3), 2002 (pp. 319–56), with contributions by Connell, Yates, Thrupp and Arnot.

29 See http://www.education.qld.gov.au/corporate/new basics; and Lingard *et al.* (2001); Lingard, Hayes and Mills (2002); Lingard, Hayes, Mills and Christie (2003); and Yates (2002).

References

Anderson, G. L. (2002) Reflecting on research for doctoral students in education, *Educational Researcher* 31(7):22–5.

Apple, M. (2000) *Educating the 'Right' Way: Markets, Standards, God and Inequality*. New York: Routledge.

Arnot, M. (1982) Male hegemony, social class and women's education, *Journal of Education* 164(1):64–89.

Arnot, M., David, M. and Weiner, G. (1999) *Closing the Gender Gap: Postwar Education and Social Change*. Cambridge: Polity Press.

Australia, Department of Education, Training and Youth Affairs. Higher Education Division Research Evaluation Programme (2000) *The Impact of Educational Research*. Canberra: Commonwealth of Australia.

Ball, S. (1994) *Educational Reform: A Critical and Post-structural Approach*. Buckingham: Open University Press.

Ball, S. J., Bowe, R. and Gerwirte, S. (1996) School choice, social class and distinction: the realisation of social advantage in education, *Journal of Education Policy* 11(1):89–112.

Ball, S. J. and Gewirtz, S. (1997) Is research possible? A rejoinder to Tooley's 'On school choice and social class', *British Journal of Sociology of Education* 18(4):575–86.

Bennett, N. S. (1976) *Teaching Styles and Pupil Progress*. London: Open Books.

Berge, B.-M. with Ve, H. (2000) *Action Research for Gender Equity*. Buckingham: Open University Press.

Berliner, D. C. (2002) Educational Research: the hardest science of all, *Educational Researcher* 31(8):18–20.

Bessant, B. and Holbrook, A. (1995) *Reflections on Educational Research in Australia: A History of the Australian Association for Research in Education*. Coldstream: Australian Association for Research in Education.

Bibby, M. (ed.) (1997) *Ethics in Educational Research*. Coldstream: Australian Association for Research in Education.

Bourdieu, P. (1984) *Distinction: A Social Critique of the Judgement of Taste*. London: Routledge.

Bourdieu, P. (1998) *The State Nobility*. Cambridge: Polity Press.

Brennan, M. (1997) Struggles over the definition and practice of the educational doctorate in Australia, *Australian Educational Researcher* 25(1):71–89.

Brennan, M., Kenway, J., Thomson, P. and Zipin, L. (2002) Uneasy alliances: university, workplace, industry and profession in the education doctorate, *Australian Educational Researcher* 29(3):63–84.

Chappell, C., Rhodes, C., Solomon, N., Tennant, M. and Yates, L. (2003), *Reconstructing the Lifelong Learner: Pedagogy and Identity in Individual, Organizational and Social Change*. London: Routledge Falmer.

Clandinin, D. J. and Connelly, E. M. (2000) *Narrative Inquiry: Experience and Story in Qualitative Research*. San Francisco: Jossey-Bass.

Coats, M. (1996) *Recognising Good Practice in Women's Education and Training*. Leicester: National Institute of Adult Continuing Education.

Cohen, D. K. and Barnes, C. A. (1999) Research and the purposes of education, in E. C. Lagemann and L. S. Shulman (eds), *Issues in Education Research*. San Francisco: Jossey-Bass.

Cohen, L., Manion, L. and Morrison, K. (2000) *Research Methods in Education*. London: Routledge/Falmer.

Collard, J. (2000), Figures and Landscapes: male and female principals in Victorian schools, PhD thesis, University of Melbourne, Faculty of Education.

Collins, C., Kenway, J. and McLeod, J. (2000) *Factors Influencing the Educational Performance of Males and Females in School and their Initial Destinations after Leaving School*. Canberra: Department of Education, Training and Youth Affairs.

Connell, R. W., Ashenden, D. J., Kessler, S. and Dowsett, G. W. (1982) *Making the Difference: Schools, Families and Social Division*. Sydney: Allen & Unwin.

Connell, W. F. (1980) *The Australian Council for Educational Research, 1930–1980*, Hawthorn: Australian Council for Educational Research.

Cunningham, J. W. (2001) The National Reading Panel Report, *Reading Research Quarterly* 36(3):326–35.

Davics, B. (1989) *Frogs and Snails and Feminist Tales: Pre-school Children and Gender*. Sydney: Allen & Unwin.

Dillion, S. (2001), The students as Maker: an examination of the meaning of music to students in a school and the ways in which we give access to meaningful music cducation, PhD thesis, La Trobe University.

Doecke, B. and Seddon, T. (2002) Research Education: whose space for learning? *Australian Educational Researcher* 29(3):85–100.

Dressman, M. (1999) On the use and misuse of research evidence: decoding two states' reading initiatives, *Reading Research Quarterly* 34(3): 258–285.

Edwards, A. (2002) Seeking uncertainty: educational research as an engaged social science. Paper presented to the Australian Association for Research in Education Annual Conference, Brisbane, December.

Erickson, F. and Gutierrez, K. (2002) Culture, rigor, and science in educational research, *Educational Researcher* 31(8):21–4.

Feuer, M. J., Towne, L. and Shavelson, R. J. (2002) Scientific culture and educational research, *Educational Researcher* 31(8):4–14.

Figgis, J., Zubrick, A., Butorac, A. and Alderson, A. (2000) Backtracking practice and policies to research, in Higher Education Division Commonwealth of

Australia (ed), *The Impact of Educational Research*, Canberra: Commonwealth of Australia.

Garrick, J. and Rhodes, C. (eds) (2000) *Research and Knowledge at Work*. London: Routledge.

Gaskell, J. (1996) One big study: the local and the national in the Exemplary Schools Project, *Alberta Journal of Educational Research* 42(2):195–209.

Gaskell, J. and McLeod, D. (forthcoming) Learning from research networks: the Western Research Network on Education and Training 1996–2001, in J. Gaskell and K. Rubenson (eds), *Educational Outcomes for the Canadian Workplace: New Frameworks for Policy and Research*. Toronto: University of Toronto Press.

Gay, L. R. and Airasian, P. (2000) *Educational Research: Competencies for Analysis and Application*. Upper Saddle River, NJ: Merrill.

Gibbons, M., Limoges, C., Nowotny, H., Schwartzman, S., Scott, P. and Trow, M. (1994) *The New Production of Knowledge: The Dynamics of Science and Research in Contemporary Societies*. London: Sage.

Gill, M. (1994) Who framed English? A case study of the media's role in curriculum change, *Melbourne Studies in Education* 1994: 96–113.

Gilligan, C. (1982) *In A Different Voice: Psychological Theory and Women's Development*. Cambridge, Mass: Harvard University Press.

Granato, L. (1991) *Reporting and Writing News*. New York: Prentice Hall.

Gregory, M. (1995) Implications of the introduction of the Doctor of Education degree in British universities: can the Ed D reach parts the PhD cannot?, *Vocational Aspects of Education* 47(2):177–88.

Hamilton, D., Jenkins, D., King, C., MacDonald, B. and Parlett, M. (eds) (1977) *Beyond the Numbers Game*. Basingstoke: Macmillan.

Hannan, B. (1985) *Democratic Curriculum: Essays on Schooling and Society*. Sydney VSTA and Allen & Unwin.

Hargreaves, D. H. (1996) Teaching as a research-based profession: possibilities and prospects (The Teacher Training Agency Annual Lecture). London: Teacher Training Agency.

Hartley, J. (1982) *Understanding News*. London: Methuen.

Henriques, J., Hollway, W., Urwin, C., Venn, C. and Walkerdine, V. (1984) *Changing the Subject: Psychology, Social Regulation and Subjectivity*. London: Methuen.

Hill, G. (2002) Reflecting on professional practice with a cracked mirror: Productive pedagogy experiences. Paper presented to Australian Association for Research in Education Annual Conference, Brisbane, December.

Hirsch, E. D. (1978) *Cultural Literacy: What Every American Needs to Know*. Boston: Houghton Mifflin.

Holbrook, A. and Johnston, S. (eds) (1999) *Supervision of Postgraduate Research in Education*. Coldstream: Australian Association for Research in Education.

Holbrook, A., Ainley, J., Bourke, S., Owen, J., McKenzie, P., Misson, S. and Johnson, T. (2000) Mapping educational research and its impact on Australian schools, in Higher Education Division Research Evaluation Programme Commonwealth of Australia (ed), *The Impact of Educational Research*. Canberra: Commonwealth of Australia.

James, P. and McQueen-Thomson, D. (2002) Abstracting knowledge formation: a report on academia and publishing, *Arena*, 17/18:183–205.

Johnson, E. (1999) Methodist Ladies College (MLC) still leading the way in learning with technology, *Teacher Learning Network* 6(3):5.

Johnson, E. (2000) 'We really started coming up with a final product' Primary practitioners' perceptions of gender inclusive curriculum, in M. Brennan (ed.) *Australian Curriculum Studies Association Conference Papers*. Canberra: ACSA.

Johnson, E. (2002a) Gender inclusive policy developments in Australia, *Journal of Education Policy* 17(5):1–14.

Johnson, E. (2002b) Implementing a culture-inclusive curriculum, in M. Singh (ed.) *Worlds of Learning*. Sydney: Common Ground.

Johnson, E. (2003) 'They don't associate it with feminism': in-service educators' conceptions of gender inclusive curriculum, *Journal of In-service Education* 29(1):31–48.

Kamler, B. and Thomson, P. (2002) Abstract art, or the politics and pedagogies of getting read. Paper presented to Australian Association for Research in Education Annual Conference, Brisbane.

Kelly, A. (ed.) (1987) *Science for Girls?* Buckingham: Open University Press.

Kenway, J. (1991) Conspicuous consumption: class, gender and private schooling, in David Dawkins (ed.) *Power and Politics in Education*. London: Falmer Press.

Kenway, J., Willis, S., Blackmore, J. and Rennie, L. (1997) *Answering Back: Girls, Boys and Feminism in Schools*. Sydney: Allen & Unwin.

Kuhn, T. S. (1996) *The Structure of Scientific Revolutions.* Chicago: University of Chicago Press.

Lagemann, E. C. (2000) *An Elusive Science: The Troubling History of Education Research*. Chicago: University of Chicago Press.

Lather, P. (1991) *Getting Smart: Feminist Research and Pedagogy With/in the Postmodern*. New York: Routledge.

Latour, B. and Woolgar, S. (1979) *Laboratory Life: The Social Construction of Scientific Facts*, Beverley Hills: Sage.

Leder, G. (1976) Contextual setting and mathematics performance, *The Australian Mathematics Teacher* 32(4):119–27.

Lee, A. (1998) Doctoral research as writing, in J. Higgs (ed.) *Writing Qualitative Research*. Sydney: Hampden Press.

Lee, A. and Williams, C. (1999) 'Forged in Fire': narratives of trauma in PhD pedagogy, *Southern Review* 32(1):6–26.

Lee, A., Green, B. and Brennan, M. (2000) Organisational knowledge, professional practice and the professional doctorate at work, in J. Garrick and C. Rhodes (eds), *Research and Knowledge at Work*. London: Routledge.

Leonard, D. (1997) Gender and doctoral studies, in N. Graves and V. Varma (eds), *Working for a Doctorate: A Guide for the Humanities and Social Sciences*. London: Routledge.

Leonard, D. (2001) *A Woman's Guide to Doctoral Studies*. Buckingham: Open University Press.

Lesko, N. (2001) *Act Your Age! A Cultural Construction of Adolescence*. New York: Routledge Falmer.

Lincoln, Y. S. and Guba, E. G. (2000) Paradigmatic controversies, contradictions, and emerging confluences, in N. K. Denzin and Y. S. Lincoln (eds) *Handbook of Qualitative Research*, 2nd edn. Thousand Oaks: Sage.

Lingard, R. *et al.* (2001) *The Queensland School Reform Longitudinal Study*. 2 vols. Brisbane: State of Queensland Department of Education.

Lingard, B., Hayes, D., Mills, M. and Christie, P. (2003) *Leading Learning: Making Hope Practical in Schools*. Buckingham: Open University Press.

Lingard, B., Mills, M. and Hayes, D. (2000) Teachers, school reform and social justice: challenging research and practice, *Australian Education Researcher* 27(3):93–109.

Loughran, J. (ed.) (1999) *Researching Teaching: Methodologies and Practices for Understanding Pedagogy*. London: Falmer Press.

Lovat, T., Holbrook, A., Bourke, S., Dally, K. and Hazel, G. (2000) Examiner comment on theses that have been revised and resubmitted. Paper presented to *Australian Association for Research in Education Annual Conference*, Brisbane, December.

Maclure, M. (2003) *Discourse in Educational and Social Research*. Buckingham: Open University Press.

Mahoney, P. and Zmroczek, C. (eds) (1997) *Class Matters: 'Working-class' Women's Perspectives on Social Class*. London: Taylor & Francis.

Martin, J. R. (1982) Excluding women from the educational realm, *Harvard Education Review* 34(4):341–53.

McLeod, J. (2003) Why we interview now–perspective and reflexivity in longitudinal study, *International Journal of Social Research Methodology* 6(3):201–212.

McLeod, J. and Yates, L. (1997) Can we find out about girls and boys today, or must we just settle for talking about ourselves? Dilemmas of a feminist, qualitative longitudinal research project, *Australian Education Researcher* 24(3):23–42.

McLeod, J. and Yates, L. (2003) Who is 'us'? Students negotiating discourses of racism and national identification in Australia, *Race, Ethnicity and Education* 6(1):29–49.

McMeniman, M., Cumming, J., Wilson, J., Stevenson, J. and Sim, C. (2000) Teacher knowledge in action, in Higher Education Division Commonwealth of Australia (ed.), *The Impact of Educational Research*, Canberra: Commonwealth of Australia.

McQueen, H. (1977) *Australia's Media Monopolies*. Camberwell: Widescope.

McWilliam, E. and Singh, P. (2002) Towards a Research Training Curriculum: what, why, how, who? *Australian Educational Researcher* 29(3):3–18.

Middleton, S. (2001) *Educating researchers: New Zealand Education PhDs 1948–1998*. Palmerston North: Massey University and New Zealand Association for Research in Education.

Oakham, M. (ed.) (1997) *Don't Bury the Lead*. Geelong: Deakin University Press.

Popkewitz, T. S. (ed.) (2000) *Educational Knowledge: Changing Relationships Between the State, Civil Society and the Educational Community*. Albany: SUNY.

Popkewitz, T. S. (2002) The non-bricks and non-mortar of an intellectual culture: my Americanization story of graduate education, *Australian Educational Researcher* 29(3):43–62.

Putnam, R. D. (2000) *Bowling Alone: The Collapse and Revival of American Community*. New York: Simon & Schuster.

Rathgen, E. (1996), On good authority: towards feminist pedagogies, PhD thesis, University of Canterbury, New Zealand.

Readance, J. E. and Barone, D. M. (2002) Editing RRQ 1994–2002: a retrospective, *Reading Research Quarterly* 37(4):368–70.

Rhedding-Jones, J. (1997) The writing on the wall: doing a feminist post-structural doctorate, *Gender and Education* 9(2):193–206.

Richardson, L. (2000) Writing: a method of inquiry, in N. K. Denzin and Y. S. Lincoln (eds) *Handbook of Qualitative Research*, 2nd edn. Thousand Oaks: Sage.

Rigby, K. (1996) *Bullying in Schools and What To Do About It*. Hawthorn: Australian Council for Educational Research.

Rist, R. C. (2000) Influencing the policy process with qualitative research, in N. K. Denzin and Y. S. Lincoln (eds) *Handbook of Qualitative Research*, 2nd edn. Thousand Oaks: Sage.

Rudner, L. M., Miller-Whitehead, M. and Gellmann, J. S. (2002) Who is reading online education journals? Why? And what are they reading?, *D-Lib Magazine [online journal]* 8, no. 12, http://www.dlib.org/dlib/december02/rudner/12rudner, accessed 28 May 2003 1:55.

Rutter, M., Maughan, B., Mortimore, P. and Ouston, J. (1979) *Fifteen Thousand Hours: Secondary Schools and their Effects on Children*. London: Open Books.

Scheeres, H. and Solomon, N. (2000a) Research partnerships at work: new identities for new times, in J. Garrick and C. Rhodes (eds) *Research and Knowledge at Work*. London: Routledge.

Scheeres, H. and Solomon, N. (2000b) Whose text? Methodological dilemmas in collaborative research practice, in A. Lee and C. Poynton (eds) *Culture and Text*. Sydney: Allen & Unwin.

Scott, J. (1990) Deconstructing equality-versus-difference: or the uses of post-structuralist theory for feminism, in M. Hirsch and E. Fox Keller (eds) *Conflicts in Feminism*, New York: Routledge.

Slavin, R. R. (2002) Evidence-based education policies: transforming educational practice and research, *Educational Researcher* 31(7):15–21.

Solomon, N. (2000) Reconstructing the subject: tactical textual uptakes, PhD thesis, University of Technology, Sydney.

Steedman, C., Urwin, C. and Walkerdine, V. (1985) *Language, Gender and Childhood*. London: Routledge.

Strauss, S. L. (2001) An open letter to Reid Lyon, *Educational Researcher* 30(5):26–33.

Teese, R. (2000) *Academic Success and Social Power: Examinations and Inequality*. Carlton South: Melbourne University Press.

Tooley, J., with Darby, D. (1998) Educational research: a critique. London: Office for Standards in Education.

Tooley, J. (2001) The quality of educational research: a perspective from Great Britain, *Peabody Journal of Education* 76(3/4):122–40.

Thomson, P. (2002) *Schooling the Rustbelt Kids: Making the Difference in Changing Times*. Sydney: Allen & Unwin.

Tsolidis, G. (2001) *Schooling, Diaspora and Gender: Being Feminist and Being Different*. Buckingham: Open University Press.

Vinson, T. C. (2002) *Report of the Independent Inquiry into Public Education in NSW*. Sydney: Pluto Press and NSW Teachers Federation.

Walden, R. and Walkerdine, V. (1982) *Girls and Mathematics: The Early Years*. Bedford Way Papers No. 8. London: Institute of Education, University of London.

Walkerdine, V. (1988) *The Mastery of Reason: Cognitive Development and the Production of Rationality*. London: Routledge.

Willinsky, J. (2002) Education and democracy: the missing link may be ours, *Harvard Educational Review* 72(3):367–92.

Willinsky, J. (2003) Scholarly associations and the economic viability of open access publishing, *Journal of Digital Information* 4(2). http://jodi.ecs.soton.ac.uk/Articles/v04/02/Willin, accessed 28 May 2003.

Wyse, D. (2000) Phonics – the whole story? A critical review of empirical evidence, *Educational Studies* 26(3):355–64.

Yates, L. and Leder, G. C. (1996) *Student Pathways: A Review and Overview of National Databases on Gender Equity*. Canberra: ACT Dept of Education and Training.

Yates, L. (1997a) Gender equity and the boys debate: what sort of challenge is it?, *British Journal of Sociology of Education* 18(3):337–47.

Yates, L. (1997b) Research methodology, education, and theoretical fashions: constructing a methodology course in an era of deconstruction, *International Journal of Qualitative Studies in Education* 10, (4): pp.487–98.

Yates, L. (1997c) Who are girls and what are we trying to do to them in schools? Changing assumptions and visions in contemporary education reforms, in J. Gill and M. Dyer (eds) *School Days: Past, Present and Future. Education of Girls in 20th Century Australia*, Research Centre for Gender Studies: University of South Australia.

Yates, L. (1998) Constructing and deconstructing 'girls' as a category of concern, in I. Elgqvist-Saltzman, A. Prentice and A. Mackinnon (eds) *Education into the 21st Century: Dangerous Terrain for Women?* London: Falmer Press.

Yates, L. (1999a) Feminisms' fandango with the state revisited: reflections on Australia, feminism, education and change, *Women's Studies International Forum* 22(5):555–62.

Yates, L. (1999b) Revisiting Durkheim's morality, democracy and collective spirit of education in an era of instrumentalism, pluralism and competition, *Pedagogy, Culture and Society* 7(1):165–74.

Yates, L. (1999c) Subject positions and the evolving PhD: some further thoughts, *Southern Review* 32(3):179–85.

Yates, L. (2000) Representing 'class' in qualitative research, in J. McLeod and K. Malone (eds) *Researching Youth*. Hobart: Australian Clearinghouse for Youth Research.

Yates, L. and McLeod, J. (2000) Social justice and the middle, *Australian Education Researcher* 27(3):59–77.

Yates, L. (2001a) Negotiating methodological dilemmas in a range of chilly climates – a story of pressures, principles and problems, *Asia-Pacific Journal of Teacher Education* 29(2):187–96.

Yates, L. (2001b) Selves, social factors, school sites and the tricky issue of 'school effects', *Change: Transformations in Education* 4(2):15–29.

Yates, L. (2002) Effectiveness, difference and sociological research, *Discourse: Studies in the Cultural Politics of Education*, 23(3):329–38.

Yates, L. (2003) Interpretive claims and methodological warrant in small number qualitative longitudinal research, *International Journal of Social Research Methodology*, 6(3): 223–232.

INDEX